Collins

PUB QUIZ

HarperCollins Publishers
Westerhill Road
Bishopbriggs
Glasgow
G64 2QT

First Edition 2012

Reprint 10 9 8 7 6 5 4 3 2 1 0

ISBN 978-0-00-747997-9

www.collinslanguage.com

A catalogue record for this book is
available from the British Library

Typeset by Davidson Publishing
Solutions, Glasgow

Printed in Great Britain by Clays Ltd,
St Ives plc

Acknowledgements
We would like to thank those authors
and publishers who kindly gave
permission for copyright material
to be used in the Collins Corpus.
We would also like to thank Times
Newspapers Ltd for providing
valuable data.

AUTHOR
Chris Bradshaw

EDITOR
Gerry Breslin
Freddy Chick

FOR THE PUBLISHER
Lucy Cooper
Julianna Dunn
Kerry Ferguson
Elaine Higgleton

Introduction

Pubs and pub quizzes go together like ovens and oven chips, like unicyclists and juggling, daytime TV and napping. Once one was invented, the other was sure to follow. No one knows exactly when the pub first appeared in Britain, it was probably about a week after beer was discovered. No one knows when the first pub quiz was held after that, although it can't have been much more than a month. What we do know is that the pub quiz is the natural offshoot of the pub, along with darts, table football, peanuts, Sky Sports News, outdoor heaters and weekends (designed to give people more time to spend in pubs).

After all, what is the main reason that people visit pubs? To drink, okay, sure, but what is it after that? It is to sit down with friends and talk absolute nonsense to each other. Drinks flow, tongues loosen and eventually arguments break out over who is right about some odd piece of trivia. Something like whether a fox is a dog or a cat, or how many times Uruguay have won the World Cup. At this point, people turn to the group beside them to ask for an adjudication over who's correct. Normally, that group will be in the middle of a trivial argument of their own. The two groups will merge and debate obscure facts together. Eventually, the whole pub will be at it. The pub quiz is just a way of formalising this.

At the centre of every good pub quiz lies an excellent quizmaster, and the secret to being a top-grade quizmaster is having knock-out questions. That's where *Collins Pub Quiz* comes in. *Collins Pub Quiz* is designed to give you, the potential quizmaster, the questions that will guarantee everyone in the pub cheers your name and hails you as their leader. Turn over to find out how it works.

The quizzes

There are two hundred quizzes in this book. Half of them are themed with classic pub quiz themes. There are animal quizzes, movie quizzes, written word, sport, soap opera and history quizzes. Astronomy and space are covered. So too is food and drink, and the human body. Everything you could want really. The other half of the quizzes are pot luck rounds, because you can never have enough of these.

The quizzes are grouped together according to how tricky they are. First come the easy ones, then medium and finally the difficult quizzes.

Easy

The easy questions should not have you scratching your head for very long. If they do, you need to wonder if there's anything inside it. A few of them are trickier than others and might even be labelled as 'challenging' by some judges. These have been included to add the frisson of mental sweat to an easy round. If things are too simple people switch off.

Medium

The medium-grade quizzes will get a good buzz of conferring going in each team. Someone will be sure of the answer, someone else will be sure that person is wrong but won't quite be able to remember the right answer themselves. Someone else will think it begins with a 'b'.

Difficult

These questions are tricky. Tricky, tricky, tricky. Tricky as the fifth entry in an alphabetical list of skateboard stunts: trick E. Anyone who gets all of these questions right you should immediately suspect of cheating. Ask to see their smartphone's browser history and be ready for a nasty showdown. You might not want to throw too many of this level into your quiz, but they are great for spicing things up or as tie-breaker questions.

The answers

The answers to each quiz are printed at the end of the following quiz. For example, the answers to Quiz 1-Pot Luck appear at the bottom of Quiz 2-Flags. The exception to this rule is the last quiz in every level. The answers to these quizzes appear at the end of the very first quiz in the level.

Running a quiz

Running a pub quiz is a difficult business. The guy in your local only makes it look easy through years of practice and finessing of technique. If you're gearing yourself up to take the challenge, then there are a few essential preparations to be made.

❖ Rehearse: don't just pick this book up and read out the questions cold. Go through all the quizzes you're going to use by yourself beforehand. Note down all the questions (notes look better in a quiz environment than reading from a book) and answers. Although every effort has been made to ensure that all the answers in *Collins Pub Quiz* are correct, despite our best endeavours, mistakes may still appear. If you see an answer you are not sure is right, or if you think there is more than one possible answer, then check.

❖ Paper and writing implements: do yourself a favour and prepare enough sheets of paper for everyone to write on. The aim of the game here is to stop the mad impulse certain people feel to 'help'. They will spend ten minutes running around looking for 'scrap' paper, probably ripping up your latest novel in the process. The same problem applies to pens. Ideally, have enough for everyone. Remember, though, that over half of them will be lost forever once you've given them out.

❖ Prizes: everyone likes a prize. No matter how small, it's best to have one on offer.

Good luck! We hope you enjoy *Collins Pub Quiz*!

Contents

Easy Quizzes

Medium Quizzes

Difficult Quizzes

EASY QUIZZES

Quiz 1: Pot Luck

1. Which ocean covers approximately one third of the earth's surface?

2. What part of the body is the patella more commonly known as?

3. Which American city is known as the Windy City?

4. Which actor sings the theme tune to New Tricks?

5. George Orwell's Homage to Catalonia is set in which conflict?

6. Jacob Marley was the partner of which literary character?

7. Which comedy duo presented TV gameshow Shooting Stars?

8. Lady Godiva rode naked through which English city?

9. Sofia is the capital city of which European country?

10. Who was the first man to walk on the moon?

11. Who wrote the Harry Potter novels?

12. What sign of the zodiac is represented by a set of scales?

13. In the nursery rhyme Hey Diddle Diddle, which animal jumped over the moon?

14. Which Irish comedian hosts Mock The Week?

15. Granny Smith is a variety of which type of fruit?

16. Which cartoon character works for the Slate and Gravel Company?

17. In 1933, Percy Shaw invented what road safety device?

18. Which London thoroughfare is traditionally associated with newspapers?

19. At their nearest points, how far apart are Russia and America?
    a) 4km
    b) 40km
    c) 400km

20. According to singer Katie Melua, how many bicycles are in Beijing?
    a) 8 million
    b) 9 million
    c) 10 million

EASY

Answers to Quiz 68: Births, Marriages and Deaths

1. California
2. Arthur Miller
3. Daniel Radcliffe
4. Buddy Holly
5. Mozart
6. Paul McCartney
7. Katy Perry
8. Seve Ballesteros
9. David Walliams
10. Wallace and Gromit
11. Peter Crouch
12. Spencer Perceval
13. 23rd Apr
14. James Brown
15. India
16. Taxes
17. Eight
18. Tupac Shakur
19. Ruby
20. Slippy

Quiz 2: Flags

1. Old Glory is the nickname for the flag of which country?

2. Which country's flag features the Star of David?

3. What sort of leaf appears on the flag of Canada?

4. A white cross on a black background is the flag of which English county?

5. A wheel appears in the flag of which Asian country?

6. What is the system of communication using flags called?

7. The flags of which three saints make up the Union Flag?

8. What flag is waved at the end of a motor racing Grand Prix?

9. What colour of flag is flown to indicate surrender?

10. What do the rings on the Olympic flag represent?

11. How many stars are on the flag of China?

12. What is the flag traditionally flown by pirates?

13. Which three colours are common to the flags of Luxembourg, Netherlands, Czech Republic and Slovenia?

14. In which branch of the armed services is the White Ensign flown?

15. What do the 13 stripes on the American flag represent?

16. Which country's flag is known as the blue saltire?

17. What flag is flown by British merchant ships?

18. The yin and yang symbols feature on the flag of which Asian country?

19. What is the study of flags known as?
    a) Angrology
    b) Ragology
    c) Vexillology

20. What colour appears on around 75% of national flags?
    a) Blue
    b) Red
    c) White

Answers to Quiz 1: Pot Luck

1. Pacific
2. The kneecap
3. Chicago
4. Dennis Waterman
5. The Spanish Civil War
6. Ebeneezer Scrooge
7. Vic Reeves and Bob Mortimer
8. Coventry
9. Bulgaria
10. Neil Armstrong
11. JK Rowling
12. Libra
13. The cow
14. Dara O Briain
15. Apple
16. Fred Flintstone
17. Cat's eyes
18. Fleet Street
19. 4km
20. 9 million

Quiz 3: Pot Luck

EASY

1. John Lennon Airport is in which city?

2. What fruit is used to describe a third party on a date?

3. Who is the patron saint of Wales?

4. George Formby is associated with which musical instrument?

5. Someone who discloses a secret is said to have let what out of the bag?

6. How many points is the yellow worth in a game of snooker?

7. Sasquatch is another name for which mythical creature?

8. What is the name of the counting device consisting of columns of beads strung on wires?

9. What word represents Z in the NATO Phonetic Alphabet?

10. How many years are in a millennium?

11. What is the art of clipping hedges more commonly known as?

12. What two elements combine to make water?

13. Zeta, iota and kappa are letters in which alphabet?

14. The word karaoke originates from what language?

15. Which classic comedy was set in Walmington-on-Sea?

16. Radio drama The Archers is set in which fictional village?

17. What are Daphne Fowler, Kevin Ashman, CJ de Mooi, Chris Hughes, Judith Keppel, Barry Simmons and Pat Gibson collectively known as?

18. What is the square root of 49?

19. If something is the genuine article it is said to be the real?
    a) McCoy
    b) McGrath
    c) McGrain

20. A gazetteer is a dictionary of what?
    a) newspapers
    b) places
    c) people called Gary

Answers to Quiz 2: Flags

1. USA
2. Israel
3. Maple Leaf
4. Cornwall
5. India
6. Semaphore
7. St George, St Andrew and St Patrick
8. Chequered Flag
9. White flag
10. Continents
11. Five
12. Jolly Roger
13. Red, white and blue
14. Royal Navy
15. The 13 original colonies
16. Scotland
17. Red Ensign
18. South Korea
19. Vexillology
20. Red

Quiz 4: Silver and Gold

1. In the song The 12 Days of Christmas, what was sent on the fifth day?

2. What awards are decided each year by the Hollywood Foreign Press Association?

3. What sort of gold did the Stone Roses sing about in 1989?

4. What nickname is given to an older person who spends a lot of time on the Internet?

5. After how many years is a Golden Jubilee celebrated?

6. Which footballer was nicknamed Goldenballs?

7. Who had a top ten hit in 1980 with Silver Dream Machine?

8. What is the third film in the James Bond series?

9. Which fictional character had a parrot called Captain Flint?

10. Which actor originally played TV's Sergeant Bilko?

11. What type of primate is a Silverback?

12. What is the chemical symbol for silver?

13. Which author wrote Lord of the Flies?

14. In which American city will you find the Golden Gate Bridge?

15. Which ancient king turned everything he touched into gold?

16. Which American state is nicknamed The Golden State?

17. What is the mineral pyrite more commonly known as?

18. Which circuit has hosted the British Grand Prix since 2010?

19. The Golden Temple in India is an important place of
    worship in which religion?
    a) Islam
    b) Judaism
    c) Sikhism

20. Which African country was formerly known as Gold Coast?
    a) Nigeria
    b) Ghana
    c) Botswana

EASY

Answers to Quiz 3: Pot Luck

1. Liverpool	11. Topiary
2. Gooseberry	12. Hydrogen and oxygen
3. St David	13. Greek
4. Ukulele	14. Japanese
5. Cat	15. Dad's Army
6. Two	16. Ambridge
7. The Abominable Snowman (Big Foot)	17. The Eggheads
	18. Seven
8. Abacus	19. McCoy
9. Zulu	20. Places
10. One thousand	

Quiz 5: Pot Luck

1. On a radio, what does FM stand for?

2. What is the technical term for stamp collecting?

3. Which football team won the 2012 FA Cup final?

4. Rhodesia was the former name of which African country?

5. What is measured using the Richter Scale?

6. What does a cartographer draw?

7. What was famously banned in America between 1920 and 1933?

8. Bergamot is used to flavour which type of tea?

9. Mount Everest is part of which mountain range?

10. Which British monarch abdicated in 1936?

11. Which country hosted the World Cup in 2006?

12. Old Bill is a slang term for what?

13. A trimester is a period of how many months?

14. Which spiritualist device takes its name from the French and German words for yes?

15. What is the first letter of the Greek alphabet?

16. On a dart board, what number lies between one and five?

17. In which TV soap could you have something to eat at Roy's Rolls?

18. Which county cricket team play their home matches at Headingley?

EASY

19. What would you do with lederhosen?
    a) eat them
    b) play them
    c) wear them

20. Another name for a voyeur is a Peeping...?
    a) John
    b) Tom
    c) Ron

Answers to Quiz 4: Silver and Gold

1. Five Gold Rings
2. Golden Globes
3. Fool's Gold
4. Silver Surfer
5. Fifty
6. David Beckham
7. David Essex
8. Goldfinger
9. Long John Silver
10. Phil Silvers
11. Gorilla
12. Ag
13. William Golding
14. San Francisco
15. Midas
16. California
17. Fool's Gold
18. Silverstone
19. Sikhism
20. Ghana

Quiz 6: Pop Music part 1

1. Which group topped the charts for the first time in 1993 with Pray?

2. Which indie rockers take their name from a South African football team?

3. Push The Button, Freak Like Me and Round Round were number one hits for which female group?

4. Who represented Switzerland in the 1988 Eurovision Song Contest?

5. Robbie Williams' first solo top ten single was a cover of which George Michael song?

6. Don't Shoot Me I'm Only The Piano Player was a number one album for which bespectacled singer and pianist?

7. Parachutes was the debut album from which group?

8. Flea is the bass player with which American rock band?

9. What title provided hits for Depeche Mode in 1981 and Black Eyed Peas in 2011?

10. Swagger Jagger was the debut single from which female X Factor singer?

11. Aston Merrygold and Marvin Humes are members of which British band?

12. Which American Idol winner recorded the album Stronger?

13. Who is Shawn Carter more commonly known as?

14. Complete the title of the 2010 hit by Tinie Tempah featuring Eric Turner: Written In The ...?

15. Who went In For The Kill in 2009?

16. Whose debut single was Chasing Pavements?

17. What sort of face did Lady Gaga show on her 2008 number one?

18. The Boss is the nickname of which American rocker?

19. What appeared on the front cover of Nirvana's album Nevermind?
    a) a baby
    b) a dog
    c) a cat

20. You Keep Me Hangin' On was a 1966 hit for which Motown group?
    a) The Four Tops
    b) The Supremes
    c) The Temptations

Answers to Quiz 5: Pot Luck

1. Frequency Modulation
2. Philately
3. Chelsea
4. Zimbabwe
5. The intensity of earthquakes
6. Maps
7. Alcohol
8. Earl Grey
9. The Himalayas
10. Edward VIII
11. Germany
12. The Police
13. Three
14. Ouija Board
15. Alpha
16. Twenty
17. Coronation Street
18. Yorkshire
19. Wear them
20. Tom

Quiz 7: Pot Luck

1. What is the second largest continent in the world?

2. Which UK city has the dialling code 0131?

3. What is the only country whose name doesn't appear on its postage stamps?

4. Old Joanna is cockney rhyming slang for which musical instrument?

5. Craven Cottage is the home ground of which Premier League football club?

6. Which TV comedy was set at a paper merchant called Wernham Hogg?

7. In June 1949, a monkey called Albert II was the first to travel where?

8. According to the proverb, what cannot be taught new tricks?

9. William Shakespeare was born in which Warwickshire town?

10. Which architect designed St Paul's Cathedral?

11. Which Swedish group's name is derived from the first letter of its members' Christian names?

12. What is the name of the newsagent in Coronation Street?

13. The Seine is the principal waterway in which European capital city?

14. 'As if by magic, a shopkeeper would appear' in which children's TV programme?

15. What is the capital city of Croatia?

16. Who did David Cameron succeed to become British Prime Minister?

17. On which continent would you find the Cape of Good Hope?

18. What was the former name of Zimbabwe?

19. The end of a day's shooting on a film set is known as?
    a) can
    b) wrap
    c) baguette

20. England play Scotland at rugby union for which trophy?
    a) Calcutta Cup
    b) Delhi Cup
    c) Bombay Cup

EASY

Answers to Quiz 6: Pop Music part 1

1. Take That
2. Kaiser Chiefs
3. Sugababes
4. Celine Dion
5. Freedom
6. Elton John
7. Coldplay
8. Red Hot Chili Peppers
9. Just Can't Get Enough
10. Cher Lloyd
11. JLS
12. Kelly Clarkson
13. Jay Z
14. Stars
15. La Roux
16. Adele
17. Poker Face
18. Bruce Springsteen
19. A baby
20. The Supremes

Quiz 8: Mottos and Catchphrases

1. 'Come on down!' was the catchphrase on which TV gameshow?

2. 'Be prepared' is the motto of which organisation?

3. In which TV quiz show can a player 'ask the audience'?

4. The phrase 'big brother' comes from which novel?

5. The founder of which department store coined the phrase 'the customer is always right'?

6. 'If it's up there I'll give you the money myself' was said by the host of which TV gameshow?

7. 'Here's looking at you, kid' is a line from which classic film?

8. Which TV character 'loves it when a plan comes together'?

9. Which department store is said to be 'never knowingly undersold'?

10. Which magician's catchphrase is 'Now that's magic'?

11. 'Don't be evil' is the informal motto of which global company?

12. 'It's a cracker' was the catchphrase of which comedian who died in 2012?

13. Which TV comedienne coined the catchphrase 'Am I bovvered?'?

14. On which TV show will you hear the phrase 'No likey, no lighty'?

15. The phrase 'Vorsprung durch Technik' is associated with which German car manufacturer?

16. 'Because I'm worth it' is the motto of which beauty company?

17. What is the motto of the SAS?

18. Who, after collecting an Oscar for Chariots of Fire, famously said that 'The British are coming'?

19. Which US president is associated with the phrase 'If you can't stand the heat, get out of the kitchen'?
    a) Harry Truman
    b) Richard Nixon
    c) Bill Clinton

20. Think Different is an advertising slogan for which technology company?
    a) Apple
    b) Facebook
    c) Microsoft

Answers to Quiz 7: Pot Luck

1. Africa
2. Edinburgh
3. Great Britain
4. Piano
5. Fulham
6. The Office
7. Space
8. An old dog
9. Stratford-upon-Avon
10. Sir Christopher Wren
11. Abba
12. The Kabin
13. Paris
14. Mr Benn
15. Zagreb
16. Gordon Brown
17. Africa
18. Rhodesia
19. Wrap
20. Calcutta Cup

EASY

Quiz 9: Pot Luck

EASY

1. Tripoli is the capital city of which African country?

2. Which musician was murdered outside his New York apartment by Mark Chapman in 1980?

3. Loftus Road is the home ground of which football club?

4. Which English county is famous for its pasties?

5. Claret, soave and liebfraumilch are all types of which drink?

6. Proverbially, how long does a wonder last?

7. Shylock is a character in which Shakespeare play?

8. In what country would you catch a Bullet Train?

9. In 79AD the city of Pompeii was destroyed after an eruption from which volcano?

10. Tiger, bull and great white are types of what marine animal?

11. Richard of York gave battle in vain is a mnemonic to remember what?

12. What is the sum of money paid to ensure that a person turns up to a court case?

13. Who topped the the UK singles chart for a record 16 weeks in 1991 with (Everything I Do) I Do It For You?

14. Michael Stipe was the lead singer with which band?

15. Which actor wrote the script for the boxing movie Rocky?

16. Who was the leader of the British Union of Fascists?

17. Crockett and Tubbs appeared in which US cop drama?

18. What was the name of the court set up by the Roman Catholic Church in the 13th century to try cases of heresy?

19. What is the highest out of these voices?
    a) bass
    b) baritone
    c) tenor

20. What word describes a government run on religious lines?
    a) theocracy
    b) plutocracy
    c) meritocracy

Answers to Quiz 8: Mottos and Catchphrases

1. The Price Is Right
2. The Boy Scouts
3. Who Wants To Be A Millionaire
4. 1984
5. Selfridge's (H Gordon Selfridge?
6. Family Fortunes
7. Casablanca
8. Hannibal from The A Team
9. John Lewis
10. Paul Daniels
11. Google
12. Frank Carson
13. Catherine Tate
14. Take Me Out
15. Audi
16. L'Oreal
17. Who Dares Wins
18. Colin Welland
19. Harry Truman
20. Apple

Quiz 10: Written Word

1. Who wrote The Da Vinci Code?

2. What is the first book in the Harry Potter series?

3. According to the novel by Lauren Weisberger, who wears Prada?

4. The His Dark Materials fantasy trilogy was written by which author?

5. Which US president wrote Dreams of My Father?

6. Twisting My Melon is the autobiography of which Manchester musician?

7. Who wrote the legal thrillers A Time To Kill, The Pelican Brief and The Litigators?

8. Charlie and the Chocolate Factory, The Twits and Fantastic Mr Fox are by which author?

9. Helen Fielding wrote whose famous fictional diary?

10. Round The Bend, How Hard Can It Be and Driven To Distraction are by which controversial broadcaster?

11. Dear Fatty is by which actress and comedian?

12. The Sebastian Faulks novel Birdsong is set during which conflict?

13. Who created the fictional detective Inspector Maigret?

14. What is the spy writer David Cornwell better known as?

15. What nationality is the fictional detective Hercule Poirot?

16. Hemingway's For Whom The Bell Tolls is set during which European war?

17. According to the title of a book by John Gray, Men Are From Mars, Women Are From...?

18. Who wrote the American classic Of Mice and Men?

19. Captain Corelli's Mandolin is set in which country?
    a) Greece
    b) Italy
    c) Spain

20. Man and Boy, Men From The Boys and My Favourite Wife are novels by which author?
    a) Jonathan Coe
    b) Nick Hornby
    c) Tony Parsons

EASY

Answers to Quiz 9: Pot Luck

1. Libya
2. John Lennon
3. QPR
4. Cornwall
5. Wine
6. Nine days
7. The Merchant of Venice
8. Japan
9. Vesuvius
10. Shark
11. Colours of the rainbow
12. Bail
13. Bryan Adams
14. REM
15. Sylvester Stallone
16. Oswald Mosley
17. Miami Vice
18. Spanish Inquisition
19. Tenor
20. Theocracy

Quiz 11: Pot Luck

1. Who, in 2004, founded the social network Facebook?

2. Cairo is the capital city of which country?

3. Which American city is known as The Big Apple?

4. According to the proverb, a bird in the hand is worth how many in the bush?

5. Who You Are was the debut album by which female singer?

6. In computing, what does the acronym RAM stand for?

7. What classic horse race was first run on 4 May 1780?

8. What type of aircraft has wings but no motor?

9. What does the DC in Washington DC stand for?

10. Which South American capital city translates as River of January?

11. Which poem starts 'I wandered lonely as a cloud'?

12. Which composer wrote the European Union anthem, Ode To Joy?

13. Mountaineer Sir Edmund Hillary is from which Commonwealth country?

14. The holder of which political office is also First Lord of the Treasury?

15. On what date do the French celebrate Bastille Day?

16. Which group's first UK top ten hit was It Only Takes A Minute?

17. What did America purchase from Russia for 2 cents an acre in March 1867?

18. Which actress appeared in the video to Bruce Springsteen's Dancing In The Dark?

19. What is the largest frog in the world?
    a) Giant frog
    b) Goliath frog
    c) Whopper frog

20. Who trained 15 boxing world champions including Muhammad Ali?
    a) Angelo Aberdeen
    b) Angelo Dundee
    c) Angelo Motherwell

EASY

Answers to Quiz 10: Written Word

1. Dan Brown
2. Harry Potter and The Philosopher's Stone
3. The Devil Wears Prada
4. Philip Pullman
5. Barack Obama
6. Shaun Ryder
7. John Grisham
8. Roald Dahl
9. Bridget Jones's
10. Jeremy Clarkson
11. Dawn French
12. First World War
13. Georges Simenon
14. John Le Carre
15. Belgian
16. Spanish Civil War
17. Venus
18. John Steinbeck
19. Greece
20. Tony Parsons

Quiz 12: Movies

1. David Prowse, James Earl Jones and Sebastian Shaw played which classic screen baddie?

2. My Name Is Tallulah, Fat Sam's Grand Slam and You Give A Little Love are songs from which film musical?

3. Who plays Edward Cullen in the Twilight films?

4. 'Louis, I think this is the start of a beautiful friendship' is the last line of which wartime classic?

5. Who is the ruler of the planet Mongo?

6. George Bailey is the central character in which Christmas classic?

7. Who played Hannibal in the 2010 film version of The A Team?

8. Which restaurant critic directed the original Death Wish film?

9. Who provides the voice of Buzz Lightyear in the Toy Story films?

10. What is the name of the character played by Bruce Willis in the Die Hard films?

11. 'Fear can set you prisoner. Hope can set you free' is the tagline to which 1994 film?

12. Which English comedian played Flash Harry in the 2007 St Trinian's film?

13. Who is the bumbling English spy played by Rowan Atkinson?

14. Which island in the Indian Ocean gives its name to a 2005 animation?

EASY

15. Who played The Hatter in the 2010 version of Alice In Wonderland?

16. Which former Neighbour played King Edward VIII in The King's Speech?

17. Who directed Inception?

18. The 2011 film Puss In Boots was a spin-off from which film series?

19. What was the call sign of the character played by Tom Cruise in Top Gun?
    a) Iceman
    b) Maverick
    c) Viper

20. Complete the title of the 2011 film: Me and...?
    a) Orson Welles
    b) Alfred Hitchcock
    c) Billy Wilder

Answers to Quiz 11: Pot Luck

1. Mark Zuckerberg
2. Egypt
3. New York
4. Two
5. Jessie J
6. Random Access Memory
7. The Derby
8. Glider
9. District of Columbia
10. Rio de Janeiro
11. Daffodils
12. Beethoven
13. New Zealand
14. The Prime Minister
15. 14th July
16. Take That
17. Alaska
18. Courtney Cox
19. Goliath Frog
20. Angelo Dundee

Quiz 13: Pot Luck

1. Who is the patron saint of Scotland?

2. What are the Islas Malvinas known as in English?

3. The opposite sides of a die always add up to what number?

4. What is the only metal that is liquid at room temperature?

5. Paddington Bear arrived in London as a stowaway from which country?

6. In the Bible, Judas betrayed Jesus for how many pieces of silver?

7. How many feet are in a yard?

8. Which naturalist sailed on a survey ship called The Beagle?

9. What is the square root of 144?

10. Chris Collins is the real name of which stand-up comedian?

11. Ashley Banjo is the leader of which dance troupe?

12. In mythology, Jason and the Argonauts were searching for a golden what?

13. Which cricketer won I'm a Celebrity...Get Me Out of Here in 2003?

14. Which dart player is nicknamed The Power?

15. What name links a character from Only Fools and Horses and horses ridden by Roy Rogers and Benny Hill?

16. Which actor plays Mr Bean?

17. Which branch of mathematics is concerned with lines, points, surfaces and solids?

18. The dish goulash is traditionally associated with which country?

19. What ship is docked on the South Bank of the River Thames at Symon's Wharf?
    a) HMS London
    b) HMS Edinburgh
    c) HMS Belfast

20. Another name for a police informant is?
    a) stool dove
    b) stool eagle
    c) stool pigeon?

Answers to Quiz 12: Movies

1. Darth Vader
2. Bugsy Malone
3. Robert Pattinson
4. Casablanca
5. Ming the Merciless
6. It's A Wonderful Life
7. Liam Neeson
8. Michael Winner
9. Tim Allen
10. John McClane
11. The Shawshank Redemption
12. Russell Brand
13. Johnny English
14. Madagascar
15. Johnny Depp
16. Guy Pearce
17. Christopher Nolan
18. Shrek
19. Maverick
20. Orson Welles

Quiz 14: Politics

1. Who lives at 11 Downing Street?

2. Which long-serving MP is nicknamed The Beast of Bolsover?

3. What colour are the benches in the House of Commons?

4. The Dail is the name of the parliament in which country?

5. Who delivers the Mansion House Speech?

6. In the UK parliament, what do the initials EDM stand for?

7. On what day of the week are elections traditionally held in Britain?

8. Members of which UK political body have the letter AM after their name?

9. What is the minimum age at which people in the UK can vote?

10. Which Prime Minister wrote The Downing Street Years and The Path to Power?

11. Which politician was nicknamed The Prince of Darkness?

12. Which former Lib Dem MP was romantically linked with one of the Cheeky Girls?

13. What is the name of David Cameron's wife?

14. What are the two chambers of the US Congress?

15. Which Scottish politician pretended to be a cat alongside actress Rula Lenska in Celebrity Big Brother?

16. Who was the last Prime Minister who didn't go to university?

17. What assent is needed for an Act of Parliament to become law?

18. Who was the Prime Minister when England won the 1966 World Cup?

19. In what year was David Cameron elected into the House of Commons?
    a) 1997
    b) 2001
    c) 2005

20. Who did Margaret Thatcher succeed as Prime Minister?
    a) James Callaghan
    b) Harold Wilson
    c) Neil Kinnock

Answers to Quiz 13: Pot Luck

1. St Andrew	11. Diversity
2. The Falkland Islands	12. Fleece
3. 7	13. Phil Tufnell
4. Mercury	14. Phil Taylor
5. Peru	15. Trigger
6. Thirty	16. Rowan Atkinson
7. Three	17. Geometry
8. Charles Darwin	18. Hungary
9. 12	19. HMS Belfast
10. Frank Skinner	20. Stool pigeon

Quiz 15: Pot Luck

EASY

1. Which pair lost their jobs at Sky Sports in a row over sexism?

2. Television soap Neighbours is set in which Australian city?

3. The thistle is the national symbol of which country?

4. The black keys on a piano are traditionally made from which type of wood?

5. How many furlongs are in a mile?

6. What type of animal is a dachshund?

7. In the nursery rhyme Hey Diddle Diddle what instrument did the cat play?

8. The character Holly Golightly appears in which book and film?

9. What was the last state to join the United States of America?

10. Who presented the first and last episodes of Top of the Pops?

11. Which Disney character has a sister called Dumbella?

12. Which actor and comedian hosts TV quiz show The Chase?

13. Cirrhosis affects which organ of the body?

14. Copacabana Beach is in which South American country?

15. Hell In A Handbasket is a 2012 album by which veteran rocker?

16. Complete the title of the 2011 film: My Week With...?

17. Which comedian's autobiography is called Small Man in a Book?

Answers - page 33

EASY

18. Michael Eavis is the founder of which music festival?

19. Which of the following is a comedy award?
    a) The Laftas
    b) The Gagstas
    c) The Titters

20. In Texas Hold'em poker which is the best of the three following hands?
    a) trips
    b) a flush
    c) a straight

Answers to Quiz 14: Politics

1. The Chancellor of the Exchequer
2. Dennis Skinner
3. Green
4. Republic of Ireland
5. The Chancellor of the Exchequer
6. Early Day Motion
7. Thursday
8. Welsh Assembly
9. 18
10. Margaret Thatcher
11. Peter Mandelson
12. Lembit Opik
13. Samantha
14. Senate and House of Representatives
15. George Galloway
16. John Major
17. Royal Assent
18. Harold Wilson
19. 2001
20. James Callaghan

Quiz 16: Art and Architecture

1. What is the central aisle of a church called?

2. Which British artist painted The Blue Boy?

3. In which Italian city would you find the Uffizi Gallery?

4. 'If you seek his memorial, look about you' is written on the tomb of which architect?

5. What is the vertical iron gate of a castle called?

6. George Stubbs is associated with paintings of what animals?

7. What name describes the fine plaster used for coating wall surfaces into architectural decorations?

8. Burne-Jones, Millais, Holman Hunt and Dante Gabriel Rossetti were members of which artistic movement?

9. The Baltic Centre for Contemporary Art is in which British town?

10. A Rake's Progress and A Harlot's Progress were works by which 18th-century British artist?

11. Jack Hoggan is the real name of which Scottish painter?

12. Canaletto is associated with paintings of which Italian city?

13. Who painted the ceiling of the Sistine Chapel?

14. Where is a fresco painted?

15. Which Dutch artist painted Girl with a Pearl Earring?

16. Which sculptor created The Angel of the North?

17. Who painted Starry Night and Sunflowers?

EASY

18. Poppy Field and Water Lillies are paintings by which French Impressionist?

19. What is the painting of inanimate objects known as?
    a) motionless life
    b) statuesque life
    c) still life

20. What is missing from the Mona Lisa?
    a) eyebrows
    b) nostrils
    c) eyeballs

Answers to Quiz 15: Pot Luck

1. Richard Keys and Andy Gray
2. Melbourne
3. Scotland
4. Ebony
5. Eight
6. Dog
7. The fiddle
8. Breakfast at Tiffany's
9. Hawaii
10. Sir Jimmy Savile
11. Donald Duck
12. Bradley Walsh
13. Liver
14. Brazil
15. Meat Loaf
16. Marilyn
17. Rob Brydon
18. Glastonbury
19. The Laftas
20. Flush

Quiz 17: Pot Luck

1. Buenos Aires is the capital city of which country?

2. Sprouts are associated with which European capital city?

3. Awards founder Alfred Nobel invented which explosive material?

4. One swallow doesn't make a what?

5. Which French queen said, 'Let them eat cake'?

6. In a theatre, it is considered bad luck to mention which Shakespeare play?

7. Named after textiles workers who destroyed their machinery in the early 1800s, what name describes opponents of technological change?

8. US President John F Kennedy was assassinated in which city?

9. Norman Stanley were the Christian names of which legendary sitcom character?

10. Which team won the Champions League for the first time in 2012?

11. Who served as US Vice President alongside Bill Clinton?

12. In 2012, which former politician made her debut at London's Royal Opera House in La Fille Du Regiment?

13. Boston is the largest city in which US state?

14. Which rag and bone men had a horse called Hercules?

15. What type of animal is the Disney character Goofy?

EASY

16. Bramley, Braeburn and Laxton's Superb are varieties of which fruit?

17. Which country hosted the World Cup in 2010?

18. On what side of the road do they drive in Australia?

19. Jesse J topped the charts in 2012 with?
    a) Domino
    b) Draught
    c) Checker

20. Which of these three groups had the most number one singles?
    a) Oasis
    b) The Spice Girls
    c) McFly

Answers to Quiz 16: Art and Architecture

1. Nave
2. Thomas Gainsborough
3. Florence
4. Sir Christopher Wren
5. Portcullis
6. Horses
7. Stucco
8. Pre-Raphaelite Brotherhood
9. Gateshead
10. William Hogarth
11. Jack Vettriano
12. Venice
13. Michelangelo
14. On a wall
15. Jan Vermeer
16. Anthony Gormley
17. Vincent Van Gogh
18. Claude Monet
19. Still life
20. Eyebrows

Quiz 18: Astronomy and Space

1. Which planet is closest to the Sun?

2. The big red spot is a feature of which planet?

3. Who was the second man to walk on the Moon?

4. Which planet is named after the Roman goddess of love and beauty?

5. What is the second largest planet in our Solar System?

6. Which composer wrote an orchestral suite called The Planets?

7. What is the hottest planet in the Solar System?

8. Which Greek and Roman god gave his name to the American moon landing programme?

9. What is the distance 5,865,696,000,000 miles more commonly known as?

10. Which constellation appears on the flag of Australia?

11. Astronaut Alan Shepard played what ball game on the moon?

12. What was the name of the space shuttle that exploded, killing seven astronauts?

13. What did astronauts James S Voss and Susan J Helms do for 8 hours 56 minutes in March 2001?

14. What is the largest body in the Solar System?

15. Which musician-turned-scientist presented the TV series The Wonders of the Solar System?

16. What celestial event occurs when the Moon passes between the Sun and the Earth?

17. What is the constellation Ursa Major also known as?

18. Which planet is nicknamed The Red Planet?

19. Canis Major, the brightest star in the sky, is also known as?
    a) cat star
    b) dog star
    c) goat star

20. Which planet has 63 moons?
    a) Jupiter
    b) Saturn
    c) Neptune

EASY

Answers to Quiz 17: Pot Luck

1. Argentina
2. Brussels
3. Dynamite
4. Summer
5. Marie Antoinette
6. Macbeth
7. Luddites
8. Dallas
9. Fletcher from Porridge
10. Chelsea
11. Al Gore
12. Ann Widdecombe
13. Massachusetts
14. Steptoe and Son
15. Dog
16. Apple
17. South Africa
18. Left
19. Domino
20. The Spice Girls

Quiz 19: Pot Luck

1. Seville oranges are the main ingredient in which popular British condiment?

2. Which poet wrote Daffodils?

3. Sicily is the largest island in which sea?

4. Mylo Xyloto was a number one album by which UK group?

5. La Manche is another name for what?

6. What is the second letter of the Greek alphabet?

7. Fifteen is the flagship restaurant of which British chef?

8. Which philosopher and mathematician is noted for his theorem concerning right angled triangles?

9. According to the proverb, what type of stone never gathers moss?

10. What was the only passenger plane to fly faster than the speed of sound?

11. What do Americans call nappies?

12. Which English monarch was killed at the Battle of Hastings?

13. Scarface was the nickname of which American gangster?

14. Fish can breathe under water thanks to what organs?

15. What is the largest city in the US state of California?

16. Which modern-day country was formerly known as Persia?

17. In The Jungle Book, what type of animal was Kaa?

18. The painters Vermeer and Frans Hals were from which country?

19. What is the longest river in Northern Ireland?
    a) Bann
    b) Cann
    c) Dann

20. What was the name of Arkwright's shop boy in the sitcom Open All Hours?
    a) Granville
    b) Grenville
    c) Greville

Answers to Quiz 18: Astronomy and Space

1. Mercury	11. Golf
2. Jupiter	12. Challenger
3. Buzz Aldrin	13. Spacewalk
4. Venus	14. The Sun
5. Saturn	15. Professor Brian Cox
6. Gustav Holst	16. Solar Eclipse
7. Venus	17. The Great Bear
8. Apollo	18. Mars
9. A light year	19. Dog star
10. Southern Cross (or Crux)	20. Jupiter

Quiz 20: Colours

1. Which English football club is nicknamed The Red Devils?

2. What was Coldplay's first top ten single?

3. Which group represented the UK in the 2011 Eurovision Song Contest?

4. Which horse won the Grand National in 1973, 1974 and 1977?

5. What article of clothing is given to the winner of the US Masters golf tournament?

6. Jennifer Aniston played which character in Friends?

7. What is Scary Spice's real name?

8. What is the Royal Air Force Aerobatic Team more commonly known as?

9. What colour is usually associated with envy?

10. What sort of crush did REM sing about in 1989?

11. In snooker, how many points is the black ball worth?

12. Which author wrote the Father Brown mystery novels?

13. Back To Black was a best-selling album by which female singer?

14. What is the name of the girls' gang in the film Grease?

15. What was landscape gardener Lancelot Brown more commonly known as?

16. Which group had hits with Agadoo, Superman and Do The Conga?

17. Which actress played Dot Cotton in EastEnders?

18. Purple Rain was a top ten hit single for which diminutive musician?

19. Clean beaches are signified by what colour flag?
    a) Blue
    b) Green
    c) Yellow

20. What colour of door did Shakin' Stevens sing about in his 1981 chart topper?
    a) Blue Door
    b) Green Door
    c) Red Door

EASY

Answers to Quiz 19: Pot Luck

1. Marmalade
2. William Wordsworth
3. Mediterranean
4. Coldplay
5. The English Channel
6. Beta
7. Jamie Oliver
8. Pythagoras
9. A rolling stone
10. Concorde
11. Diapers
12. Harold
13. Al Capone
14. Gills
15. Los Angeles
16. Iran
17. Snake
18. Netherlands
19. Bann
20. Granville

Quiz 21: Pot Luck

1. The Yangtze is the longest river in which country?

2. Proverbially, who is the king of the kingdom of the blind?

3. What is the opposite of nocturnal?

4. The New Deal is associated with which US President?

5. What is the fruit of the oak tree?

6. Acoustics is the study of what?

7. The Montgolfier brothers are associated with which form of transport?

8. Which banker was stripped of his knighthood in January 2012?

9. In TV comedy Absolutely Fabulous, what is the name of Edina's sensible daughter?

10. Who flies in a plane called Air Force One?

11. The sword of Damocles was suspended by a single what?

12. The Tigers are a rugby union team in which English city?

13. A heptagon has how many sides?

14. Lesley Hornby is the real name of which sixties icon?

15. What occupation links Glyn Purnell, Jason Atherton and Richard Corrigan?

16. Which England cricket captain was a skipper on TV quiz show They Think It's All Over?

17. Napoleon was born on which island?

18. Is the Tropic of Cancer north or south of the equator?

EASY

19. What word describes defaming someone in writing?
    a) slander
    b) libel
    c) trespass

20. In the Samuel Beckett play, the two tramps are Waiting For...?
    a) mercy
    b) Godot
    c) rescue

Answers to Quiz 20: Colours

1. Manchester United
2. Yellow
3. Blue
4. Red Rum
5. Green Jacket
6. Rachel Green
7. Melanie Brown
8. The Red Arrows
9. Green
10. Orange Crush
11. Seven
12. GK Chesterton
13. Amy Winehouse
14. The Pink Ladies
15. Capability Brown
16. Black Lace
17. June Brown
18. Prince
19. Blue
20. Green Door

Quiz 22: Sport part 1

EASY

1. What colour of jersey does the leader of the Tour de France wear?

2. What trophy is awarded to the winners of the Rugby World Cup?

3. Sheffield's Crucible Theatre is the venue for which annual sporting event?

4. What nationality is footballer Lionel Messi?

5. Mo Farah won a gold medal at the 2011 World Athletics Championships at what distance?

6. Bramall Lane is the home ground of which Yorkshire football club?

7. In American football, how many points are awarded for scoring a touchdown?

8. Which Olympic gold medallist was a runner-up in Strictly Come Dancing?

9. How long is an Olympic swimming pool?

10. In 2011, which county won its first cricket County Championship title since 1950?

11. What is the last event of a decathlon?

12. What is the first tennis major of the year?

13. Which driver won the 2010 and 2011 Formula One World Drivers' Championship?

14. Which country won the 2011 Rugby World Cup?

15. In what month does horse racing's Cheltenham Festival take place?

EASY

16. The first World Cup was held in which country?

17. Which Northern Irishman won the 2011 Open Golf Championship?

18. What is the maximum possible score in a game of ten pin bowling?

19. Record breaking sprinter Usain Bolt is from which country?
    a) USA
    b) Jamaica
    c) Trinidad

20. Which city has not hosted the Olympic Games?
    a) Amsterdam
    b) Antwerp
    c) Brussels

Answers to Quiz 21: Pot Luck

1. China
2. The one eyed man
3. Diurnal
4. Franklin D Roosevelt
5. Acorn
6. Sound
7. Hot air balloons
8. Fred Goodwin
9. Saffron
10. President of the USA
11. Hair
12. Leicester
13. Seven
14. Twiggy
15. Chefs
16. David Gower
17. Corsica
18. North
19. Libel
20. Godot

Quiz 23: Pot Luck

1. Which American city was once known as New Amsterdam?

2. What is the capital of the Falkland Islands?

3. On what date is St George's Day celebrated?

4. Lily Savage is the alter ego of which Liverpudlian comedian?

5. What French phrase describes a sudden, violent, change of government?

6. What is the last letter of the Greek alphabet?

7. Which nursery rhyme character runs through the town, upstairs and downstairs in his night gown?

8. Somebody who is disgusted is typically associated with which Kent town?

9. Selhurst Park is the home ground of which London football club?

10. Gregg Wallace and John Torode are judges on which culinary TV show?

11. The richest man in the world, Carlos Slim Helu, is from which country?

12. Scafell Pike is located in which UK National Park?

13. Tom Chaplin is the lead singer with which band?

14. The island Madeira belongs to which country?

15. What is measured using the pH scale?

16. In which county would you find the Eden Project?

17. How many points are there on the Star of David?

EASY

18. Who is Alan Sugar's right-hand man on The Apprentice?

19. In politics, what name is used to describe a public relations expert?
    a) spin doctor
    b) spin surgeon
    c) spin master

20. The giant Tomatina festival takes place in which country?
    a) Italy
    b) Portugal
    c) Spain

Answers to Quiz 22: Sport part 1

1. Yellow
2. The Webb-Ellis Cup
3. The World Snooker Championship
4. Argentine
5. 5,000 metres
6. Sheffield United
7. 6
8. Denise Lewis
9. 50m
10. Lancashire
11. 1500 metres
12. Australian Open
13. Sebastian Vettel
14. New Zealand
15. March
16. Uruguay
17. Darren Clarke
18. 300
19. Jamaica
20. Brussels

Quiz 24: Musicals

EASY

1. My Favourite Things, Climb Ev'ry Mountain and Do-Re-Mi are songs from which musical?

2. Which Liverpool playwright wrote Blood Brothers?

3. All That Jazz, Cell Block Tango and We Both Reached For The Gun are songs from which musical?

4. Cats is based on a book of poems by which author?

5. Who played the Phantom in the original 1986 stage version of The Phantom of the Opera?

6. Springtime For Hitler is a song from which musical?

7. Who wrote the lyrics to Joseph and the Amazing Technicolor Dreamcoat and Jesus Christ Superstar?

8. Evita is based on the life of which Argentine political leader?

9. Les Miserables is based on a novel by which author?

10. Which pair recorded the original of the duet I Know Him So Well?

11. Who is the Demon Barber of Fleet Street?

12. I'd Do Anything is a song from which musical?

13. Spamalot is a musical based on which comedy group?

14. What is the name of the musical based on Frankie Valli and the Four Seasons?

15. Who played Tallullah in the 1976 film version of Bugsy Malone?

16. Fiddler on the Roof is set in which country?

17. Matilda The Musical is based on a book by which author?

18. Which Aussie soap star played the title role in the 1991 revival of Joseph and the Amazing Technicolor Dreamcoat?

19. In what year did Les Miserables make its West End debut?
    a) 1975
    b) 1985
    c) 1995

20. Which musical features music by Elton John?
    a) Chess
    b) The Lion King
    c) Mary Poppins

EASY

Answers to Quiz 23: Pot Luck

1. New York
2. Stanley
3. 23rd April
4. Paul O'Grady
5. Coup d'état
6. Omega
7. Wee Willie Winkie
8. Tunbridge Wells
9. Crystal Palace
10. Masterchef
11. Mexico
12. The Lake District
13. Keane
14. Portugal
15. Acidity or alkalinity
16. Cornwall
17. Six
18. Nick Hewer
19. Spin doctor
20. Spain

Quiz 25: Pot Luck

1. Apples and pears is cockney rhyming slang for what?

2. Greenback is slang for which currency?

3. Boy George was the front man for which 80s pop band?

4. Which comedian created the characters Paul and Pauline Calf and Tommy Saxondale?

5. Which country were runners-up in the 2011 Rugby World Cup final?

6. Jeroboam, methusaleh and nebuchadnezzar are sizes of what?

7. The Occupy movement protest took place outside which famous London landmark?

8. Which British actor plays Sheriff Rick Grimes in zombie series The Walking Dead?

9. If it rains on St Swithin's Day what is said to happen for the next 40 days?

10. Which pair were the first to climb Mount Everest?

11. Magwitch and Herbert Pocket are characters in which novel by Charles Dickens?

12. Mrs Hudson is the landlady of which fictional sleuth?

13. It's Not About The Bike is the autobiography of which legendary cyclist?

14. In The Simpsons, what is the first name of Mr Burns's assistant Smithers?

15. The ICC is the governing body of which sport?

16. Who is the host of property restoration show Grand Designs?

17. What is the top award at the dog show Crufts?

18. Brian Lane, Gerry Standing and Jack Halford are characters in which TV drama?

19. Which of the following countries has the euro as its currency?
    a) Denmark
    b) Finland
    c) Sweden

20. What is the name of London's insurance market?
    a) Lloyd's
    b) Smithfield
    c) Billingsgate

EASY

Answers to Quiz 24: Musicals

1. The Sound of Music
2. Willy Russell
3. Chicago
4. TS Eliot
5. Michael Crawford
6. The Producers
7. Tim Rice
8. Eva Peron
9. Victor Hugo
10. Elaine Paige and Barbara Dickson
11. Sweeney Todd
12. Oliver!
13. Monty Python's Flying Circus
14. Jersey Boys
15. Jodie Foster
16. Russia
17. Roald Dahl
18. Jason Donovan
19. 1985
20. The Lion King

Quiz 26: Geography

EASY

1. What is the capital city of Hungary?

2. In which European city would you find the Bridge of Sighs?

3. What is the longest river in Scotland?

4. In meteorology, what line connects points of equal atmospheric pressure?

5. A giant statue of Christ overlooks which South American city?

6. The Spanish Riding School is in which city?

7. Honshu is the largest island of which country?

8. The Suez Canal connects which two seas?

9. Which landlocked country is bordered by France, Germany, Austria, Italy and Liechtenstein?

10. What is the name of the Welsh-speaking part of Argentina?

11. East Pakistan is the former name of which country?

12. The Clifton Suspension Bridge spans which river?

13. What is the most westerly capital city in Europe?

14. The symbol of which English county is a rampant white horse?

15. Which city is further north – Birmingham or Norwich?

16. How many countries make up the United Kingdom?

17. The River Tamar separates which two English counties?

18. The classical Inca site of Macchu Picchu is in which country?

19. What is the capital of the US state of Texas?
    a) Austin
    b) Dallas
    c) Houston

20. What is the longest river in France?
    a) Rhine
    b) Loire
    c) Seine

EASY

Answers to Quiz 25: Pot Luck

1. Stairs
2. US Dollar
3. Culture Club
4. Steve Coogan
5. France
6. Champagne bottles
7. St Paul's Cathedral
8. Andrew Lincoln
9. It will rain
10. Edmund Hilary and Tenzing Norgay
11. Great Expectations
12. Sherlock Holmes
13. Lance Armstrong
14. Waylon
15. Cricket
16. Kevin McCloud
17. Best In Show
18. New Tricks
19. Finland
20. Lloyd's

Quiz 27: Pot Luck

1. Which radio DJ's autobiography was called Memoirs of a Fruitcake?

2. Bill Adama is the captain of which fictional spaceship?

3. What is the name of the beer served in The Simpsons?

4. 'It is a truth universally acknowledged, that a single man in possession of a good fortune, must be in want of a wife' is the opening line of which classic novel?

5. What letter usually represents the vertical axis on a graph?

6. Phasmophobia is the fear of what?

7. Alaska and Hawaii joined the United States of America in which decade?

8. The news agency AFP is based in which country?

9. Who rush in where angels fear to tread?

10. Which country won the 2011 Cricket World Cup?

11. Tony Blair was Prime Minister for how many years?

12. Which district of London is the location of a disused power station and a home for dogs and cats?

13. What character does Robert Pattinson play in the Twilight films?

14. Which US President said, 'Read my lips, no new taxes'?

15. Charles de Gaulle Airport is in which city?

16. In which English county is Stonehenge?

17. In relation to time, what do the initials AM stand for?

18. The imaginary world of Rohan was created by which author?

19. What was the name of the plane Charles Lindbergh flew on the maiden solo flight across the Atlantic?
    a) Spirit of Los Angeles
    b) Spirit of New York
    c) Spirit of St Louis

20. Complete the title of this sci-fi classic: Blake's...?
    a) 7
    b) 8
    c) 9

Answers to Quiz 26: Geography

1. Budapest
2. Venice
3. River Tay
4. Isobar
5. Rio de Janeiro
6. Vienna
7. Japan
8. Red Sea and Mediterranean Sea
9. Switzerland
10. Patagonia
11. Bangladesh
12. River Avon
13. Lisbon
14. Kent
15. Norwich
16. Four
17. Cornwall and Devon
18. Peru
19. Austin
20. Loire

Quiz 28: Britain

1. Which Wiltshire town was granted Royal Patronage in 2011?

2. Devon shares borders with which three counties?

3. What is the name of the bridge over the Thames that links Tate Modern with St Paul's?

4. The seaside resort of Bognor Regis is in which county?

5. Which city has railway stations called Temple Meads and Parkway?

6. What are Clackett Lane, Hilton Park and Newport Pagnell?

7. The Bull Ring is a shopping centre in which city?

8. In which British city will you find St Mungo's Cathedral?

9. The city of Durham lies on which river?

10. 0161 is the dialling code for which city?

11. Cheddar Gorge is in which county?

12. People from which city are nicknamed Jacks?

13. The Tomb of the Unknown Warrior is in which London place of worship?

14. The University Boat Race starts from which bridge on the River Thames?

15. Which racecourse holds the St Leger?

16. What is the name of the Welsh national anthem?

17. The bands Pulp, Arctic Monkeys and ABC are from which city?

EASY

18. John Moores University is in which city?

19. What is the southernmost point of mainland Britain called?
    a) Snake Point
    b) Lizard Point
    c) Newt Point

20. Would you find a Bridge of Sighs in
    a) Oxford
    b) Cambridge
    c) Both

Answers to Quiz 27: Pot Luck

1. Chris Evans
2. Battlestar Galactica
3. Duff
4. Pride and Prejudice by Jane Austen
5. Y
6. Ghosts
7. 1950s
8. France
9. Fools
10. India
11. 10
12. Battersea
13. Edward Cullen
14. George H W Bush
15. Paris
16. Wiltshire
17. Ante Meridiem
18. JRR Tolkien
19. Spirit of St Louis
20. 7

Quiz 29: Pot Luck

EASY

1. What is the only city in Cornwall?

2. The son of which aviator was kidnapped and killed in 1932?

3. Who succeeded Bamber Gascoigne as presenter of University Challenge?

4. On the stock exchange, what do the initials AIM stand for?

5. What nationality is actress Cate Blanchett?

6. Siamese, Ragdoll and Birman are breeds of what domestic animal?

7. Which poet wrote The Rime of the Ancient Mariner?

8. Cool Runnings was a film about a bobsleigh team from which country?

9. How often does a leap year occur?

10. Which black and white mammal is noted for its foul-smelling spray?

11. Who was the ship's captain during the Mutiny on the Bounty?

12. The Saints are a top-flight rugby union team from which Midlands city?

13. In The Lion, The Witch and the Wardrobe, what is the name of the Lion?

14. In text speak, what does MYOB stand for?

15. In what decade was the United Nations founded?

16. What mountain range is nicknamed the Backbone of England?

17. What school did Harry Potter attend?

18. What fruit is traditionally used to make a tarte tatin?

19. Regicide is the killing of what sort of person?
    a) brother
    b) father
    c) king

20. What name is given to a fraction where the numerator is larger than the denominator?
    a) proper fraction
    b) improper fraction
    c) mixed fraction

EASY

Answers to Quiz 28: Britain

1. Royal Wootton Bassett
2. Cornwall, Dorset and Somerset
3. Millennium Bridge
4. West Sussex
5. Bristol
6. Motorway service stations
7. Birmingham
8. Glasgow
9. River Wear
10. Manchester
11. Somerset
12. Swansea
13. Westminster Abbey
14. Putney Bridge
15. Doncaster
16. Land of My Fathers
17. Sheffield
18. Liverpool
19. Lizard Point
20. Both

Quiz 30: Television part 1

1. Ash Morgan, Albert Stroller and Mickey Stone are the main characters in which drama?

2. Which actor, who found fame in The Office, plays Dr Watson in Sherlock?

3. The Dog in the Pond is a pub in which TV soap?

4. David Suchet plays which dapper detective?

5. What was the name of the antiques dealer played by Ian McShane?

6. Who played George Smiley in the TV version of Tinker, Tailor, Soldier, Spy?

7. What series features a Miami Police forensics expert who moonlights as a serial killer?

8. Dr Who was born on which fictional planet?

9. How many single women appear at the start of Take Me Out?

10. Wild At Heart is set in which country?

11. Who played the eponymous detective in the British version of Wallander?

12. In The Simpsons, what is the name of the school caretaker?

13. Craig Phillips was the first winner of which reality TV series?

14. Who did Karen Brady succeed in the boardroom on The Apprentice?

15. What are the first names of detective duo Scott and Bailey?

16. Children's drama Byker Grove was set in which city?

17. Who comes next in this list – Arthur Negus, Hugh Scully, Michael Aspel?

18. Complete the title of the BBC3 show: Don't Tell The...?

19. US comedy Frasier was set in which city?
    a) Boston
    b) San Francisco
    c) Seattle

20. What is the name of the ITV sitcom set in a Spanish holiday resort?
    a) Benidorm
    b) Magaluf
    c) Torremolinos

Answers to Quiz 29: Pot Luck

1. Truro
2. Charles Lindbergh
3. Jeremy Paxman
4. Alternative Investment Market
5. Australian
6. Cat
7. Samuel Taylor Coleridge
8. Jamaica
9. Every 4 years
10. Skunk
11. Captain Bligh
12. Northampton
13. Aslan
14. Mind Your Own Business
15. 1940s
16. The Pennines
17. Hogwarts School of Witchcraft and Wizardry
18. Apple
19. King
20. Improper fraction

Quiz 31: Pot Luck

EASY

1. What is the capital city of Switzerland?

2. On a French train, what do the initials TGV stand for?

3. Wishing I Was Lucky was the debut single by which Scottish group?

4. Sidewalk is the American word for what?

5. On what date is St Patrick's Day celebrated?

6. Standing On The Shoulders of Giants is written on which British coin?

7. How many faces does a cube have?

8. According to the nursery rhyme, which child 'is loving and giving'?

9. What saint's day is celebrated on 30th November?

10. What word represents the letter M in the NATO phonetic alphabet?

11. The Bodleian Library is in which city?

12. In dating, what do the initials WLTM stand for?

13. The Baker Street Irregulars were a group of street urchins that occasionally assisted which fictional detective?

14. Ich liebe dich is I love you in which language?

15. What is the condition tinea pedis more commonly known as?

16. On a graph, what letter usually represents the horizontal axis?

17. Which two of Henry VIII's wives were beheaded?

18. In technology, what is app short for?

19. Hay-on-Wye is famous for what type of shops?
    a) antique shops
    b) book shops
    c) furniture shops

20. Cricketer Ashley Giles was nicknamed the King of where?
    a) Warwick
    b) Spain
    c) England

Answers to Quiz 30: Television part 1

1. Hustle
2. Martin Freeman
3. Hollyoaks
4. Hercule Poirot
5. Lovejoy
6. Alec Guinness
7. Dexter
8. Gallifrey
9. 30
10. South Africa
11. Kenneth Branagh
12. Groundskeeper Willie
13. Big Brother
14. Margaret Mountford
15. Janet and Rachel
16. Newcastle
17. Fiona Bruce (hosts of Antiques Roadshow)
18. Bride
19. Seattle
20. Benidorm

Quiz 32: Law and Order

1. What was the name of the prison in TV comedy Porridge?

2. In which city was Martin Luther King murdered?

3. Which country singer recorded albums in San Quentin and Folsom Prison?

4. What is the highest rank in the Metropolitan Police?

5. What French name is given to a soldier who is employed on civilian police duties?

6. Who was the cricket-loving Texas financier found guilty of running a $7bn Ponzi scheme?

7. Criminal organisation the Camorra is based in which Italian city?

8. Which serial killer lived at 25 Cromwell Street?

9. Who famously disappeared after the family nanny was murdered in 1974?

10. In the Metropolitan police, what rank comes between constable and inspector?

11. One of Britain's most notorious prisoners shares his name with which actor?

12. Which singer was jailed in 2008 for the false imprisonment of a male escort?

13. What criminal organisation loosely translates into English as 'our thing'?

14. Gangster Al Capone was eventually convicted of what crime?

15. The statue of justice outside the Old Bailey has a sword in one hand but what is in the other?

16. 'We always get our man' is the unofficial motto of which crime-fighting organisation?

17. What is the Japanese mafia called?

18. 'Say hello to my friend' is a famous line from which classic gangster film?

19. Ned Kelly was a notorious outlaw in which country?
    a) America
    b) Australia
    c) England

20. Alcatraz Prison is off the coast of which city?
    a) San Diego
    b) San Francisco
    c) Los Angeles

Answers to Quiz 31: Pot Luck

1. Berne
2. Train a Grand Vitesse (High Speed Train)
3. Wet Wet Wet
4. Pavement
5. 17th March
6. £2
7. Six
8. Friday's child
9. St Andrew's
10. Mike
11. Oxford
12. Would Like To Meet
13. Sherlock Holmes
14. German
15. Athlete's foot
16. X
17. Anne Boleyn and Catherine Howard
18. Application
19. Book shops
20. Spain

Quiz 33: Pot Luck

1. The last finisher in a contest is awarded the wooden...?

2. Bob Cratchit was a character in which novel by Charles Dickens?

3. The Crimson Haybailer, Turbo Terrific and the Buzzwagon were vehicles in which cartoon series?

4. Belle Époque describes the era before which conflict?

5. Which fictional detective made her debut in Murder at the Vicarage?

6. What do Americans call a curriculum vitae?

7. In pre-decimal currency, how many shillings were in a guinea?

8. What was the name of Tintin's dog?

9. Which TV personality has a production company called Harpo?

10. According to the proverb, who makes work for idle hands?

11. On a wage slip, what do the initials PAYE stand for?

12. Which American author wrote Breakfast At Tiffany's and In Cold Blood?

13. Fe is the symbol for which element of the Periodic Table?

14. What French phrase is used to describe a road with one end blocked off?

15. What does the S in UNESCO stand for?

16. Ornithology is the study of what type of animals?

17. Who captained England to victory in the 2010/11 Ashes cricket series?

18. What nationality is racing driver Sebastian Vettel?

19. In motorcycling, a minger is another term for what action?
    a) a crash
    b) a u-turn
    c) a wheelie

20. If something is said 'sotto voce' in what manner is it spoken?
    a) very softly
    b) very loudly
    c) very quickly

EASY

Answers to Quiz 32: Law and Order

1. Slade
2. Memphis
3. Johnny Cash
4. Commissioner
5. Gendarme
6. Allen Stanford
7. Naples
8. Fred West
9. Lord Lucan
10. Sergeant
11. Charles Bronson
12. Boy George
13. Cosa Nostra
14. Tax evasion
15. Scales
16. The Royal Canadian Mounted Police
17. Yakuza
18. Scarface
19. Australia
20. San Francisco

Quiz 34: Pop Music part 2

1. Fergie, Will.I.Am and Taboo are members of which band?

2. Whose acceptance speech was controversially cut short at the 2012 Brit Awards ceremony?

3. Complete the title of the number one by X Factor winner Matt Cardle: When We...?

4. Cannonball was a hit for which Irish singer-songwriter?

5. Brothers In Arms is a best-selling album by which group?

6. Kelly Jones is the lead singer with which Welsh group?

7. What was Kylie Minogue's first number one single?

8. What song connects Frankie Goes To Hollywood, Jennifer Rush and Huey Lewis and the News?

9. How many Red Balloons did Nena sing about in her 1984 number one?

10. Kevin Rowland was the lead singer with which group?

11. Which music producer was noted for his Wall of Sound?

12. What sort of Love did Leona Lewis sing about in her 2007 best-seller?

13. Alexandra Burke topped the charts in 2008 with a cover of which Leonard Cohen song?

14. Back To Bedlam was a best-selling album for which former soldier?

15. Mama Do, Boys and Girls and All About Tonight were chart toppers for which female singer?

16. Which female vocalist appeared in the film Austin Powers: Goldmember?

17. Boy In Da Corner is an award-winning album by which rapper?

18. On which day of the week is the UK singles chart announced?

19. What is Stefani Joanne Angelina Germanotta better known as?
    a) Lady Gaga
    b) Madonna
    c) Pink

20. The biggest-selling UK album of all time is the Greatest Hits of which group?
    a) Abba
    b) Spice Girls
    c) Queen

Answers to Quiz 33: Pot Luck

1. Spoon
2. A Christmas Carol
3. The Wacky Races
4. World War One
5. Miss Marple
6. A résumé
7. 21
8. Snowy
9. Oprah Winfrey
10. The Devil
11. Pay As You Earn
12. Truman Capote
13. Iron
14. Cul de sac
15. Scientific
16. Birds
17. Andrew Strauss
18. German
19. Wheelie
20. Very softly

Quiz 35: Pot Luck

1. What name describes a person who doesn't eat meat but does eat fish?

2. Who was elected Russian president in March 2012?

3. In 2012, which Spice Girl designed a special, limited edition Range Rover?

4. Which TV cook is known as The Naked Chef?

5. The Grand Canyon is in which US state?

6. What nationality is teen sensation Justin Bieber?

7. What substance makes blood red?

8. LL Zamenhof is the creator of which international language?

9. Who was elected President of France in May 2012?

10. Which scientist has made cameo appearances in The Simpsons, Red Dwarf and The Big Bang Theory?

11. What are arial, comic sans and garamond?

12. Who was the third wife of Henry VIII?

13. Which novelist's only full-length play was called Beat Generation?

14. According to the proverb, March winds and April showers bring what?

15. Elland Road is the home ground of which football team?

16. Which encyclopaedia ceased publishing a print edition in 2012, 244 years after its first edition was published?

Answers - page 73

EASY

17. Which country was granted Test cricket status in 2000?

18. What French phrase describes someone who incites another?

19. Complete the title of the book and film: We Need To Talk About...?
    a) Darren
    b) Kevin
    c) Lewis

20. Someone working for the enemy within a country at war is said to be a...?
    a) third column
    b) fourth column
    c) fifth column

Answers to Quiz 34: Pop Music part 2

1. The Black Eyed Peas
2. Adele
3. When We Collide
4. Damien Rice
5. Dire Straits
6. Stereophonics
7. I Should Be So Lucky
8. The Power of Love
9. 99
10. Dexys Midnight Runners
11. Phil Spector
12. Bleeding Love
13. Hallelujah
14. James Blunt
15. Pixie Lott
16. Beyonce Knowles
17. Dizzee Rascal
18. Sunday
19. Lady Gaga
20. Queen

Quiz 36: Song Opening Lines

Identify the songs from the following opening lines:

EASY

1. You were working as a waitress in a cocktail bar

2. You never close your eyes any more when I kiss your lips

3. Hello Darkness, my old friend

4. I am an antichrist

5. Why do birds suddenly appear every time you are near?

6. Well, she was just seventeen / You know what I mean?

7. I met her in a club down in old Soho/Where they drink champagne and it tastes just like cherry cola

8. Please allow me to introduce myself, I'm a man of wealth and taste

9. A Wop Bop a Loo Bop a Lop Bam Boom

10. Is this the real life? / Is this just fantasy?

11. Oh baby baby, how was I supposed to know /That something wasn't right here

12. We skipped the light fandango /Turned cartwheels 'cross the floor

13. When the day is dawning / On a Texas Sunday morning

14. Naughty boys in nasty schools / Headmaster's breaking all the rules / Having fun and playing fools / Smashing up the woodwork tools

15. At first I was afraid / I was petrified / Kept thinking I could never live / without you by my side

16. I've never seen you looking so lovely as you did tonight

17. You can dance, you can jive, having the time of your life

18. Street's like a jungle / So call the police / Following the herd / Down to Greece

19. People say I'm the life of the party / Cause I tell a joke or two

20. It's been seven hours and fifteen days / Since you took your love away

EASY

Answers to Quiz 35: Pot Luck

1. Pescatarian
2. Vladimir Putin
3. Victoria Beckham
4. Jamie Oliver
5. Arizona
6. Canadian
7. Haemoglobin
8. Esperanto
9. François Hollande
10. Steven Hawking
11. Typefaces
12. Jane Seymour
13. Jack Kerouac
14. May flowers
15. Leeds United
16. Encyclopaedia Britannica
17. Bangladesh
18. Agent provocateur
19. Kevin
20. Fifth column

Quiz 37: Pot Luck

1. The words angst, kitsch and schmalz derive from which language?

2. What is the name of the official printed transcripts of debates in the Houses of Parliament?

3. What animal represents the star sign Cancer?

4. According to the proverb, many hands make?

5. Which German philosopher said, 'God is dead'?

6. In the nursery rhyme, on what day did Solomon Grundy get married?

7. Which football club is nicknamed The Rams?

8. What is a barista?

9. FRA is the code for which European airport?

10. Which Turner Prize-winning artist has an alter ego called Claire?

11. What is the Hawaiian word for hello and goodbye?

12. When You Wish Upon A Star is a song from which animated Disney film?

13. What was the name of King Arthur's famous sword?

14. Which political leader said paint me 'warts and everything'?

15. Phil Drabble was the long-time presenter of which animal-related TV programme?

16. Earl Grey, Ceylon and Darjeeling are varieties of what type of drink?

17. Where would you find an aglet?

18. What did the F in John F Kennedy stand for?

EASY

19. Which of the following is a shipping forecast area?
    a) Thirties
    b) Forties
    c) Fifties

20. What former clause in the Labour Party constitution called for the 'common ownership of the means of production, distribution and exchange'?
    a) Clause 3
    b) Clause 4
    c) Clause 5

Answers to Quiz 36: Song Opening Lines

1. Don't You Want Me by the Human League
2. You've Lost That Lovin' Feelin' by The Righteous Brothers
3. Sound of Silence by Simon and Garfunkel
4. Anarchy In The UK by The Sex Pistols
5. Close To You by The Carpenters
6. I Saw Her Standing There by The Beatles
7. Lola by The Kinks
8. Sympathy for the Devil by The Rolling Stones
9. Tutti Frutti by Little Richard
10. Bohemian Rhapsody by Queen
11. Baby One More Time by Britney Spears
12. A Whiter Shade of Pale by Procol Harum
13. Amarillo by Tony Christie
14. Baggy Trousers by Madness
15. I Will Survive by Gloria Gaynor
16. The Lady In Red by Chris de Burgh
17. Dancing Queen by Abba
18. Boys and Girls by Blur
19. Tracks of My Tears by Smokey Robinson and the Miracles
20. Nothing Compares 2 U by Sinead O'Connor

Quiz 38: History

1. Who led the Scottish army that beat the English in the Battle of Bannockburn?

2. What scandal forced US President Richard Nixon to resign?

3. Who did Tony Blair succeed as British Prime Minister?

4. Jawaharlal Nehru was the first Prime Minister of which country?

5. The Siege of Sevastopol and the Battle of Balaclava were events in which conflict?

6. In what year did the Gunpowder Plot take place?

7. Who did Barack Obama beat to win the 2008 US Presidential election?

8. Which two countries were involved in the Hundred Years War?

9. Who was the leader of the Free French during World War II?

10. Whose tomb was discovered by Howard Carter and Lord Carnarvon in 1922?

11. The Tet Offensive was an attack during which war?

12. Ceausescu was the Communist leader in which country?

13. Which French monarch was executed in 1793?

14. East Pakistan is the former name of which country?

15. In what year was the Act of Union between England and Scotland signed?

16. Who did The Praetorian Guard protect?

Answers - page 79

EASY

17. What name was given to the period of industrial unrest in late 1978 and early 1979?

18. In what country did the so-called Long March take place?

19. Who makes sure that MPs attend important votes?
a) chains
b) sticks
c) whips

20. In what year did Russia's Bolshevik Revolution happen?
a) 1907
b) 1917
c) 1927

Answers to Quiz 37: Pot Luck

1. German
2. Hansard
3. Crab
4. Light work
5. Friedrich Nietzsche
6. Wednesday
7. Derby County
8. An expert coffee maker
9. Frankfurt
10. Grayson Perry
11. Aloha
12. Pinocchio
13. Excalibur
14. Oliver Cromwell
15. One Man and His Dog
16. Tea
17. At the end of a shoelace
18. Fitzgerald
19. Forties
20. Clause 4

Quiz 39: Pot Luck

1. Entomology is the study of what type of creatures?

2. What is the name of the Prime Minister's country house residence?

3. Which land mammal has the largest brain?

4. Which Welsh female singer recorded the albums Daydream and One Fine Day?

5. In physics, what is the opposite of an insulator?

6. My Heart Will Go On was the main theme song to which film?

7. What is the national flower of England?

8. In the Harry Potter books, what is Professor Dumbledore's first name?

9. What does the prefix Mc or Mac at the beginning of a surname mean?

10. The Alhambra is in which Spanish city?

11. Charles Lynton are the middle names of which former Prime Minister?

12. In law and order, what do the initials CPS stand for?

13. In what year was the first female Prime Minister elected in Britain?

14. Who was elected as Vice President of the United States alongside Barack Obama in 2008?

15. What organisation was the predecessor of the United Nations?

16. People in what occupation are represented by the trade union Equity?

17. Ewood Park is the home ground of which football club?

18. Gouda is a cheese from which country?

19. Which Irish band had 6 UK number one singles between 1996 and 1999?
    a) Boyzone
    b) U2
    c) Westlife

20. What is Charlie's surname in Charlie and the Chocolate Factory?
    a) Bucket
    b) Broom
    c) Mopp

Answers to Quiz 38: History

1. Robert the Bruce
2. Watergate
3. John Major
4. India
5. Crimean War
6. 1605
7. John McCain
8. England and France
9. Charles de Gaulle
10. Tutankhamun's
11. Vietnam War
12. Romania
13. Louis XVI
14. Bangladesh
15. 1707
16. Roman Emperors
17. The Winter of Discontent
18. China
19. Whips
20. 1917

Quiz 40: Animals

1. By what name is the German Shepherd dog also known?

2. What is the most important dog show in Britain called?

3. How many antennae does a wasp have?

4. What name is given to a creature that eats both plants and animals?

5. Arachnophobia is the fear of what type of animals?

6. What sort of creatures would you find in an apiary?

7. What doesn't an invertebrate animal have?

8. The dingo is native to which continent?

9. What animal's name derives from the Ancient Greek for river horse?

10. What is contained in a camel's hump?

11. The nanook is another name for what animal?

12. What is a female tiger known as?

13. Which two creatures appear on the coat of arms of Britain?

14. What name links a character from Friends and a baby kangaroo?

15. What is the only species of deer where the females have antlers?

16. In the film Marley and Me, what sort of animal was Marley?

17. The spots on a ladybird are usually what colour?

EASY

18. What bird is often used to describe people from New Zealand?

19. How many legs does a crab have?
    a) 6
    b) 8
    c) 10

20. Which elephant has bigger ears?
    a) Indian
    b) African

Answers to Quiz 39: Pot Luck

1. Insects
2. Chequers
3. Elephant
4. Katherine Jenkins
5. Conductor
6. Titanic
7. Red rose
8. Albus
9. Son of
10. Granada
11. Tony Blair
12. Crown Prosecution Service
13. 1979
14. Joe Biden
15. The League of Nations
16. Actors
17. Blackburn Rovers
18. The Netherlands
19. Boyzone
20. Bucket

Quiz 41: Pot Luck

EASY

1. Who resigned as manager of the England football team in February 2012?

2. The elephant is the symbol of which US political party?

3. Who created the fictional character Adrian Mole?

4. What is the capital city of Austria?

5. Which company was founded in 1998 by Sergey Brin and Larry Page?

6. Which DJ is the host of the modern-day version of Blockbusters?

7. In The Jungle Book, what sort of animal is Shere Khan?

8. When You Believe was a Christmas number one for which X Factor winner?

9. Which author created the fictional character Tracy Beaker?

10. What shape is the Give Way road sign?

11. Who is the Irish coach on the TV talent show The Voice?

12. How many strings does a cello have?

13. Which actress won an Oscar in 2010 playing a ballet dancer in the film Black Swan?

14. What is the wife of a marquess called?

15. Who was the first wife of Henry VIII?

16. Which award-winning 2009 film was set on the planet Pandora?

17. After leaving The Jam, Paul Weller formed which band?

18. In which city will you find Magdalen Bridge?

19. Osasuna, Levante and Getafe are football teams in which country?
    a) Italy
    b) Portugal
    c) Spain

20. In what field is Karen Millen a notable name?
    a) cooking
    b) fashion design
    c) hairdressing

EASY

Answers to Quiz 40: Animals

1. Alsatian
2. Crufts
3. 2
4. Omnivore
5. Spiders
6. Bees
7. A backbone
8. Australia
9. Hippopotamus
10. Fat
11. Polar Bear
12. Tigress
13. Lion and unicorn
14. Joey
15. Reindeer
16. A dog
17. Black
18. Kiwi
19. 10
20. African

Quiz 42: Fun and Games

1. How many picture cards are there in a standard deck of cards?

2. On a standard dartboard, what number lies between 3 and 7?

3. Who is the victim in Cluedo?

4. In chess, what piece is also known as the rook?

5. What is the game Americans call Tic Tac Toe known as in Britain?

6. In the card game blackjack, players hope to gain what score?

7. Charles Darrow was the creator of which classic board game?

8. How many squares are there on a chess board?

9. Who moves first in a game of chess, black or white?

10. In Scrabble, how many points is the letter Z worth?

11. In what game would you see a flop, turn and river?

12. Which chess piece always stays on the same colour squares?

13. The world championships in which game take place every year in Ashton, Northamptonshire?

14. How many points are there on a backgammon board?

15. In a game of poker, what is the best possible hand?

16. What is the name of the Professor in Cluedo?

EASY

17. The giant El Gordo lottery takes place in which country?

18. Which board game takes its name from the Latin for 'I play'?

19. How many checkers does each player start with in a game of backgammon?
    a) 14
    b) 15
    c) 16

20. In what game would a player used a squidger?
    a) marbles
    b) chess
    c) tiddlywinks

Answers to Quiz 41: Pot Luck

1. Fabio Capello	11. Danny O'Donoghue
2. Republican Party	12. 4
3. Sue Townsend	13. Natalie Portman
4. Vienna	14. Marchioness
5. Google	15. Catherine of Aragon
6. Simon Mayo	16. Avatar
7. Tiger	17. The Style Council
8. Leon Jackson	18. Oxford
9. Jacqueline Wilson	19. Spain
10. Triangular	20. Fashion design

Quiz 43: Pot Luck

1. Which former newspaper editor was loaned a horse for two years by the Metropolitan Police?

2. Which actor provided the voice of Danger Mouse in the animated series of the same name?

3. Lionel Richie was the lead singer with which Motown band?

4. In Fawlty Towers, what city was Manuel from?

5. All My Sons and Death of a Salesman are works by which playwright?

6. Which former Strictly Come Dancing winner joined the judging panel of Britain's Got Talent in 2012?

7. Which animal provided the name for a 2012 hit by Alexandra Burke?

8. Iago is a character in which Shakespeare play?

9. In the TV comedy Gavin and Stacey, what Essex town was Gavin from?

10. What is a palindrome?

11. In the song The Twelve Days of Christmas, there are how many 'lords-a-leaping'?

12. In online dating, what do the initials WTR stand for?

13. What word describes the distance between the centre and the circumference of a circle?

14. Who was the first serving Pope to visit Britain after the reformation?

15. Who is the patron saint of children?

16. The Hawthorns is the home ground of which football club?

17. What website was launched in January 2001 by Jimmy Wales and Larry Sanger?

18. The Inca site of Macchu Picchu is in which country?

19. Which political party was founded in 1981 by the so-called 'Gang of Four'?

20. What creatures did St Patrick supposedly drive from Ireland?

EASY

Answers to Quiz 42: Fun and Games

1. 12
2. 19
3. Dr Black
4. Castle
5. Noughts and crosses
6. 21
7. Monopoly
8. 64
9. White
10. 10
11. Poker
12. Bishop
13. World Conker Championships
14. 24
15. Royal Flush
16. Professor Plum
17. Spain
18. Ludo
19. 15
20. Tiddlywinks

Quiz 44: Nursery Rhymes

1. According to the nursery rhyme, what are little girls made of?

2. Who ran away with the dish in Hey Diddle Diddle?

3. How many men did the Grand Old Duke of York have?

4. Which rhyme contains the line 'with rings on her fingers'?

5. Who kissed the girls and made them cry?

6. Which nursery rhyme character ate curds and whey?

7. What was the queen eating in Sing A Song Of Sixpence?

8. Which pair went up the hill to fetch a pail of water?

9. In Rub A Dub Dub, who was in the tub with the butcher and the candlestick maker?

10. Who killed Cock Robin?

11. Which three people got a bag of wool in Baa, Baa, Black Sheep?

12. Who went up to a pieman and asked to taste his ware?

13. In Oranges and Lemons, which bells say 'You owe me five farthings'?

14. Which doctor stepped in a puddle, right up to his middle?

15. Who cut off the tails of the Three Blind Mice with a carving knife?

16. In Monday's Child, on what day is a child who is 'bonny and blithe and good and gay' born?

17. What did the Old Woman Who Lived In A Shoe do to the children before she put them to bed?

EASY

18. Who found Lucy Locket's lost pocket?

19. What sort of pie did Little Jack Horner eat?
    a) Christmas pie
    b) mince pie
    c) shepherd's pie

20. How many fiddlers did Old King Cole have?
    a) 2
    b) 3
    c) 4

Answers to Quiz 43: Pot Luck

1. Rebekah Brooks
2. David Jason
3. The Commodores
4. Barcelona
5. Arthur Miller
6. Alesha Dixon
7. Elephant
8. Othello
9. Billericay
10. A word that reads the same forwards and backwards
11. Ten
12. Willing To Relocate
13. Radius
14. John Paul II
15. St Nicholas
16. West Bromwich Albion
17. Wikipedia
18. Peru
19. The Social Democratic Party (SDP)
20. Snakes

Quiz 45: Pot Luck

1. What is the plural of the word radius?

2. In slang, how much money is a pony?

3. The Ring Cycle is a collection of operas by which German composer?

4. What German city gives its name to a type of aftershave?

5. How many dots are on a six-sided die?

6. What is the maximum number of characters allowable in a Twitter message?

7. In darts, how much is the outer part of the bullseye worth?

8. What animal is used to describe a falling stock market?

9. Davy Crockett was killed at which famous battle?

10. What is the name of Apu's shop in The Simpsons?

11. The Jorvik Viking Museum is in which English city?

12. What tennis grand slam is hosted at Flushing Meadows?

13. What is the national parliament of Germany called?

14. What actor connects the TV shows The Sweeney, Minder and New Tricks?

15. I Dreamed a Dream is a song from which musical?

16. What is the medical name for the voicebox?

17. Actor Charlie Sheen was axed from which sitcom?

18. Who is the main character in the movie comedy Anchorman?

19. Who played a wicked witch in the 2012 film Mirror, Mirror?
    a) Halle Berry
    b) Julia Roberts
    c) Hilary Swank

20. The Fat Duck restaurant in Bray is run by which famous chef?
    a) Gordon Ramsay
    b) Heston Blumenthal
    c) Michel Roux Jr

EASY

Answers to Quiz 44: Nursery Rhymes

1. Sugar and spice and all things nice
2. The spoon
3. 10,000
4. Banbury Cross
5. Georgie Porgie
6. Little Miss Muffet
7. Bread and honey
8. Jack and Jill
9. Baker
10. The sparrow
11. The master, the dame and the little boy who lives down the lane
12. Simple Simon
13. St Martin's
14. Dr Foster
15. The farmer's wife
16. On the Sabbath
17. She whipped them all soundly
18. Kitty Fisher
19. Christmas
20. 3

Quiz 46: Firsts and Lasts

1. Who was the first footballer to score a hat trick in a World Cup final?

2. Compo, Clegg and Foggy were characters in which long-running TV comedy?

3. What is the first word in the Bible?

4. William Hartnell was the first actor to play which time traveller?

5. Who topped the charts in 1974 with You're The First, The Last, My Everything?

6. What is the last word in the Bible?

7. Which boxer's last fight was a defeat at the hands of Trevor Berbick in December 1981?

8. In 1896, which city hosted the first modern Olympic Games?

9. What piece of music is traditionally played at military funerals?

10. Which group's last album was called Let It Be?

11. In a pub, what announcement is made shortly before closing time?

12. According to the 1977 song by Rod Stewart, The First Cut Is The...?

13. Matthew Webb was the first person to swim which body of water?

14. A clip entitled Me at the Zoo was the first video to appear on which website?

EASY

15. Eugene Cernan was the last person to walk where?

16. Which disgraced former politician wrote the novel First Among Equals?

17. What nationality was the first man to reach the South Pole?

18. Who was the first man to run a mile in under four minutes?

19. According to the Book of Revelation, what is the last Horseman of the Apocalypse?
    a) famine
    b) disease
    c) death

20. Which actor played 007 in the first James Bond film?
    a) Sean Connery
    b) George Lazenby
    c) Roger Moore

Answers to Quiz 45: Pot Luck

1. Radii
2. £25
3. Richard Wagner
4. Cologne
5. 21
6. 140
7. 25
8. Bear
9. The Battle of the Alamo
10. Kwik-E-Mart
11. York
12. US Open
13. Bundestag
14. Dennis Waterman
15. Les Miserables
16. Larynx
17. Two and a Half Men
18. Ron Burgundy
19. Julia Roberts
20. Heston Blumenthal

Quiz 47: Pot Luck

1. Which broadcaster and retailer produced a 2011 report on the future of the British high street?

2. Liverpool paid a record-breaking £35m for which striker in January 2011?

3. I Dreamed A Dream is the title of a musical about which reality TV star?

4. What is the lowest score in darts that cannot be made with a single dart?

5. O'Hare Airport is in which American city?

6. What sporting event is held annually at the Georgia National Club?

7. Do more people live in the northern or southern hemisphere?

8. Which football team won the FA Cup in 2011?

9. What is the largest of the Greek islands?

10. Which city hosted the 1968 Olympic Games?

11. What is a doctor who specialises in heart conditions called?

12. Tim Campbell was the first winner of which reality TV show?

13. North, South, Chatham and Stewart are the main islands of which country?

14. What mythical creature has the body of a lion and the head and wings of an eagle?

15. What is the name of the massive shopping centre located between Sheffield and Rotherham?

Answers - page 97

16. What dance represents the letter T in the in the NATO phonetic alphabet?

17. In what century was William Shakespeare born?

18. Conjunctivitis is a disease affecting what part of the body?

19. Who in 2011 became the coach of the England rugby union team?
    a) Stuart Lancaster
    b) Stuart Derbyshire
    c) Stuart Yorkshire

20. Which of the following was a British Prime Minister?
    a) Lord Adelaide
    b) Lord Melbourne
    c) Lord Brisbane

EASY

Answers to Quiz 46: Firsts and Lasts

1. Sir Geoff Hurst
2. Last of the Summer Wine
3. In
4. Dr Who
5. Barry White
6. Amen
7. Muhammad Ali
8. Athens
9. Last Post
10. The Beatles
11. Last orders
12. Deepest
13. The English Channel
14. YouTube
15. On the Moon
16. Jeffrey Archer
17. Norwegian
18. Sir Roger Bannister
19. Death
20. Sean Connery

Quiz 48: Sport part 2

EASY

1. Ibrox is the home ground of which football club?

2. In which sport would you use an epee or a foil?

3. Which city hosted the 2008 Olympic Games?

4. Which heavyweight boxing champion was known as The Real Deal?

5. The Claret Jug is awarded to the winner of which golf tournament?

6. In snooker, how many points does a player get for potting the brown?

7. Which athlete won four gold medals in the 1936 Olympic Games?

8. Benfica are a football team from which country?

9. How many events are in a heptathlon?

10. Lakeside in Frimley Green is the venue for the World Championships of which sport?

11. Who won the 2011 Men's Singles Championship at Wimbledon?

12. The 2010 Commonwealth Games were hosted in which country?

13. What nationality is record-breaking athlete Haile Gebrselassie?

14. Horse racing classics the 1,000 and 2,000 Guineas are run at which course?

15. In which city will you find a rugby league team called the Rhinos?

16. Which jockey won the BBC Sports Personality of the Year Award in 2010?

17. Ben Ainslie is an Olympic champion in which sport?

18. Which country won the 2010 FIFA World Cup?

19. In ten pin bowling, what name is given to three consecutive strikes?
    a) chicken
    b) turkey
    c) gobbler

20. Which goalkeeper has not appeared on Strictly Come Dancing?
    a) Peter Schmeichel
    b) David Seaman
    c) Peter Shilton

Answers to Quiz 47: Pot Luck

1. Mary Portas
2. Andy Carroll
3. Susan Boyle
4. 23
5. Chicago
6. The US Masters golf tournament
7. Northern
8. Manchester City
9. Crete
10. Mexico City
11. A cardiologist
12. The Apprentice
13. New Zealand
14. Griffin
15. Meadowhall
16. Tango
17. 16th
18. The eye
19. Stuart Lancaster
20. Lord Melbourne

Quiz 49: Pot Luck

EASY

1. A Salopian is someone from which English county?

2. Which author's works include On Chesil Beach, Amsterdam and Enduring Love?

3. Which city hosted the 1976 Summer Olympics?

4. How many of the Queen's grandchildren tied the knot in 2011?

5. What is the name of the church minister in The Simpsons?

6. Which actor plays Alfie Moon in EastEnders?

7. What river flows through the city of Gloucester?

8. Colman's Mustard comes from which English city?

9. Nigel Farage is the leader of which political party?

10. Which city in New Zealand suffered a massive earthquake in February 2011?

11. Dance With Me Tonight was a number one single for which X Factor runner up?

12. Wisden is a book about which sport?

13. Acrophobia is a fear of what?

14. In the Bible, who was the mother of John the Baptist?

15. The samba is a dance which originates from which country?

16. Gangster Al Capone was based in which American city?

17. The Scilly Isles lie off the coast of which English county?

18. Which Northern Irish golfer won the 2011 US Open?

19. What was the name of the best-selling album by Susan Boyle?
    a) The Present
    b) The Gift
    c) The Prize

20. What is the second event of a decathlon?
    a) high jump
    b) long jump
    c) javelin

Answers to Quiz 48: Sport part 2

1. Rangers
2. Fencing
3. Beijing
4. Evander Holyfield
5. The Open Championship
6. 4
7. Jesse Owens
8. Portugal
9. Seven
10. Darts

11. Novak Djokovic
12. India
13. Ethiopian
14. Newmarket
15. Leeds
16. Tony McCoy
17. Sailing
18. Spain
19. Turkey
20. David Seaman

Quiz 50: Transport

1. Which Doctor controversially shut down thousands of miles of Britain's railway network in the 1960s?

2. Belfast City Airport is named after which person?

3. Which fictional detective solved the case of the Murder on the Orient Express?

4. Sir Alec Issigonis designed which car?

5. Which motorway crosses the Pennines to link Liverpool and Hull?

6. Who directed the classic 1951 film Strangers on a Train?

7. What does Vespa mean in Italian?

8. In which city is Schiphol Airport?

9. What is the car manufacturer Fabbrica Italiana Automobili Torino more commonly known as?

10. Which city has railway stations called Piccadilly, Victoria and Oxford Road?

11. Heathrow Airport has how many terminals?

12. In 1934, which steam train was the first to be officially recorded travelling at 100mph?

13. El Al is the flag-carrying airline of which country?

14. In what country is the Škoda motor company based?

15. Who wrote the novel The Railway Children?

16. What is the name of the tilting trains that run on the West Coast Mainline?

EASY

17. Which car manufacturer has produced models called Leon, Toledo and Alhambra?

18. What is the name of the exam taken by London Black Cab drivers?

19. Who designed and built the first motorcycle?
    a) Karl Benz
    b) Gottfried Daimler
    c) Ferdinand Porsche

20. What was the world's fastest steam engine called?
    a) Drake
    b) Mallard
    c) Goose

Answers to Quiz 49: Pot Luck

1. Shropshire
2. Ian McEwan
3. Montreal
4. Two (William and Zara)
5. Reverend Lovejoy
6. Shane Richie
7. Severn
8. Norwich
9. United Kingdom Independence Party
10. Christchurch
11. Olly Murs
12. Cricket
13. Heights
14. Elizabeth
15. Brazil
16. Chicago
17. Cornwall
18. Rory McIlroy
19. The Gift
20. Long jump

Quiz 51: Pot Luck

1. What is a myocardial infarction more commonly known as?

2. Which Asian city hosted the 1988 Olympic Games?

3. What is the only vowel that isn't on the top row of a standard QWERTY keyboard?

4. Which X Factor star topped the charts in 2010 with a cover of the Miley Cyrus song, The Climb?

5. Melbourne is the capital city of which Australian state?

6. On the London Underground map, what colour is the Central Line?

7. Which city will host the 2016 Olympic Games?

8. What animal is affected by the disease myxomatosis?

9. In the nursery rhyme The Queen of Hearts, who stole the tarts?

10. Shakespeare's Romeo and Juliet is set in which Italian city?

11. The Estoril Formula One circuit is in which country?

12. Which South American capital features in the NATO phonetic alphabet?

13. In what decade did Fred Perry last win the Wimbledon men's singles title?

14. JD, Elliot Reid and Christopher Turk are characters in which medical comedy?

15. Which three colours feature on the flag of Belgium?

16. Madras is the former name of which Indian city?

Answers - page 105

17. The Whitsun Weddings is a collection of poems by which British poet?

18. What is the musician Gordon Sumner better known as?

19. Which Canadian city hosted the 2010 Winter Olympics?
    a) Montreal
    b) Quebec
    c) Vancouver

20. In which park is London Zoo located?
    a) Green Park
    b) Hyde Park
    c) Regent's Park

EASY

Answers to Quiz 50: Transport

1. Dr Beeching
2. George Best
3. Hercule Poirot
4. The Mini
5. M62
6. Alfred Hitchcock
7. Wasp
8. Amsterdam
9. Fiat
10. Manchester
11. Five
12. Flying Scotsman
13. Israel
14. Czech Republic
15. Edith Nesbit
16. Pendolino
17. SEAT
18. The Knowledge
19. Gottfried Daimler
20. Mallard

Quiz 52: Movie Taglines

Identify the films from the following taglines:

EASY

1. A long time ago in a galaxy far, far away.

2. He is afraid, he is totally alone, he is 3 million light years from home.

3. What if Peter Pan grew up?

4. Houston, we have a problem.

5. Just when you thought it was safe to go back in the water...

6. Eight legs, two fangs, and an attitude.

7. You'll really believe a man can fly.

8. Love means never having to say you're sorry.

9. The true story of a real fake.

10. One dream. Four Jamaicans. Twenty below zero.

11. For Harry and Lloyd, every day is a no-brainer.

12. There are 3.7 trillion fish in the ocean. They're looking for one.

13. Earth. Take a good look. It could be your last.

14. If Nancy doesn't wake up screaming, she won't wake up at all.

15. The list is life.

16. An undercover cop in a class by himself.

17. He's the only kid ever to get into trouble before he was born.

18. An offer you can't refuse.

19. The classic story of power and the press.

Answers to Quiz 51: Pot Luck

1. Heart attack
2. Seoul
3. A
4. Joe McElderry
5. Victoria
6. Red
7. Rio de Janeiro
8. Rabbit
9. The Knave of Hearts
10. Verona
11. Portugal
12. Lima
13. 1930s
14. Scrubs
15. Black, yellow and red
16. Chennai
17. Philip Larkin
18. Sting
19. Vancouver
20. Regent's Park

Quiz 53: Pot Luck

1. Otalgia is pain afflicting what part of the body?

2. On a standard QWERTY keyboard, what key is directly to the right of D?

3. Bizarre is the name of a showbiz column in which newspaper?

4. What Shakespearean character also represents the letter R in the NATO phonetic alphabet?

5. Wentworth Detention Centre was the setting for which TV soap?

6. Edward Smith was the captain of which ill-fated ship?

7. A dermatologist is a doctor who specialises in treating what part of the body?

8. Which actor has played Brian Clough, Tony Blair and David Frost on film?

9. Which reggae band reached number one in 1988 with Don't Turn Around?

10. Whatever People Say I Am, That's What I'm Not is an album by which Sheffield band?

11. Which veteran American actor played Albert Stroller in TV drama Hustle?

12. What herb is traditionally used in the pie and mash accompaniment liquor?

13. Which country won its third World Cup in 1970?

14. In computing, what does the acronym ROM stand for?

15. Glamis Castle is in which part of the UK?

16. What motorway stretches from Exeter to Birmingham?

17. Which author created TV's Inspector Morse?

18. Martin Luther King delivered his 'I Have a Dream' speech in which city?

19. What did Queen want to do in their 1984 hit?
    a) Break Free
    b) Get Rich
    c) Fall Down

20. What is decompression sickness more commonly known as?
    a) the bends
    b) the twirls
    c) the shakes

Answers to Quiz 52: Movie Taglines

1. Star Wars
2. ET
3. Hook
4. Apollo 13
5. Jaws II
6. Arachnophobia
7. Superman
8. Love Story
9. Catch Me If You Can
10. Cool Runnings
11. Dumb and Dumber
12. Finding Nemo
13. Independence Day
14. A Nightmare on Elm Street
15. Schindler's List
16. Kindergarten Cop
17. Back To The Future
18. The Godfather
19. Citizen Kane

Quiz 54: Food and Drink

1. What is the main ingredient of the Spanish dish paella?

2. What herb is used to make pesto sauce?

3. Pancetta comes from which country?

4. Conchiglie, perciatelli and bucatini are types of what?

5. Kedgeree is usually eaten at what time of day?

6. What is a madeleine?

7. Profiteroles are made using what type of pastry?

8. Bearnaise sauce usually contains which herb?

9. What meat is traditionally eaten by Americans on Thanksgiving day?

10. What is chorizo?

11. Moussaka is a dish from which country?

12. The juice of which fruit is used in Hollandaise sauce?

13. What is the principal ingredient in hummus?

14. Savoy, Late Flat Dutch and Early Jersey Wakefield are varieties of which vegetable?

15. Pecorino cheese is made from the milk of which animal?

16. What shape is fusili pasta?

17. What is the main ingredient of the the Indian dish daal?

18. What spirit is added to make an Irish coffee?

19. Nasi goreng is a dish commonly found in which country?
    a) India
    b) Indonesia
    c) Italy

20. A Wiener Schnitzel is usually made using which meat?
    a) beef
    b) chicken
    c) pork

Answers to Quiz 53: Pot Luck

1. Ear
2. F
3. The Sun
4. Romeo
5. Prisoner Cell Block H
6. Titanic
7. The skin
8. Michael Sheen
9. Aswad
10. Arctic Monkeys
11. Robert Vaughn
12. Parsley
13. Brazil
14. Read Only Memory
15. Scotland
16. M5
17. Colin Dexter
18. Washington DC
19. Break Free
20. The bends

Quiz 55: Pot Luck

EASY

1. Which boy band recorded the album Outta This World?

2. Feta cheese comes from which country?

3. What is the capital city of Vietnam?

4. What spirit is used in a mojito cocktail?

5. Life Thru a Lens was the debut album from which boy band star?

6. Ilex aquifolium is the Latin name of which popular Christmas plant?

7. Who played Sergeant George Carter in The Sweeney and Gerry Standing in New Tricks?

8. An oenophile is a lover of what type of drink?

9. Which left-handed golfer won his first Major at the 2004 Masters?

10. Mr MacGregor, Love & Dr Devon and Only Dad are novels by which TV gardener?

11. Dappy, Tulisa and Fazer are members of which band?

12. According to the proverb, birds of a feather flock…?

13. Which Spanish football club play at the Bernabeu Stadium?

14. What is the boiling point of water in Celsius?

15. Which politician won the 2009 Nobel Peace Prize?

16. Which actress has played Queen Elizabeth I, Queen Elizabeth II, Queen Charlotte as well as providing the voice of the Snow Queen?

17. What is sodium chloride more commonly known as?

18. Prime Minister David Cameron went to which famous school?

19. Someone who gets away with something is said to go
    a) Irish free
    b) Welsh free
    c) Scot free

20. Singer songwriter Paolo Nutini was born in which country?
    a) Australia
    b) Italy
    c) Scotland

Answers to Quiz 54: Food and Drink

1. Rice
2. Basil
3. Italy
4. Pasta
5. Breakfast
6. Sponge cake
7. Choux
8. Tarragon
9. Turkey
10. Spicy sausage
11. Greece
12. Lemon
13. Chickpeas
14. Cabbage
15. Sheep
16. Spiral
17. Lentils
18. Whiskey
19. Indonesia
20. Pork

Quiz 56: Anatomy and Medicine

1. What tendon connects the calf muscles to the heel bone?

2. Halitosis is another name for what?

3. Scurvy is caused by a lack of which vitamin?

4. What is thrombosis?

5. Opthalmology is a branch of medicine relating to which part of the body?

6. What name is given to a pill with no medicinal value that is used in place of a drug?

7. In which part of the body is there a stirrup-shaped bone called stapes?

8. What is the largest artery of the body?

9. What is the coloured part of the eye called?

10. How many lungs does the human body have?

11. Trichology is the branch of science that deals with the study of what part of the body?

12. What is the outside layer of human skin called?

13. What are the smallest blood vessels in the human body?

14. What disease is represented by the initials CFS?

15. What type of headache takes its name from the Greek for 'pain on one side of the head'?

16. What is the medical name for the thighbone?

17. Which British physician was the pioneer of immunisation?

18. What is the trachea also known as?

EASY

19. The biceps and triceps are muscles in which part of the body?
    a) arms
    b) legs
    c) stomach

20. Haematology is the branch of medicine that is concerned with what?
    a) blood
    b) bones
    c) brain

Answers to Quiz 55: Pot Luck

1. JLS
2. Greece
3. Hanoi
4. White rum
5. Robbie Williams
6. Holly
7. Dennis Waterman
8. Wine
9. Phil Mickelson
10. Alan Titchmarsh
11. N-Dubz
12. Together
13. Real Madrid
14. 100C
15. Barack Obama
16. Helen Mirren
17. Salt
18. Eton
19. Scot free
20. Scotland

Quiz 57: Pot Luck

EASY

1. A jester appears on which playing card?

2. What is the home ground of football club Sheffield Wednesday?

3. Who is the host of TV quiz Breakaway?

4. In the song The Twelve Days of Christmas, how many geese were a-laying?

5. What old coin was nicknamed a bob?

6. How is 900 written in Roman numerals?

7. What berries are used to flavour gin?

8. What does the word 'amen' mean?

9. Which actor provided the voice of Shrek?

10. Who went 'Bonkers' with Armand van Helden in 2009?

11. The novel All Quiet On The Western Front was set during which conflict?

12. On a flat-screen TV, what do the initials LCD stand for?

13. Which Shakespearean king said, 'A horse! a horse! my kingdom for a horse!'?

14. Who played Baldrick in Blackadder?

15. The character Sherlock Holmes was created by which author?

16. Classic horse race The Derby is run at which course?

17. What are Furi, Poppet, Luvli, Katsuma, Diavlo, and Zommer?

18. Which TV news programme celebrated its 40th birthday in 2012?

19. David Barbie, Philip Serrell and James Braxton are TV experts on what subject?
    a) antiques
    b) astronomy
    c) food

20. The Social Network was a film centred on which technology company?
    a) Bebo
    b) Facebook
    c) Twitter

EASY

Answers to Quiz 56: Anatomy and Medicine

1. Achilles tendon
2. Bad breath
3. Vitamin C
4. The formation of a blood clot in a blood vessel
5. The eyes
6. Placebo
7. Ear
8. Aorta
9. Iris
10. Two
11. Hair
12. Epidermis
13. Capillaries
14. Chronic Fatigue Syndrome
15. Migraine
16. Femur
17. Dr Edward Jenner
18. Windpipe
19. Arms
20. Blood

Quiz 58: Books

1. To Kill A Mockingbird was the only novel by which author?

2. The Bennet family appear in which novel by Jane Austen?

3. 'These two very old people are the father and mother of Mr Bucket' is the opening line from which children's classic?

4. Roddy Doyle's Barrytown Trilogy is set in which city?

5. Which author created the characters Lisbeth Salander and Mikael Blomkvist?

6. In The Lord of the Rings, what type of creature is Gollum?

7. At My Mother's Knee and The Devil Rides Out are books by which Liverpudlian comedian, presenter and DJ?

8. Gabriel Oak and Bathsheba Everdene are characters in which novel by Thomas Hardy?

9. What day of the week was the title of a 2005 novel by Ian McEwan?

10. In George Orwell's Animal Farm, what sort of animal was Napoleon?

11. Who wrote East of Eden and Travels with Charley?

12. What city in Florida is also the name of a novel by Virginia Woolf?

13. Ernest Hemingway's A Farewell To Arms is set during which conflict?

14. The Kite Runner is mostly set in which country?

15. Hilary Mantell's 2009 novel Wolf Hall is set during the reign of which monarch?

16. Which writer and broadcaster's books include Pies and Prejudice and Adventures on the High Teas?

17. Which actor's 2009 autobiography was called The Time Of My Life?

18. A Study In Scarlet marked the first appearance of which fictional sleuth?

19. Which borough of New York was the title of a novel by Colm Toibin?
    a) Brooklyn
    b) Manhattan
    c) Queens

20. Complete the title of the bestseller by SJ Watson: Before I Go To...?
    a) Bed
    b) America
    c) Sleep

Answers to Quiz 57: Pot Luck

1. The joker
2. Hillsborough
3. Nick Hancock
4. Six
5. Shilling
6. CM
7. Juniper
8. So be it
9. Mike Myers
10. Dizzee Rascal
11. World War One
12. Liquid Crystal Display
13. Richard III
14. Tony Robinson
15. Arthur Conan Doyle
16. Epsom
17. Moshi Monsters
18. Newsround
19. Antiques
20. Facebook

Quiz 59: Pot Luck

1. Lard is the fat of which animal?

2. What was the Indian city of Mumbai formerly known as?

3. In slang, how much money is a monkey?

4. Budapest is the capital city of which country?

5. Who provided the voice of Lightning McQueen in the animated films Cars and Cars 2?

6. Whose only number one hit was When You're In Love With A Beautiful Woman?

7. Somebody being given cross examination is being given what degree?

8. In EastEnders, who killed Archie Mitchell?

9. Which football team play at Goodison Park?

10. Who played Mark Zuckerberg in the award-winning film The Social Network?

11. James Bond actor Pierce Brosnan was born in which country?

12. Who topped the charts in 2011 with What's My Name?

13. 'Water, water, every where, And all the boards did shrink' is a line from which poem?

14. What is the name of the brewery in Coronation Street?

15. Which country's name means Little Venice in Spanish?

16. Penfold was the sidekick of which animated superhero?

17. What is the nickname of Newcastle United football club?

18. What was the first name of the Russian leader Lenin?

19. What would you do with a Glengarry?
    a) drink it
    b) eat it
    c) wear it

20. In what year did Christopher Columbus discover America?
    a) 1392
    b) 1492
    c) 1592

EASY

Answers to Quiz 58: Books

1. Harper Lee
2. Pride and Prejudice
3. Charlie and the Chocolate Factory
4. Dublin
5. Stieg Larsson
6. A hobbit
7. Paul O'Grady
8. Far From The Madding Crowd
9. Saturday
10. Pig
11. John Steinbeck
12. Orlando
13. World War One
14. Afghanistan
15. Henry VIII
16. Stuart Maconie
17. Patrick Swayze
18. Sherlock Holmes
19. Brooklyn
20. Sleep

Quiz 60: Radio Times

1. In radio broadcasting, what do the initials DAB stand for?

2. The Pop Master quiz is a regular feature on whose Radio 2 show?

3. Which former Scottish international footballer presents the breakfast show on Talk Sport?

4. 'I'd sit alone and watch your light, my only friend through teenage nights' is the opening line of what song?

5. What 2009, pirate radio-inspired film had the tagline 'On air. Off shore. Out of control'?

6. Which national radio station broadcasts on 90-93FM?

7. Who is the host of long-running panel show Just A Minute?

8. Who joins Simon Mayo every Friday on 5 Live to review the week's films?

9. What was the former name of Absolute Radio?

10. Peter Donaldson, Charlotte Green and Kathy Clugston do what on Radio 4?

11. Which national station hit the airwaves for the first time on 7 September 1992?

12. One For The Radio was a number 2 hit in 2008 for which band?

13. Eric Robson, Matthew Wilson, Chris Beardshaw and Bob Flowerdew are regulars on which panel show?

14. Local radio station BBC WM is based in which city?

15. Which Tube station is also the name of a game on panel show I'm Sorry I Haven't A Clue?

16. Who is the Scottish broadcaster famous for reading the football scores on BBC Radio 5 Live?

17. Lynn Bowles, Bobbie Pryor and Sally Boazman regularly report on what?

18. Johnny Vaughan, Christian O'Connell, Nick Hancock and Colin Murray have all hosted which 5 Live panel show?

19. Who did Chris Moyles succeed as host of the Radio One Breakfast Show?
    a) Zoe Ball
    b) Sara Cox
    c) Mark and Lard

20. On My Radio was a top ten hit for which Two Tone group?
    a) The Beat
    b) The Selecter
    c) The Specials

Answers to Quiz 59: Pot Luck

1. Pig
2. Bombay
3. £500
4. Hungary
5. Owen Wilson
6. Dr Hook
7. Third
8. Stacey Slater
9. Everton
10. Jesse Eisenberg
11. Ireland
12. Rihanna featuring Drake
13. The Rime of the Ancient Mariner
14. Newton and Ridley
15. Venezuela
16. Danger Mouse
17. The Magpies
18. Vladimir
19. Wear it (it's a type of hat)
20. 1492

Quiz 61: Pot Luck

1. In the Bible, who had sons called Ham, Shem and Japeth?

2. Dry ice is the solid form of which gas?

3. The blood of which animal is usually used to make black pudding?

4. The Fame was a best selling 2010 album by which artist?

5. Prince William and Kate Middleton got engaged while on holiday in which African country?

6. What nationality was the Formula One driver Ayrton Senna?

7. What word represents the letter K in the NATO phonetic alphabet?

8. Which South African golfer is nicknamed The Big Easy?

9. What is the square root of 121?

10. Xenophobia is a fear of what?

11. In snooker, how many points is the pink ball worth?

12. Victoria Pendleton and Rebecca Romero are Olympic champions in which sport?

13. Which country has the international dialing code +353?

14. Who is the only US President to be elected for four terms?

15. James Bourne, Matt Willis and Charlie Simpson were members of which boy band?

16. Henning Wehn is the so-called comedy ambassador for which country?

Answers - page 125

17. Robert Mugabe is the long-time leader of which country?

18. Peter Hernandez is the real name of which Hawaiian-born chart topper?

19. Moor Street, New Street and Snow Hill are railway stations in which city?
    a) Birmingham
    b) Bristol
    c) Manchester

20. What is the first name of fashion designer Versace?
    a) Davina
    b) Donatella
    c) Dominga

Answers to Quiz 60: Radio Times

1. Digital Audio Broadcasting
2. Ken Bruce
3. Alan Brazil
4. Radio GaGa by Queen
5. The Boat That Rocked
6. BBC Radio 3
7. Nicholas Parsons
8. Mark Kermode
9. Virgin Radio
10. Read the news
11. Classic FM
12. McFly
13. Gardeners' Question Time
14. Birmingham
15. Mornington Crescent
16. James Alexander Gordon
17. Travel
18. Fighting Talk
19. Sarah Cox
20. The Selecter

Quiz 62: Television part 2

EASY

1. Who presents TV gameshow The Cube?

2. Which radio DJ hosts his own TV Quiz Night?

3. Liz Bonnin, Jem Stansfield and Dallas Campbell are the presenters of which science programme?

4. The fictional sleuth Jessica Fletcher appears in which programme?

5. Jake, Ben and Karen are children in which TV comedy?

6. Which chef appears on The F Word?

7. Dave Lamb provides sarcastic commentary on which culinary contest?

8. Jason Manford, Jon Richardson, Dave Spikey and Sean Lock have been captains on which comedy panel show?

9. The Mill Health Centre is the setting for which British medical drama?

10. Who was the original host of Have I Got News For You?

11. Which Aussie soap is set in Summer Bay?

12. Which children's programme is set in the fictional Welsh town of Pontypandy?

13. Beckindale was the original setting for which long-running soap?

14. TV scientist Brian Cox played keyboards for which chart-topping group?

15. Which actress played Zoe Reynolds in Spooks, Alex Drake in Ashes to Ashes and Agnes Holland in Upstairs, Downstairs?

E A S Y

16. Endeavour was a prequel to which long-running detective drama?

17. Nick Hancock, Paul Merton and Frank Skinner have all hosted which show, which takes its name from George Orwell's 1984?

18. Holby City is set in which city?

19. In EastEnders, who shot Phil Mitchell?
    a) Lisa Shaw
    b) Kathy Mitchell
    c) Melanie Healy

20. Mock The Week host Dara Ó Briain studied what at university?
    a) English
    b) economics
    c) theoretical physics

Answers to Quiz 61: Pot Luck

1. Noah
2. Carbon dioxide
3. Pig
4. Lady Gaga
5. Kenya
6. Brazilian
7. Kilo
8. Ernie Els
9. 11
10. Foreigners
11. 6
12. Cycling
13. Republic of Ireland
14. Franklin D Roosevelt
15. Busted
16. Germany
17. Zimbabwe
18. Bruno Mars
19. Birmingham
20. Donatella

Quiz 63: Pot Luck

1. What is the capital city of Turkey?

2. Clark Kent is a reporter on which fictional newspaper?

3. Mansion House is the official residence of the holder of which office?

4. What animal is used to describe a falling stock market?

5. What black and white sweets share their name with a Premier League football club?

6. Which French singer was nicknamed the Little Sparrow?

7. Queso is the Spanish word for what type of food?

8. Who played TV detective Spender?

9. In which European country is the volcano Santorini located?

10. Au is the chemical symbol for which metal?

11. Before finding solo success, Beyonce Knowles was in which band?

12. Who played The Joker in the 2008 film Batman The Dark Knight?

13. Bangkok is the capital city of which country?

14. Who was the Egyptian god of the sun?

15. Spud is the colloquial name for which vegetable?

16. Actor Jon Voight is the father of which Hollywood superstar?

17. Who is the patron saint of France?

18. Jenny Frost replaced Kerry Katona in which band?

19. What occupation is a leprechaun said to have?
    a) dressmaker
    b) shoemaker
    c) watchmaker

20. Complete the title of Don Henley's 1984 hit: Boys of
    a) Summer
    b) Autumn
    c) Winter

EASY

Answers to Quiz 62: Television part 2

1. Philip Schofield
2. Chris Moyles
3. Bang Goes The Theory
4. Murder She Wrote
5. Outnumbered
6. Gordon Ramsay
7. Come Dine With Me
8. 8 out of 10 Cats
9. Doctors
10. Angus Deayton
11. Home and Away
12. Fireman Sam
13. Emmerdale
14. D:Ream
15. Keeley Hawes
16. Inspector Morse
17. Room 101
18. Bristol
19. Lisa Shaw
20. Theoretical physics

Quiz 64: Sport part 3

1. Which haulage company sponsors rugby league's Super League?

2. How many holes are in a ten-pin bowling ball?

3. Headingley cricket ground is in which city?

4. What bird describes a two under par score on a golf hole?

5. At what event was Daley Thompson a double Olympic gold medallist?

6. What number sits between 2 and 3 on a standard dart board?

7. Who knocked both England and Wales out of the 2011 Rugby World Cup?

8. Which two countries hosted the World Cup in 2002?

9. Jamie Staff, Jason Kenney and Chris Hoy are Olympic gold medallists in which sport?

10. In rugby league, how many points are awarded for a try?

11. What nickname is shared by both Bristol City and Swindon Town?

12. What colour is the centre portion of an archery target?

13. What nickname links a rugby league team in Brisbane and an NFL team in Denver?

14. Sumo wrestling is the national sport of which country?

15. Who, in 2008, became Britain's first swimming gold medallist since 1988?

16. Upton Park is the home ground of which football club?

17. The Dunhill Cup is a competition in which sport?

18. Which bearded thrower won the BDO World Darts Championship in Frimley Green in 2007, 2010 and 2011?

19. In what year was the first Rugby Union World Cup held?
    a) 1983
    b) 1987
    c) 1991

20. What game is the culmination of the American football season?
    a) Amazing Bowl
    b) Great Bowl
    c) Super Bowl

Answers to Quiz 63: Pot Luck

1. Ankara
2. The Daily Planet
3. Lord Mayor of London
4. Bear
5. Everton mints
6. Edith Piaf
7. Cheese
8. Jimmy Nail
9. Greece
10. Gold
11. Destiny's Child
12. Heath Ledger
13. Thailand
14. Ra
15. Potato
16. Angelina Jolie
17. St Denis
18. Atomic Kitten
19. Shoemaker
20. Summer

Quiz 65: Pot Luck

EASY

1. Which city hosts a Fringe Festival every August?

2. How many cards is a player dealt in a game of Texas Hold'em poker?

3. In which science fiction series will you find Autons, Silurians and Cybermen?

4. Which legendary broadcaster hosted TV gameshow Through The Keyhole?

5. In Internet chat, what do the initials BRB stand for?

6. D is the international vehicle registration code for which country?

7. Archbishop Thomas Becket was killed at which cathedral?

8. Mary Robinson was the first female president of which country?

9. The song Money appeared on which album by Pink Floyd?

10. Who played fearsome magazine editor Miranda Priestly in the 2006 film The Devil Wears Prada?

11. What nationality is the fashion designer Karl Lagerfeld?

12. Bobby Fischer and Garry Kasparov were world champions in which game?

13. What type of animal is a mamba?

14. Denise Lewis won Olympic gold in which event?

15. What was the first adhesive postage stamp?

16. Which brothers are said to have founded the city of Rome?

17. Edgbaston cricket ground is in which city?

18. An even number is a whole number that can be exactly divided by what number?

19. In TV drama Downton Abbey, what is the occupation of Matthew Crawley?
    a) doctor
    b) accountant
    c) lawyer

20. Someone looking to enter into something throws their what into the ring?
    a) hat
    b) scarf
    c) shoe

EASY

Answers to Quiz 64: Sport part 3

1. Eddie Stobart
2. Three
3. Leeds
4. Eagle
5. Decathlon
6. 17
7. France
8. Japan and South Korea
9. Cycling
10. Four
11. The Robins
12. Gold
13. Broncos
14. Japan
15. Rebecca Adlington
16. West Ham United
17. Golf
18. Martin Adams
19. 1987
20. Super Bowl

Quiz 66: Christmas Time

EASY

1. What does the word advent mean?

2. Which Oscar-winning actor starred in The Muppet Christmas Carol?

3. What is traditionally hidden in a Christmas pudding?

4. What kind of Christmas was Bing Crosby hoping for?

5. Which character, created by Dr Seuss, stole Christmas?

6. 'Joyful, all ye nations rise / Join the triumph of the skies' is a line from which Christmas carol?

7. On what date are Christmas trees usually taken down?

8. In Charles Dickens' A Christmas Carol, who was Scrooge's underpaid clerk?

9. Feliz navidad is Merry Christmas in which language?

10. December 26 is the feast day of which saint?

11. Which monarch popularised Christmas trees in Britain?

12. Which Irish singer, responsible for one of the most popular Christmas songs ever, was born on Christmas Day in 1957?

13. Which Christmas character is known in France as le petit renne au nez rouge?

14. What fruit is usually used to make a christingle?

15. The Trafalgar Square Christmas tree is a gift from which country?

16. Which group had consecutive Christmas number ones in 1996, 1997 and 1998?

17. In the song The 12 Days of Christmas, how many maids were a-milking?

18. Tom Smith invented which Christmas dinner favourite?

19. What was the name of the character played by Macaulay Culkin in Home Alone?
    a) Kevin
    b) George
    b) Harry

20. Complete the title of the classic Christmas film: Miracle on...?
    a) 24th Street
    b) 34th Street
    c) 44th Street

EASY

Answers to Quiz 65: Pot Luck

1. Edinburgh
2. Two
3. Dr Who
4. Sir David Frost
5. Be right back
6. Germany
7. Canterbury
8. Republic of Ireland
9. The Dark Side of the Moon
10. Meryl Streep
11. German
12. Chess
13. Snake
14. Heptathlon
15. Penny Black
16. Romulus and Remus
17. Birmingham
18. 2
19. Lawyer
20. Hat

Quiz 67: Pot Luck

1. Who was the first female Chancellor of Germany?

2. Which Coventry-born author created the fictional military policeman Jack Reacher?

3. The wife of which Biblical character was turned into a pillar of salt?

4. What is the name of the river that flows through the centre of Glasgow?

5. What is musician Paul Hewson more commonly known as?

6. Which actor plays the Earl of Grantham in Downton Abbey?

7. The Triceratops dinosaur had three what?

8. Who were runners up in the 2012 Champions League final?

9. Which British musician is sometimes known as The Modfather?

10. Patrick Cox and Jimmy Choo are noted designers of what type?

11. Idi Amin was the leader of which African country?

12. What is the German word for motorway?

13. The Sierra Nevada mountains are in which European country?

14. Clavicle is the medical name for which bone of the body?

15. Osama Bin Laden was killed by American forces in which country?

16. Sir Hallam and Lady Agnes Holland are the central characters in which contemporary TV drama?

EASY

17. What do the initials RADA stand for?

18. What are the first names of TV detectives Lewis and Hathaway?

19. What colour chip describes a good investment?
    a) blue chip
    b) green chip
    c) red chip

20. On what day of the week does the monarch hand out Maundy money?
    a) Tuesday
    b) Wednesday
    c) Thursday

Answers to Quiz 66: Christmas Time

1. The coming
2. Michael Caine
3. A coin
4. A White Christmas
5. The Grinch
6. Hark! The Herald Angels Sing
7. 6th January
8. Bob Cratchit
9. Spanish
10. St Stephen
11. Queen Victoria
12. Shane MacGowan
13. Rudolph the Red Nosed Reindeer
14. Orange
15. Norway
16. The Spice Girls
17. 8
18. The Christmas cracker
19. Kevin
20. 34th Street

Quiz 68: Births, Marriages and Deaths

1. In which American state is Death Valley?

2. Which playwright and former husband of Marilyn Monroe wrote Death of a Salesman?

3. Which Harry Potter star was born on 23 July 1989?

4. Who had a 1959 hit with Peggy Sue Got Married?

5. The Marriage of Figaro is an opera by which composer?

6. In 2011, Nancy Shevell became the third wife of which musician?

7. Which American singer, who famously kissed a girl, was born Kathryn Hudson?

8. The first Spanish golfer to win the Open Championship died in 2011. What was his name?

9. Which water loving comedian married Lara Stone in 2010?

10. Which plasticine pair were the stars of A Matter of Loaf and Death?

11. Which Premier League footballer is married to model Abby Clancy?

12. Who is the only British Prime Minister to have been assassinated?

13. William Shakespeare was born and died on which date?

14. Which Godfather of Soul died on Christmas Day 2006?

15. Politician Paddy Ashdown, actress Joanna Lumley and comedian Spike Milligan were all born in which country?

16. According to the proverb, nothing is certain but death and...?

17. How many times did Elizabeth Taylor marry?

18. Which hip hop star, who died in 1996, was named after a Peruvian revolutionary?

19. What gemstone is associated with a 40th wedding anniversary?
    a) Diamond
    b) Pearl
    c) Ruby

20. Complete the title of a 1996 hit by Underworld: Born...?
    a) Free
    b) Lucky
    c) Slippy

Answers to Quiz 67: Pot Luck

1. Angela Merkel
2. Lee Child
3. Lot
4. River Clyde
5. Bono
6. Hugh Bonneville
7. Horns
8. Bayern Munich
9. Paul Weller
10. Shoes
11. Uganda
12. Autobahn
13. Spain
14. Collar bone
15. Pakistan
16. Upstairs, Downstairs
17. Royal Academy of Dramatic Arts
18. Robbie and James
19. Blue chip
20. Thursday

MEDIUM QUIZZES

Quiz 69: Pot Luck

1. In law and order, what do the initials ACPO stand for?

2. Phnom Penh is the capital city of which Asian country?

3. Someone born on St Valentine's Day would have what star sign?

4. James Earl Ray shot and killed which US Civil Rights leader?

5. Which Italian politician and statesman, born in 1469, wrote The Prince?

6. Cabernet Sauvignon, Muscat and Pinot Noir are varieties of which fruit?

7. Which Tudor ship was raised off the coast of Portsmouth in 1982?

8. Who was sacked as manager of Chelsea in March 2012?

9. What German word describes taking delight in the misfortune of another?

10. Which group were named after a leisure centre in Swindon?

11. What is the male, reproductive part of a flower called?

12. Which comedy group provided the voices for children's TV show Bananaman?

13. In which country is there a cricket ground called The Gabba?

14. What religious organisation produces a newspaper called the War Cry?

15. Who did John Bercow succeed as Speaker of the House of Commons?

16. What was the name of William Shakespeare's wife?

17. Which US president appears on a $5 bill?

18. Luxembourg shares borders with which three countries?

19. Which group has had the most UK number one singles?
    a) The Beatles
    b) Westlife
    c) Take That

20. Albert Pierrepoint was a well known what?
    a) policeman
    b) judge
    c) hangman

MEDIUM

Answers to Quiz 134: Famous Daves

1. Dave Grohl
2. David Essex
3. David Miliband
4. Dave Gorman
5. David Duchovny
6. David Gilmour
7. David Dickinson
8. David Trimble
9. David Arquette
10. Dave Gahan
11. David Guetta
12. David Puttnam
13. Dave Eggers
14. David Koresh
15. David Mamet
16. David Bernstein
17. David Cronenberg
18. David Platt
19. David Gower
20. Dave Ulliott

Quiz 70: Colours part 1

1. Which long-running TV programme was created by Biddy Baxter?

2. What is the longest river in South Africa?

3. What is the name of the clothing label founded by Liam Gallagher?

4. Which jazz record label was founded by Alfred Lion and Max Margulis in 1939?

5. Jake Papageorge and Elwood Delaney are the Christian names of which fictional movie brothers?

6. Which group was formerly known as The Frantic Elevators?

7. What colour is present on the flags of all five members of the UN Security Council?

8. What is singer Alecia Moore better known as?

9. Which 1985 film, starring Whoopi Goldberg and Oprah Winfrey, was nominated for 11 Oscars but won none?

10. What is the puppet TV character Paul Metcalfe better known as?

11. Who was known as the Nine Days' Queen?

12. Eleanor Rigby by The Beatles was a double A side. What was the other song on the record?

13. Guy Secretan, Alan Statham and Kim Alabaster were characters in which medically inspired TV comedy?

14. What is the name of the professional baseball team in Cincinnati?

15. The Tangerines is a nickname of which English football club?

16. Dave Lister, Holly and Arnold J Rimmer were characters in which TV comedy?

17. What colour of jersey does the leader of the Giro d'Italia bike race wear?

18. Who wrote the novel Oranges Are Not The Only Fruit?

19. In heraldry, what colour is sable?
    a) Black
    b) Red
    c) White

20. What is the second full moon of a calendar month more usually known as?
    a) blue moon
    b) grey moon
    c) red moon

Answers to Quiz 69: Pot Luck

1. Association of Chief Police Officers
2. Cambodia
3. Aquarius
4. Martin Luther King
5. Niccolo Machiavelli
6. Grape
7. Mary Rose
8. André Villas-Boas
9. Schadenfreude
10. Oasis
11. Stamen
12. The Goodies
13. Australia
14. Salvation Army
15. Michael Martin
16. Anne Hathaway
17. Abraham Lincoln
18. Germany, France and Belgium
19. The Beatles
20. Hangman

Quiz 71: Pot Luck

1. What was the last album recorded by The Beatles?

2. Which two actors have played DI John Rebus on television?

3. Accra is the capital city of which African country?

4. Which 18th-century Scottish philosopher's major works include A Treatise of Human Nature and Dialogues Concerning Natural Religion?

5. All Kinds of Everything was a Eurovision Song Contest winning entry for which Irish singer?

6. Shakespeare's birthday is on the same day as what other celebration?

7. Providence is the capital of which US state?

8. Scandinavian popsters The Cardigans are from which country?

9. Who was the first US president to visit China?

10. Alec Guinness played eight characters in which Ealing classic?

11. In 1953 Lita Roza became the first British woman to do what?

12. A supercentenarian describes someone who has reached what age?

13. What is the largest of the Great Lakes?

14. What connects Gordon Banks, Sammy Davis Jr, Sir Rex Harrison and Ry Cooder?

15. When in the House of Commons what do MPs call the House of Lords?

16. Kurt Cobain, Jimi Hendrix and Amy Winehouse were how old when they died?

17. J Wellington Wimpy is the best friend of which cartoon character?

18. Who wrote The Wizard of Oz?

19. In which palace was Winston Churchill born?
    a) Blenheim Palace
    b) Buckingham Palace
    c) The Palace of Westminster

20. What river flows through the city of Hereford?
    a) Severn
    b) Trent
    c) Wye

MEDIUM

Answers to Quiz 70: Colours part 1

1. Blackpool
2. The Orange River
3. Pretty Green
4. Blue Note Records
5. The Blues Brothers
6. Simply Red
7. Red
8. Pink
9. The Color Purple
10. Captain Scarlet
11. Lady Jane Grey
12. Yellow Submarine
13. Green Wing
14. Cincinnati Reds
15. Blackpool
16. Red Dwarf
17. Pink
18. Jeanette Winterson
19. Black
20. blue moon

Quiz 72: Family Ties

1. Who is actor Tony Booth's famous son-in-law?

2. Norah Jones is the daughter of which musician?

3. Who is Shirley Maclaine's actor brother?

4. What relation is Queen Elizabeth II to Queen Victoria?

5. Elizabeth and Zacharias were the parents of which Biblical prophet?

6. Who wrote country classic Islands in the Stream?

7. Who is the famous father of film director Duncan Jones?

8. Which father and daughter combo topped the charts in 1967 with Somethin' Stupid?

9. Who is the father of musicians Martha and Rufus Wainwright?

10. What are the first names of the movie-producing Weinstein Brothers?

11. Which brothers directed the 2010 film True Grit?

12. In the comedy Frasier, what is the name of the title character's dad?

13. Aaron was the brother of which Old Testament prophet?

14. Which magician has a daughter called Moxie Crimefighter?

15. Which musical brothers played the Kray twins in the 1990 film about the London mobsters?

16. What are the first names of TV's Chuckle Brothers?

MEDIUM

17. Which musician is the father of twin boys called John Paul and Bowie?

18. Which of the 12 disciples was the brother of John?

19. Richard Griffiths played which uncle in Withnail and I?
    a) Uncle Manny
    b) Uncle Maurice
    c) Uncle Monty

20. Rose Red is the sister of which fairy tale character?
    a) Rapunzel
    b) Snow White
    c) Cinderella

MEDIUM

Answers to Quiz 71: Pot Luck

1. Abbey Road
2. John Hannah and Ken Stott
3. Ghana
4. David Hume
5. Dana
6. St George's Day
7. Rhode Island
8. Sweden
9. Richard Nixon
10. Kind Hearts and Coronets
11. Have a UK number 1 hit
12. 110
13. Superior
14. They've all lost an eye
15. The other place
16. 27
17. Popeye
18. Frank Baum
19. Blenheim Palace
20. Wye

Quiz 73: Pot Luck

1. What is the capital city of Lithuania?

2. Which fishy-sounding group had a hit with Tom Hark in 1980?

3. In December 1963, Idlewild Airport in New York changed its name to what?

4. The so-called Velvet Revolution occurred in which country?

5. What are the four official languages of Switzerland?

6. What was the first video shown on MTV?

7. Kislev, Tevet and Iyyar are months in which calendar?

8. Bob Hope, Cary Grant and Boris Karloff were born in which country?

9. Which British actor played Loki in the hit 2012 film Avengers Assemble?

10. What name is given to a word that is formed by combining two words, for example, the word 'brunch'?

11. In a right angled triangle, what name is given to the side opposite the right angle?

12. Exiled Russian revolutionary leader Leon Trotsky was assassinated in which country?

13. Barack Obama was born in which US state?

14. Which city hosted the final of football's Euro 2012 tournament?

15. What is the technical name for a tightrope walker?

16. What is the name of a French military cap with a circular top and a horizontal peak?

17. Audere est facere is the Latin motto of which football club?

18. Fashion designer Yves St Laurent and author Albert Camus were born in which country?

19. The band Heaven 17 take their name from which novel?
    a) 1984
    b) Catch 22
    c) A Clockwork Orange

20. The Nobel Peace Prize is awarded by a committee from which country?
    a) Denmark
    b) Norway
    c) Sweden

MEDIUM

Answers to Quiz 72: Family Ties

1. Tony Blair
2. Ravi Shankar
3. Warren Beatty
4. Great-great-grand-daughter
5. John the Baptist
6. The Bee Gees
7. David Bowie
8. Frank and Nancy Sinatra
9. Loudon Wainwright III
10. Bob and Harvey
11. Joel and Ethan Coen
12. Martin Crane
13. Moses
14. Penn Jillette
15. Martin and Gary Kemp
16. Barry and Paul
17. Paul Weller
18. James
19. Uncle Monty
20. Snow White

Quiz 74: Silver and Gold

1. Agent Ari Gold is a character in which American TV show?

2. Which superhero's real name is Norrin Radd?

3. Hi Ho Silver by Jim Diamond was the theme tune to which 1980s TV drama?

4. Which British comedian hosted the TV gameshow Goldenballs?

5. The Golden Bear award is given to the best film at which European film festival?

6. Which British singer had a top ten hit in 1975 with Golden Years?

7. Who was the host of European quiz show Going For Gold?

8. What is the atomic number of gold?

9. Who is the chief executive of the Ann Summers chain?

10. Henry Fonda and Katherine Hepburn won Oscars in 1981 for their performances in which film?

11. Which golfer is nicknamed the Golden Bear?

12. Which Canadian rock band topped the UK album charts in 2002 with Silver Side Up?

13. What was the name of the 1990s TV series starring Samantha Morton and Cathy Tyson that was set in Bradford's red light district?

14. Which train gave its name to a 1976 film starring Gene Wilder and Richard Pryor?

15. What is the carassius auratus auratus more commonly known as?

16. Sir Francis Drake circumnavigated the globe sailing on which ship?

17. Who was the first female Prime Minister of Israel?

18. Aravinda de Silva was a notable name in which sport?

19. Which indie band were Going For Gold in 1996?
    a) The Bluetones
    b) Blur
    c) Shed Seven

20. Which US state is nicknamed The Silver State?
    a) North Dakota
    b) Colorado
    c) Nevada

MEDIUM

Answers to Quiz 73: Pot Luck

1. Vilnius
2. The Piranhas
3. John F Kennedy Airport
4. Czechoslovakia
5. French, German, Italian, Romansch
6. Video Killed the Radio Star by Buggles
7. Jewish
8. England
9. Tom Hiddleston
10. Portmanteau
11. Hypotenuse
12. Mexico
13. Hawaii
14. Kiev
15. A funambulist
16. Kepi
17. Tottenham Hotspur
18. Algeria
19. A Clockwork Orange
20. Norway

Quiz 75: Pot Luck

1. What was the name of the police station in TV drama The Bill?

2. Bacon is wrapped around what in the dish Angels on Horseback?

3. In what sport do teams compete for The Vince Lombardi Trophy?

4. The largest malt whisky distillery in the world is in which country?

5. The continent of Asia makes up approximately how much of the earth's surface area?
   a) 20%
   b) 30%
   c) 40%

6. Kemal Ataturk was the founder of which country?

7. Mt Rushmore is located in which American state?

8. Which city will host the 2014 Commonwealth Games?

9. What is the name of the mountain that overlooks Cape Town?

10. Who is the heroine of the video game Tomb Raider?

11. Which English cheese can only be made in the counties of Derbyshire, Leicestershire and Nottinghamshire?

12. Minsk is the capital city of which country?

13. Which comedian hosts TV panel show 8 Out of 10 Cats?

14. Which river forms the boundary between Mexico and Texas?

15. Talk That Talk, Rated R and Loud are albums by which singer?

16. Who captained England to victory in cricket's 2009 Ashes series?

17. Which UK company produced computers called the ZX80, ZX81 and ZX Spectrum?

18. Which science fiction writer created the Scientology movement?

19. Which of the following wasn't a pilgrim from Chaucer's Canterbury Tales?
    a) Baker
    b) Miller
    c) Shipman

20. A gerontocracy is ruled by which section of society?
    a) the young
    b) the old
    c) the insane

MEDIUM

Answers to Quiz 74: Silver and Gold

1. Entourage
2. The Silver Surfer
3. Boon
4. Jasper Carrott
5. Berlin
6. David Bowie
7. Henry Kelly
8. 79
9. Jacqueline Gold
10. On Golden Pond
11. Jack Nicklaus
12. Nickelback
13. Band of Gold
14. Silver Streak
15. Goldfish
16. Golden Hind
17. Golda Meir
18. Cricket
19. Shed Seven
20. Nevada

Quiz 76: Pop Music

1. Who had a number 4 hit in 1996 with The Day We Caught The Train?

2. Guy Garvey is the lead singer with which group?

3. The Defamation of Strickland Banks is an album by which British singer and rapper?

4. What sort of animal provided the title of a 2012 hit single by Alexandra Burke and Erick Morillo?

5. The Piper at the Gates of Dawn was the debut album by which group?

6. Martin Fry is the lead singer with which band?

7. Whose 2011 autobiography was called Le Freak: An Upside Down Story of Family, Disco and Destiny?

8. Which soul singer had a posthumous Christmas number one in 1986?

9. Complete the title of the 2010 number two hit by Willow Smith: Whip My...?

10. Who sang the theme tune to the James Bond film Nobody Does It Better?

11. Which band takes its name from UFOs reported by allied pilots during World War Two?

12. Jealous Guy was the only number one hit for which group?

13. Coal Miner's Daughter was a film biopic about which country singer?

14. What were the duo of Bill Medley and Bobby Hatfield better known as?

15. Caleb, Nathan, Jared and Matthew Followill are members of which group?

16. Which group enjoyed a Fantastic Day in 1982?

17. Steve Van Zandt, who played Silvio in TV drama The Sopranos, was a member of which rocker's backing band?

18. Dreams and Rise were the two number one hit singles by which British female singer?

19. Complete the title of the 2011 hit by Lady Gaga: Born This...?
    a) Year
    c) Day
    c) Way

20. According to a 1985 hit by Pat Benatar Love Is A what?
    a) Battlefield
    b) Journey
    c) Adventure

MEDIUM

Answers to Quiz 75: Pot Luck

1. Sun Hill
2. Oysters
3. American football
4. Japan
5. 30%
6. Turkey
7. South Dakota
8. Glasgow
9. Table Mountain
10. Lara Croft
11. Stilton
12. Belarus
13. Jimmy Carr
14. Rio Grande
15. Rihanna
16. Andrew Strauss
17. Sinclair
18. L Ron Hubbard
19. Baker
20. The old

Quiz 77: Pot Luck

1. Celery, apples, mayonnaise and walnuts are the main ingredients in what type of salad?

2. Cape Horn lies at the tip of which country?

3. Who topped the charts in 2010 with an album called Teenage Dream?

4. Who assassinated American President Abraham Lincoln?

5. What was the name of the 2011 political thriller starring George Clooney, Ryan Gosling and Philip Seymour Hoffman?

6. Monrovia is the capital city of which African country?

7. Which long running animated series is set in the fictional American town of Quahog, Rhode Island?

8. What is the longest river in China?

9. The Carnation Revolution occurred in which European country?

10. Turf Moor is the home ground of which English football club?

11. Which French philosopher coined the phrase 'I think therefore I am'?

12. Which Pole won the 1983 Nobel Peace Prize?

13. Which US President is associated with the phrase 'The buck stops here'?

14. What sort of train were the O'Jays riding in their 1973 top 40 hit?

15. A spaceship called Nostromo appears in which film?

16. Which comedy duo starred in the remake of Randall and Hopkirk (Deceased)?

17. Paradise City was the first UK top ten single for which rock group?

18. In what year did the first modern Olympic Games take place?

19. A man of Kent is born on which side of the River Medway?
    a) east
    b) west

20. What would you do with a Polynesian Lei?
    a) eat it
    b) wear it
    c) smoke it

MEDIUM

Answers to Quiz 76: Pop Music

1. Ocean Colour Scene
2. Elbow
3. Plan B
4. Elephant
5. Pink Floyd
6. ABC
7. Nile Rodgers
8. Jackie Wilson with Reet Petite
9. Whip My Hair
10. Carly Simon
11. Foo Fighters
12. Roxy Music
13. Loretta Lynn
14. The Righteous Brothers
15. Kings of Leon
16. Haircut One Hundred
17. Bruce Springsteen
18. Gabrielle
19. Way
20. Battlefield

Quiz 78: Back to School

1. Princes Philip and Charles both attended which school?

2. What is the name of the school in the film Grease?

3. Which group had a top 5 hit in 2002 with What I Go To School For?

4. Children from which fictional school carried out a Great Train Robbery in a 1969 film?

5. Which Premier League football club is nicknamed the School of Science?

6. Jason Schwartzmann, Bill Murray and Olivia Williams starred in which 1998 school-based comedy drama?

7. Welton Academy is the school in which 1989 film starring Robin Williams?

8. Which American teen drama is set at William McKinley High School?

9. Adele, Jessie J and Amy Winehouse all attended which Croydon school?

10. Which American sitcom was set in Bayside High School?

11. What school did Billy Bunter attend?

12. What is the name of Bart Simpson's teacher at Springfield Elementary?

13. Michael Williams, Daniel Fitzgerald and Priya Kapoor have all been principals at which fictional school?

14. Which hirsute movie hero attended Beacontown High School?

15. Which heavy metal legend, whose real name is Chaim Witz, had a spell as a teacher in New York before finding fame?

16. Which comic book superheroes attend Xavier Institute for Higher Learning?

17. Summerdown Comprehensive and Wattkins School were the locations for which British drama staring Andrew Lincoln?

18. In which American drama will you find The Harbor School?

19. What school did The Inbetweeners attend?
    a) Rudge Park Comprehensive
    b) Adams Park Comprehensive
    c) Gannon Park Comprehensive

20. Which teen comedy was set in Angel Beach High?
    a) American Pie
    b) Porky's
    c) Road Trip

MEDIUM

Answers to Quiz 77: Pot Luck

1. Waldorf
2. Chile
3. Katy Perry
4. John Wilkes Booth
5. The Ides of March
6. Liberia
7. Family Guy
8. The Yangtze River
9. Portugal
10. Burnley
11. Rene Descartes
12. Lech Walesa
13. Harry Truman
14. Love Train
15. Alien
16. Reeves and Mortimer
17. Guns 'n' Roses
18. 1896
19. East
20. Wear it

Quiz 79: Pot Luck

1. The dried meat biltong originates from which country?

2. Which abstract expressionist painted No. 5 1948, which sold for a then record sum of $140m in 2006?

3. Which river is longer, the Nile or the Amazon?

4. The Vuelta is a bike race in which country?

5. Vishnu is one of the three central deities in which religion?

6. Footballer Cristiano Ronaldo was born on which island?

7. In the TV comedy, The Golden Girls lived in which US city?

8. What common illness is also known as varicella?

9. Former prime minister John Major is a fan of which football club?

10. Which two TV news presenters have hosted quiz show Eggheads?

11. Since 2006, which actor has provided the voiceover for TV series Who Do You Think You Are?

12. Pequod was the name of the ship in which classic American novel?

13. Eric McCormack and Debra Messing starred as the title characters in which TV comedy?

14. What is the pH of pure water?

15. The Miami Sound Machine were the backing band for which female singer?

16. The Trooping The Colour parade marks what occasion?

17. Montevideo is the capital city of which country?

18. Which city is further north, London or New York?

19. An epistolary novel is one that is written as a series of what?
    a) letters
    b) drawings
    c) poems

20. Which team has not won football's European Cup?
    a) Aston Villa
    b) Nottingham Forest
    c) Tottenham Hotspur

MEDIUM

Quiz 80: Written Word

1. Who wrote the Booker Prize-winning novel A Sense of an Ending?

2. What was the last book in the Harry Potter series?

3. What was Charles Dickens' unfinished novel?

4. Which American author wrote The Corrections and Freedom?

5. White Teeth was the debut novel by which British author?

6. In Shakespeare's A Midsummer Night's Dream, who was king of the fairies?

7. George Orwell's 1984 is largely set in which city?

8. The Tipping Point, Outliers, Blink and What The Dog Saw are books by which author and journalist?

9. Captain Yossarian is the central character in which 1961 novel?

10. Ian McEwan won the Booker Prize in 1998 with which novel?

11. Harry Hole and Doktor Proktor are characters created by which Scandinavian author?

12. Who wrote the series of six novels known as The Barchester Chronicles?

13. What do the initials JK in JK Rowling stand for?

14. Which East London thoroughfare is also the name of a novel by Monica Ali?

15. What is the last book in the Stieg Larsson's Millennium series?

Answers - page 165

16. What nationality is the author Marian Keyes?

17. Captain Charles Ryder is the main protagonist in which Evelyn Waugh novel?

18. Which British prime minister wrote A History of the English-Speaking Peoples?

19. Salman Rushdie was born in which country?
    a) England
    b) India
    c) Trinidad

20. What was the name of the novel written by Christos Tsiolkas?
    a) The Kick
    b) The Punch
    c) The Slap

MEDIUM

Answers to Quiz 79: Pot Luck

1. South Africa
2. Jackson Pollock
3. The Nile
4. Spain
5. Hinduism
6. Madeira
7. Miami
8. Chickenpox
9. Chelsea
10. Dermot Murnaghan and Jeremy Vine
11. Mark Strong
12. Moby Dick
13. Will and Grace
14. 7
15. Gloria Estefan
16. The Queen's Official Birthday
17. Uruguay
18. London
19. Letters
20. Tottenham Hotspur

Quiz 81: Pot Luck

1. Law and Order star Jamie Bamber played Lee Adama in which sci-fi drama?

2. In international relations, what do the initials OECD represent?

3. What is only mammal that is capable of true flight?

4. Which English-born American revolutionary wrote The Rights of Man and Common Sense?

5. What is the capital city of Haiti?

6. What weapon was used to kill exiled Russian revolutionary Leon Trotsky?

7. Steven Spielberg's two Best Director Oscars were for which films?

8. Who preceded Tony Blair as leader of the Labour Party?

9. What is the name of the character played by David Caruso in CSI: Miami?

10. Which politician said, 'They should never have put me with that woman. ... She was just a sort of bigoted woman who said she used to be Labour'?

11. Which 80s group took their name from a Vulcan priestess from Star Trek?

12. In which American city will you find professional sports teams called the Dolphins and the Heat?

13. What connects Victoria Beckham and Peterborough United FC?

14. Which actor and comedian presents TV gameshow Pointless?

15. Who wrote the play, The Browning Version?

16. What is the first day of Lent?

17. What colour are the stars on the Australian flag?

18. What is the largest employer in Europe?

19. Which one of the Marx Brothers didn't speak?
    a) Groucho
    b) Harpo
    c) Zeppo

20. At the 1972 Oscars, Isaac Hayes won the Best Original Song award for his Theme From...?
    a) Shaft
    b) Superfly
    c) Dynamite?

MEDIUM

Answers to Quiz 80: Written Word

1. Julian Barnes
2. Harry Potter and the Deathly Hallows
3. The Mystery of Edwin Drood
4. Jonathan Franzen
5. Zadie Smith
6. Oberon
7. London
8. Malcolm Gladwell
9. Catch-22
10. Amsterdam
11. Jo Nesbø
12. Anthony Trollope
13. Joanne Kathleen
14. Brick Lane
15. The Girl Who Kicked The Hornets' Nest
16. Irish
17. Brideshead Revisited
18. Winston Churchill
19. India
20. The Slap

Quiz 82: Movies part 1

1. What was the sequel to Gentlemen Prefer Blondes?

2. Max Bialystock and Leo Bloom are the central characters in which film musical?

3. What was the name of the character played by Marilyn Monroe in Some Like It Hot?

4. Colonel Kurtz is a character in which Vietnam war film?

5. 'As far back as I can remember, I always wanted to be a gangster' is the opening line to which classic mafia movie?

6. Who played Jim Morrison in the 1991 film The Doors?

7. What is the surname of Dirty Harry?

8. Jeff Bridges played country singer Bad Blake in which 2009 film?

9. The novel Do Androids Dream of Electric Sheep? was adapted into which sci-fi classic?

10. 2009 film The Blind Side was about which sport?

11. What was the name of the film, set in the world of ballet, that starred Natalie Portman, Mila Kunis and Vincent Cassel?

12. Which Oscar-nominated actor, noted for his Shakespearean roles, directed the 2011 film Thor?

13. What nationality was the title character, played by Sacha Baron Cohen, in 2009 mockumentary Bruno?

14. Who played rugby player Francois Pienaar in the 2009 film Invictus?

15. Which Aussie actor hosted the 2009 Academy Awards?

16. Who directed Le Donk & Scor-zay-zee?

17. Simon Pegg played which character in the 2009 Star Trek remake?

18. The Last King Of Scotland was based on the life of which African ruler?

19. Which actor do Simon Mayo and Mark Kermode say hello to each week on their weekly radio show?
    a) Julian Sands
    b) Danny Dyer
    c) Jason Isaacs

20. Sean Bean is a fan of which football club?
    a) Leeds United
    b) Sheffield United
    c) Sheffield Wednesday

Answers to Quiz 81: Pot Luck

1. Battlestar Galactica
2. Organisation for Economic Co-operation and Development
3. Bat
4. Thomas Paine
5. Port-au-Prince
6. An ice pick
7. Schindler's List and Saving Private Ryan
8. John Smith
9. Horatio Cain
10. Gordon Brown
11. T'Pau
12. Miami
13. They are both nicknamed Posh
14. Alexander Armstrong
15. Terence Rattigan
16. Ash Wednesday
17. White
18. The NHS
19. Harpo
20. Shaft

MEDIUM

Quiz 83: Pot Luck

1. Ljubljana is the capital city of which country?

2. Who played DCI Sam Tyler in Life On Mars?

3. In a deck of cards, what ace is sometimes known as the death card?

4. Which member of David Cameron's cabinet shares his name with a character in Thackeray's Vanity Fair?

5. Which Ancient Greek philosopher wrote Republic?

6. Richard Hughes is the drummer with which band?

7. Which 1980s band took its name from the villain in sci-fi film Barbarella?

8. Who played undercover detective Murphy in BBC drama Murphy's Law?

9. Which English football club play their home games at Deepdale?

10. What was the name of the cow in the children's TV show The Magic Roundabout?

11. Which individual has won the most Oscars?

12. What is a camel with two humps called?

13. Holden Caulfield is the central character in which classic novel?

14. On which item of cutlery would you find a tine?

15. Who played Hilts aka The Cooler King in The Great Escape?

16. In what decade were Bakelite, false eyelashes and the automatic rifle invented?

17. The highest capital city in the world is situated in which country?

18. What is another name for person who makes candles?

19. Hull FC play which sport?
    a) football
    b) rugby league
    c) rugby union

20. What describes two words with an opposite meaning, eg hot and cold?
    a) antonym
    b) homonym
    c) synonym

MEDIUM

Answers to Quiz 82: Movies part 1

1. Gentlemen Marry Brunettes
2. The Producers
3. Sugar Kane
4. Apocalypse Now
5. Goodfellas
6. Val Kilmer
7. Callahan
8. Crazy Heart
9. Blade Runner
10. American Football
11. The Black Swan
12. Kenneth Branagh
13. Austrian
14. Matt Damon
15. Hugh Jackman
16. Shane Meadows
17. Scotty
18. Idi Amin
19. Jason Isaacs
20. Sheffield United

Quiz 84: Politics

1. Former Prime Minister Tony Blair was the MP for which constituency?

2. Which writer and broadcaster was MP for Chester from 1992 to 1997?

3. Who did Michael Howard succeed as leader of the Conservative Party in 2003?

4. What is the minimum age at which a UK citizen can stand for election to the House of Commons?

5. Who did John F Kennedy defeat in the 1960 US Presidential election?

6. Which former Cabinet minister appeared in the 2011 series of Strictly Come Dancing?

7. Which actor played the Prime Minister in the film Love Actually?

8. Who was the only 20th-century politician to hold the offices of Prime Minister, Chancellor, Foreign Secretary and Home Secretary?

9. What is the name of the mayor in The Simpsons?

10. What is the name of the quiz show hosted by former Tory MP Ann Widdecombe?

11. Who did Nicolas Sarkozy succeed as French President?

12. The Althing is the parliament of which country?

13. How often do elections to the European Parliament take place?

14. The UK National Lottery was introduced under which Prime Minister?

15. Who, in 2007, succeeded Gordon Brown as Chancellor of the Exchequer?

16. In 1984 Geraldine Ferraro became the first woman to run for what political office?

17. Which Conservative MP is a best-selling chick-lit author?

18. Who was the Member of Parliament for Hendon from 1959 to 1992?

19. Which of the following Prime Ministers was not born in Scotland?
    a) Gordon Brown
    b) Tony Blair
    c) Alec Douglas-Home

20. How many members sit in the Welsh Assembly?
    a) 50
    b) 60
    c) 70

MEDIUM

Answers to Quiz 83: Pot Luck

1. Slovenia
2. John Simm
3. Ace of Spades
4. George Osborne
5. Plato
6. Keane
7. Duran Duran
8. James Nesbitt
9. Preston North End
10. Ermintrude
11. Walt Disney
12. Bactrian
13. The Catcher in the Rye
14. A fork
15. Steve McQueen
16. 1910s
17. Bolivia (La Paz)
18. Chandler
19. Rugby League
20. Antonym

Quiz 85: Pot Luck

1. Sunny Side Up was a number one album by which Scottish singer?

2. What does the phrase 'Cogito ergo sum' mean in English?

3. What name is given to a person who takes x-rays?

4. Prunes are a dried version of which fruit?

5. Which battle is also known as Custer's Last Stand?

6. 'Call me Ishmael' is the opening line of which classic American novel?

7. Which Indian Prime Minister was murdered by her bodyguards in 1984?

8. According to a song by the Beatles, how many holes are in Blackburn, Lancashire?

9. Baku is the capital city of which country?

10. What thoroughfare did Eddy Grant sing about in 1983?

11. The Old Bailey was built on the site of which prison?

12. What word describes someone involved in a crime but not present when it is committed?

13. Matthew Horne and Joanne Page played the title characters in which TV comedy?

14. What was fictional sleuth Miss Marple's first name?

15. In 1968, Sirhan Sirhan shot and killed which US politician?

16. Lambeth Palace is the official London residence of which religious leader?

17. Springfield is the capital of which US state?

18. Meaning 'way of the Gods', what is the indigenous religion of Japan?

19. Which of the following isn't a Mr Man?
    a) Mr Messy
    b) Mr Magic
    c) Mr Muddle

20. The Japanese drink sake is made by fermenting what?
    a) barley
    b) potato
    c) rice

Answers to Quiz 84: Politics

1. Sedgefield
2. Gyles Brandreth
3. Ian Duncan Smith
4. 18
5. Richard Nixon
6. Edwina Currie
7. Hugh Grant
8. James Callaghan
9. Mayor Joe Quimby
10. Cleverdicks
11. Jacques Chirac
12. Iceland
13. Every five years
14. John Major
15. Alistair Darling
16. US Vice President
17. Louise Mensch (she writes as Louise Bagshawe)
18. Margaret Thatcher
19. Alec Douglas-Home
20. 60

Quiz 86: Art and Architecture

1. The Hermitage Museum is in which city?

2. Which British sculptor died in a fire in her studio in 1975?

3. Which Turner Prize winner used dried elephant dung in his paintings?

4. Diana and Callisto was painted by which Renaissance master?

5. What name is given to a bell tower that isn't attached to a church?

6. What nationality was Rene Magritte?

7. Hans Holbein (the younger) was the court painter to which English monarch?

8. What are the first names of art's Chapman Brothers?

9. The Card Players is a selection of works by which French artist?

10. What was the name of Marcel Duchamp's work that featured a urinal signed R Mutt?

11. Thieves at an Oslo gallery left a note reading 'Thanks for the poor security' after stealing which painting?

12. Which movement was founded by Georges Braque and Pablo Picasso in 1908?

13. The film Exit Through The Gift Shop was directed by which street artist?

14. Vincent Van Gogh is believed to have cut his ear off after a row with which painter?

15. Which Canadian-born architect designed the Guggenheim Museum in Bilbao?

16. Architect John Francis Bentley designed which London place of worship?

17. Which artist was married to Mexican painter Diego Rivera?

18. Fallingwater and Taliesin West were houses designed by which American architect?

19. Andy Brown created a portrait of Queen Elizabeth II using 1,000 what?
    a) dish cloths
    b) postage stamps
    c) tea bags

20. What objects appear in Salvador Dali's painting The Persistence of Memory?
    a) pocket watches
    b) grandfather clocks
    c) bracelets

Answers to Quiz 85: Pot Luck

1. Paolo Nutini
2. I think therefore I am
3. Radiographer
4. Plum
5. The Battle of the Little Bighorn
6. Moby Dick by Herman Melville
7. Indira Gandhi
8. 4000
9. Azerbaijan
10. Electric Avenue
11. Newgate Prison
12. Accessory
13. Gavin and Stacey
14. Jane
15. Bobby Kennedy
16. Archbishop of Canterbury
17. Illinois
18. Shinto
19. Mr Magic
20. Rice

MEDIUM

Quiz 87: Pot Luck

MEDIUM

1. Who created the fictional world of Lilliput?

2. What is an affidavit?

3. What was Madonna's first number 1 UK hit single?

4. What is the official anthem of the Women's Institute?

5. What day, made famous by a film starring Bill Murray, is celebrated annually on 2 February?

6. The Battle of Spion Kop took place in which war?

7. What name links the International Court of Justice, a former leader of the Conservative Party and a character from Babylon Five?

8. Which international newspaper was founded by Mary Baker Eddy?

9. Pyongyang is the capital city of which country?

10. What is the most northerly capital city in the world?

11. The Tivoli Gardens are in which Scandinavian capital?

12. Which composer wrote Clair de Lune?

13. What was the make of the Doc's car in Back to the Future?

14. What is the highest mountain in Africa?

15. Explorer Ferdinand Magellan was from which European country?

16. What was the name of Hitler's enforced unification of Germany and Austria?

17. What is the Israeli parliament called?

18. What happened in 1961 and won't happen again until 6009?

19. What word describes a government run by rich people?
    a) theocracy
    b) plutocracy
    c) meritocracy

20. What ducks quack?
    a) males
    b) females
    c) both

Answers to Quiz 86: Art and Architecture

1. St Petersburg
2. Barbara Hepworth
3. Chris Ofili
4. Titian
5. Campanile
6. Belgian
7. Henry VIII
8. Jake and Dinos
9. Paul Cezanne
10. Fountain
11. The Scream by Munch
12. Cubism
13. Banksy
14. Paul Gauguin
15. Frank Gehry
16. Westminster Cathedral
17. Frida Kahlo
18. Frank Lloyd Wright
19. Tea bags
20. Pocket watches

Quiz 88: Astronomy and Space

1. In which English county is the Jodrell Bank telescope located?

2. Triton is the largest moon of which planet?

3. Around 73% of the sun is made up of which element?

4. John Flamsteed was the first person to hold which post?

5. Which planet was discovered by William Herschel in 1781?

6. The Earth is in what galaxy?

7. What was the name of the rocket that propelled American astronauts to the moon?

8. How many stars make up the constellation The Plough?

9. What unit of length used in astronomy, is approximately equal to 3.261 light years?

10. Which ambient musician recorded the album Apollo: Atmospheres and Soundtracks?

11. How many moons does the planet Venus have?

12. Who topped the charts in 1975 with Space Oddity?

13. What were Salyut, Skylab and Mir?

14. The John F. Kennedy Space Center is in which American state?

15. Io, Europa and Ganymede are moons of which planet?

16. Maat Mons and Gula Mons are volcanoes on which planet?

17. How long does light from the sun take to reach Earth?

18. Which planet is bigger, Earth or Neptune?

Answers - page 181

19. Approximately how many Earths could fit inside the sun?
    a) 13,000
    b) 130,000
    c) 1.3 million

20. How old was John Glenn when he made his final flight into space in 1998?
    a) 57
    b) 67
    c) 77

Answers to Quiz 87: Pot Luck

1. Jonathan Swift
2. A sworn written statement
3. Into The Groove
4. Jerusalem
5. Groundhog Day
6. Boer War
7. Hague
8. Christian Science Monitor
9. North Korea
10. Reykjavik
11. Copenhagen
12. Debussy
13. DeLorean
14. Mt. Kilimanjaro
15. Portugal
16. Anschluss
17. Knesset
18. The year reads the same when written upside down and the right way up
19. Plutocracy
20. Females

Quiz 89: Pot Luck

1. What is the name of the canal that links London and Birmingham?

2. An obstetrician specialises in what branch of medicine?

3. What was Elton John's only number one hit in the 2000s?

4. Which houseplant features in the title of a 1936 novel by George Orwell?

5. Which detective drove a Jaguar Mark 2 with the registration 248 RPA?

6. Eric Twinge is the real name of which animated superhero?

7. Who succeeded Nelson Mandela as South African President?

8. The Adirondack Mountains are in which country?

9. Who was the fourth wife of Henry VIII?

10. Napoleon was exiled to which island after suffering defeat at Waterloo?

11. What is the world's most southerly capital city?

12. Tannadice Park is the home ground of which Scottish football club?

13. Which continent is larger, Australasia or Antarctica?

14. What trophy depicts a knight holding a crusader's sword, standing on a reel of film?

15. The island of Madagascar lies in which ocean?

16. Australian Prime Minister Julia Gillard was born in which country?

Answers - page 183

17. Which French monarch was known as the Sun King?

18. What is a John Dory?

19. Alan Sugar founded which computer company?
    a) Amstrad
    b) Commodore
    c) Sinclair

20. What are people who work on an oil rig called?
    a) roughnecks
    b) rowdies
    c) scrappers

MEDIUM

Answers to Quiz 88: Astronomy and Space

1. Cheshire
2. Neptune
3. Hydrogen
4. Astronomer Royal
5. Uranus
6. Milky Way
7. Saturn V
8. 7
9. Parsec
10. Brian Eno
11. None
12. David Bowie
13. Space stations
14. Florida
15. Jupiter
16. Venus
17. 8m 19s
18. Neptune
19. 1.3 million
20. 77

Quiz 90: Colours part 2

1. The Green, Green Grass was a spin-off from which TV comedy?

2. Which group topped the charts in 2010 with Green Light?

3. What type of fruit is a Pink Lady?

4. There You Go was the debut hit single from which female American singer?

5. What colour is the Teletubby Dipsy?

6. Living In America was the only top ten single for which legendary soul man?

7. What two colours make up the flag of the Vatican?

8. Christopher Trace and Leila Williams were the first presenters of which TV programme?

9. What is the biggest selling 12-inch single of all time?

10. Who directed the multiple Oscar-nominated film The Color Purple?

11. What is the nickname of the New Zealand national football team?

12. Who wrote the children's classic Green Eggs and Ham?

13. Caroline Lucas is the leader of which UK organisation?

14. What colour of jersey is worn by the Best Young Rider in the Tour de France?

15. Who was the king of England from 1689 until 1702?

16. The Orange Revolution was a series of political protests in which European country?

17. What colour is the sleeve of the Wisden Cricketers' Almanack?

18. In which North American city would you find a baseball team called the Blue Jays?

19. What book set out the political philosophies of Colonel Gaddafi?
    a) Blue Book
    b) Green Book
    c) Red Book

20. Yellow Submarine originally appeared on which album by The Beatles?
    a) Rubber Soul
    b) Revolver
    c) Sgt. Pepper's Lonely Hearts Club Band

MEDIUM

Answers to Quiz 89: Pot Luck

1. The Grand Union Canal
2. Childbirth
3. Are You Ready For Love
4. Aspidistra
5. Inspector Morse
6. Bananaman
7. Thabo Mbeki
8. USA
9. Anne of Cleves
10. St Helena
11. Wellington, New Zealand
12. Dundee United
13. Antarctica
14. The Oscar statue
15. Indian Ocean
16. Wales
17. Louis XIV
18. A type of fish
19. Amstrad
20. Roughnecks

Quiz 91: Pot Luck

1. St Piran's flag is the flag of which English county?

2. Nile Rodgers and Bernard Edwards were members of which band?

3. The Zambesi River flows into which ocean?

4. Who did Jacques Chirac succeed as President of France?

5. Lexicographer Susie Dent regularly appears on which TV quiz show?

6. Asuncion is the capital city of which South American country?

7. 'All happy families are alike, but an unhappy family is unhappy after its own fashion' is the opening line of which novel?

8. Trudie Goodwin played which character in long-running police drama The Bill?

9. The Mount of Olives overlooks which city?

10. Which opera takes place on the battleship HMS Indomitable?

11. Who was the original drummer with The Who?

12. What was the maiden name of former British Prime Minister Margaret Thatcher?

13. In 1982, which group enjoyed A Night To Remember?

14. What is the most commonly used consonant in the English language?

15. Who was ordered to leave The X Factor in 2011?

16. Which singer was the first person to get 20 million followers on Twitter?

17. Author and comedian Sandi Toksvig was born in which country?

18. Alexander Lukashenko is the president of which former Soviet republic?

19. How old was Mozart when he died?
    a) 25
    b) 35
    c) 45

20. How many years did Queen Victoria spend on the throne?
    a) 43
    b) 53
    c) 63

MEDIUM

Answers to Quiz 90: Colours part 2

1. Only Fools and Horses
2. Roll Deep
3. Apple
4. Pink
5. Green
6. James Brown
7. Yellow and white
8. Blue Peter
9. Blue Monday by New Order
10. Steven Spielberg
11. All Whites
12. Dr Seuss
13. The Green Party
14. White
15. William of Orange
16. Ukraine
17. Yellow
18. Toronto
19. Green Book
20. Revolver

Quiz 92: Sport part 1

1. Which Scottish football team play at Rugby Park?

2. What is the oldest of the five Classic horse races?

3. The winner of which sporting event is awarded the Venus Rosewater Dish?

4. The first Formula One Grand Prix of the 2012 season was held in which city?

5. Which snooker player was known as The Grinder?

6. How many players are in a volleyball team?

7. What system is used to determine the result of rain-interrupted cricket matches?

8. Which Asian city hosted the 1988 Olympic Games?

9. In what country is the Interlagos motor racing circuit?

10. Which Welshman won the first World Darts Championship?

11. In which American city will you find sporting teams called Ravens and Orioles?

12. In darts, what is the lowest number that cannot be finished with three darts?

13. Which athlete won the first six pole vault World Championships?

14. Which boxer is known as The Executioner?

15. Franklin's Gardens is the home ground of which English rugby union team?

16. Bangers was the nickname of which England cricketer?

Answers - page 189

17. How many pots are needed to make a maximum 147 break in snooker?

18. Who were the first winners of the Cricket World Cup?

19. Which boxer has not appeared on Strictly Come Dancing?
    a) Joe Calzaghe
    b) Lennox Lewis
    c) Audley Harrison

20. Ready is the motto of which Scottish football club?
    a) Celtic
    b) Dundee
    c) Rangers

MEDIUM

Answers to Quiz 91: Pot Luck

1. Cornwall
2. Chic
3. Indian
4. Francois Mitterand
5. Countdown
6. Paraguay
7. Anna Karenina by Leo Tolstoy
8. June Ackland
9. Jerusalem
10. Billy Budd
11. Keith Moon
12. Roberts
13. Shalamar
14. R
15. Frankie Cocozza
16. Lady Gaga
17. Denmark
18. Belarus
19. 35
20. 63

Quiz 93: Pot Luck

1. The phrase 'beyond the pale' originally referred to a region outside which city?

2. Which book's opening line is 'The family of Dashwood has long been settled in Sussex'?

3. Holi is a festival celebrated in which religion?

4. What is the only commonly used English word that ends with the letters -mt?

5. In betting slang, what odds are represented by the phrase Burlington Bertie?

6. What is measured using the SI unit newton?

7. Ulan Bator is the capital of which Asian country?

8. Who was President of the United States from 1929 to 1933?

9. Which Native American chief rode a horse called Blackie?

10. What line is represented by the colour pink on a London Underground map?

11. Sororicide is the murder of which relative?

12. Who succeeded Ted Hughes as Poet Laureate in 1998?

13. In astrology, what are the three air signs?

14. In American Presidential elections, which state has the most Electoral College votes?

15. John Graham Mellor was the real name of which punk musician?

16. Malus domestica is the Latin name for which fruit?

17. The False Mirror is a painting by which surrealist artist?

18. Who wrote the play Cat On A Hot Tin Roof?

19. What is the capital of the US state of Nebraska?
    a) Hull
    b) Lincoln
    c) Grantham

20. Which 7th-century saint established a church and monastery on Lindisfarne?
    a) St Aidan
    b) St Albert
    c) St Arthur

Answers to Quiz 92: Sport part 1

1. Kilmarnock
2. St Leger
3. The Ladies' Singles at Wimbledon
4. Melbourne
5. Cliff Thorburn
6. Six
7. Duckworth Lewis
8. Seoul
9. Brazil
10. Leighton Rees
11. Baltimore
12. 159
13. Sergey Bubka
14. Bernard Hopkins
15. Northampton Saints
16. Marcus Trescothick
17. 36
18. West Indies
19. Lennox Lewis
20. Rangers

Quiz 94: Movies part 2

1. Who won the Best Actor Oscar for his performance as George Valentin in The Artist?

2. Classic western The Magnificent Seven is based on which Japanese film?

3. In which film did Robert De Niro and Al Pacino share a scene for the first time?

4. Who played Stiffler in the American Pie films?

5. Which director's films include Midnight Express, Mississippi Burning and Bugsy Malone?

6. Harrison Ford played a retired police officer called Rick Deckard in which film?

7. 'Five criminals. One line up. No coincidence' was the tagline to which 1995 crime film?

8. Who played Catwoman in the 1992 film Batman Returns?

9. Which former star of children's drama Press Gang made his directorial debut with Wild Bill?

10. Who played sadistic Nazi officer Amon Göth in Schindler's List?

11. Dale Arden, Prince Barin and Prince Vultan are characters in which camp classic?

12. Which film was released first – Grease or Saturday Night Fever?

13. Rita, Sue and Bob Too was set in which Yorkshire city?

14. Who played elf queen Galadriel in the Lord of the Rings trilogy?

15. What was the name of the character played by James Stewart in Christmas classic It's A Wonderful Life?

16. Who won an Oscar for his portrayal of gay rights activist Harvey Milk?

17. What instrument does Marilyn Monroe's character play in Some Like It Hot?

18. Who played Pip in David Lean's classic 1946 version of Great Expectations?

19. Complete the title of this 2012 film: The Pirates! In an Adventure with...?
    a) Footballers
    b) Aliens
    c) Scientists

20. Which actor was originally offered the part of Indiana Jones?
    a) Tom Selleck
    b) Bruce Willis
    c) Michael Douglas

MEDIUM

Answers to Quiz 93: Pot Luck

1. Dublin
2. Sense and Sensibility by Jane Austen
3. Hinduism
4. Dreamt
5. 100/30
6. Force
7. Mongolia
8. Herbert Hoover
9. Sitting Bull
10. Hammersmith and City
11. Sister
12. Andrew Motion
13. Libra, Aquarius, Gemini
14. California
15. Joe Strummer
16. Apple
17. Rene Magritte
18. Tennessee Williams
19. Lincoln
20. St Aidan

Quiz 95: Pot Luck

1. What two animals are on the coat of arms of Australia?

2. The inhabitants of which Derbyshire town take part in an annual Shrovetide football match where the goals are three miles apart?

3. Robin Goodfellow is the other name of which Shakespearean character?

4. Who succeeded Henry VIII on the English throne?

5. What do the initials A.A. stand for in the name of Winnie The Pooh author A.A. Milne?

6. Who married Princess Margaret in 1960?

7. Hong Kong returned to Chinese rule in what year?

8. Rower Sir Steve Redgrave won his first Olympic gold at which games?

9. What are the gases helium, neon, argon, krypton, xenon and radon collectively known as?

10. What was Elvis Presley's first UK number one hit single?

11. Which actress played Felicity 'Flick' Scully in Aussie soap Neighbours?

12. Who was the first cricketer to score 100 international centuries?

13. Rickets is caused by a deficiency of which vitamin?

14. What did Norman Wisdom, Rolf Harris and Gary Glitter all do on radio programme Desert Island Discs?

15. The Sepang International motor racing circuit is in which country?

16. What is the most visited museum in the world?

17. In Glasgow, what is known as The Clockwork Orange?

18. Who was the first Scot to win the World Professional Darts championship?

19. What is the capital of the US state of Delaware?
    a) Deal
    b) Dover
    c) Folkestone

20. What does it mean if an Amish man has a beard?
    a) he is married
    b) he is single
    c) he is employed

MEDIUM

Answers to Quiz 94: Movies part 2

1. Jean Dujardin
2. Seven Samurai
3. Heat
4. Seann William Scott
5. Alan Parker
6. Blade Runner
7. The Usual Suspects
8. Michelle Pfeiffer
9. Dexter Fletcher
10. Ralph Fiennes
11. Flash Gordon
12. Saturday Night Fever
13. Bradford
14. Cate Blanchett
15. George Bailey
16. Sean Penn
17. Ukulele
18. John Mills
19. Scientists
20. Tom Selleck

Quiz 96: Musicals

1. Galileo and Scaramouche are characters in which musical?

2. Members of which band wrote the music to the musical Chess?

3. Michael Ball's number two hit Love Changes Everything was from which musical?

4. The controversial revue Oh! Calcutta! was created by which drama critic?

5. Man of La Mancha is based on which classic novel?

6. Complete the title of the West End show: Dreamboats and...?

7. Oh, What a Beautiful Mornin' is the opening song from which musical?

8. Who wrote the music and lyrics to Kiss Me, Kate, Anything Goes and Gay Divorce?

9. Nathan Detroit and Sky Masterson are characters from which musical?

10. Princeton, Kate Monster and Trekkie are characters in which musical?

11. Which musical is about a florist who raises a plant that feeds on human blood?

12. A green-skinned girl called Elphaba Thropp is the central character of which musical?

13. There Is Nothing Like a Dame is a song from which musical?

14. Complete the title: A Funny Thing Happened on the Way to the...?

15. Edna and Tracy Turnblad are the central characters in which musical?

16. Which 1980s pop star wrote the music for Taboo?

17. Tonight's The Night was a musical based on which singer?

18. What is the name of the nightclub in Cabaret?

19. Who wrote Porgy and Bess?
    a) George and Ira Gershwin
    b) Stephen Sondheim
    c) Rodgers and Hammerstein

20. Day By Day, Turn Back, O Man and By My Side are songs from which musical?
    a) Godspell
    b) Jesus Christ Superstar
    c) Joseph and The Amazing Technicolour Dreamcoat

MEDIUM

Answers to Quiz 95: Pot Luck

1. Kangaroo and emu
2. Ashbourne
3. Puck
4. Edward VI
5. Alan Alexander
6. Anthony Armstrong-Jones (Lord Snowdon)
7. 1997
8. Los Angeles 1984
9. The noble gases
10. All Shook Up
11. Holly Valance
12. Sachin Tendulkar
13. Vitamin D
14. They chose their own songs
15. Malaysia
16. The Louvre in Paris
17. The underground transport system
18. Jocky Wilson
19. Dover
20. He is married

Quiz 97: Pot Luck

MEDIUM

1. What item of clothing is named after James Thomas Brudenell, who wore said garment in the Crimean War?

2. Who was the original host of TV quiz show A Question of Sport?

3. Poet Philip Larkin was a librarian at which university?

4. Which director's films include Nashville, The Player and Gosford Park?

5. What size of bed measures 5ft by 6ft 3in?

6. Which comedian's memoir was called My Booky Wook?

7. What was the pen name of Belgian writer George Remi?

8. What is the middle name of former Prime Minister Margaret Thatcher?

9. In what year did Napoleon Bonaparte die?

10. Epidemic parotitis is the medical name for which disease?

11. What name provided the title for Amy Winehouse's 2003 debut album?

12. The award winning novel Midnight's Children was by which author?

13. Which Spanish artist painted Saint Martin and the Beggar?

14. 'What's in a name? That which we call a rose. By any other name would smell as sweet' is a line from which Shakespeare play?

15. Which American general accepted the Japanese surrender to end World War II?

16. Head was a 1968 film starring which pop group?

17. What is the longest river in North America?

18. Ribes nigrum is the Latin name for which fruit?

19. Which city is closest to London?
    a) Bangkok
    b) Beijing
    c) Los Angeles

20. What is the national theatre of Ireland called?
    a) Abbey Theatre
    b) Coliseum Theatre
    c) Wilde Theatre

MEDIUM

Answers to Quiz 96: Musicals

1. We Will Rock You
2. Abba
3. Aspects of Love
4. Kenneth Tynan
5. Don Quixote
6. Petticoats
7. Oklahoma
8. Cole Porter
9. Guys and Dolls
10. Avenue Q
11. Little Shop of Horrors
12. Wicked
13. South Pacific
14. Forum
15. Hairspray
16. Boy George
17. Rod Stewart
18. The Kit Kat Klub
19. George and Ira Gershwin
20. Godspell

Quiz 98: Geography

1. The ancient region of Babylonia is in which modern-day country?

2. Dakar is the capital city of which country?

3. Wallonia is a region of which European country?

4. What is the largest of New York's five boroughs by area?

5. Abyssinia is the former name of which country?

6. In which city would you find Ponte Vecchio?

7. The name of which South American city translates into English as good winds?

8. Mount Logan is the highest mountain in which Commonwealth country?

9. What is the county town of Rutland?

10. Dogger Bank is a large sandbank in which body of water?

11. What is the smallest city in Britain by population?

12. Skye, Mull, Jura and Islay are part of which island group?

13. The town of Timbuktu is in which African country?

14. What is the only city in the county of Somerset?

15 Lake Disappointment and Lake Surprise are in which country?

16. Dutch is the official language in which South American country?

17. Malin Head, the most northerly point on the island of Ireland, is in which county?

18. The Spanish Steps are in which city?

19. Trenton is the capital of which US state?
    a) New Hampshire
    b) New Jersey
    c) New York

20. Which Nordic capital is furthest north?
    a) Helsinki
    b) Oslo
    c) Stockholm

Answers to Quiz 97: Pot Luck

1. Cardigan (he was 7th Earl of Cardigan)
2. David Vine
3. Hull
4. Robert Altman
5. King size
6. Russell Brand
7. Hergé
8. Hilda
9. 1821
10. Mumps
11. Frank
12. Salman Rushdie
13. El Greco
14. Romeo and Juliet
15. General MacArthur
16. The Monkees
17. Missouri
18. Blackberry
19. Beijing
20. Abbey Theatre

MEDIUM

Quiz 99: Pot Luck

1. In the detective series, what was the name of Lt Columbo's dog?

2. Tashkent is the capital city of which former Soviet Republic?

3. In 1948, who became Israel's first prime minister?

4. What was The Beatles' first UK number one single?

5. An airport in which European city has the code CDG?

6. The Scottish city of Perth sits on which river?

7. What nationality were the painters Pieter Breughel, Paul Delvaux and Peter Paul Rubens?

8. Which American novelist's works include Infinite Jest and The Pale King?

9. Gynophobia is the fear of what?

10. Which soft drink was invented by American pharmacist Caleb Bradham?

11. 'You can't handle the truth' is a line from which 1992 film starring Tom Cruise and Jack Nicholson?

12. Which dinosaur's name means three-horned face?

13. What word describes words that have the same pronunciation and spelling but different meanings?

14. In the New Testament, what book comes after the four gospels?

15. What year is represented by the Roman numerals MCMLXVI?

Answers - page 203

16. The koruna is the currency of which European country?

17. Who sang the theme tune to the Bond film Tomorrow Never Dies?

18. What does the term presto mean in relation to musical tempo?

19. Coca Cola comes from which US city?
    a) Atlanta
    b) Miami
    c) Nashville

20. What nationality is the crime author Jo Nesbo?
    a) Danish
    b) Norwegian
    c) Swedish

MEDIUM

Answers to Quiz 98: Geography

1. Iraq
2. Senegal
3. Belgium
4. Queens
5. Ethiopia
6. Florence
7. Buenos Aires
8. Canada
9. Oakham
10. North Sea
11. St David's
12. Inner Hebrides
13. Mali
14. Wells
15. Australia
16. Suriname
17. Donegal
18. Rome
19. New Jersey
20. Helsinki

Quiz 100: Britain

1. Cumbria shares borders with which four English counties?

2. Which Yorkshire town has railway stations called Kirkgate and Westgate?

3. Watford Gap is in which English county?

4. What is the most northerly National Park in Britain?

5. In which city would you find the Whitworth Art Gallery?

6. Queen Margaret University is based in which city?

7. Which three towns make up Torbay?

8. What are Sizewell, Bradwell, Dungeness, Hinckley Point and Torness?

9. The motor racing circuit Brands Hatch is in which county?

10. Which city had 'so much to answer for' according to a song by The Smiths?

11. The Titanic set sail from which British port?

12. Football manager Brian Clough, comedian Bob Mortimer and former EastEnder Wendy Richard were all born in which town?

13. Which town appears as Sandbourne in the novels of Thomas Hardy?

14. Coombe Hill is the highest point in which range of hills?

15. The second ranking clergyman in the Church of England is the Bishop of which city?

16. In which city would you find shopping centres called Galleries, Broadmead and Cribbs Causeway?

17. Which poet is known as the Bard of Ayrshire?

18. Author DH Lawrence was from which Midlands city?

19. The tomb of King John is in which English cathedral?
    a) Hereford
    b) Salisbury
    c) Worcester

20. What islands are the most northerly part of the British Isles?
    a) Orkney
    b) Outer Hebrides
    c) Shetland

MEDIUM

Answers to Quiz 99: Pot Luck

1. Dog
2. Uzbekistan
3. David Ben-Gurion
4. From Me To You
5. Paris
6. Tay
7. Belgian
8. David Foster Wallace
9. Women
10. Pepsi Cola
11. A Few Good Men
12. Triceratops
13. Homonym
14. Acts of the Apostles
15. 1966
16. Czech Republic
17. Sheryl Crow
18. Very fast
19. Atlanta
20. Norwegian

Quiz 101: Pot Luck

1. TV drama The Wire was set in which US city?

2. Napoleon Bonaparte was born on which island?

3. The emperor of which country sits on the Chrysanthemum Throne?

4. The Fiat car company was founded in which Italian city?

5. What is the skin condition milaria rubra more commonly known as?

6. Which former Friend went on to star in TV drama Cougar Town?

7. The Communards topped the charts with Don't Leave Me This Way, but who recorded the original?

8. Muscat is the capital city of which country?

9. Jonathan Ive is a leading designer at which technology company?

10. In astrology, what are the three fire signs?

11. On which London Underground line will you find the stations Tooting Broadway, Oval and Archway?

12. The Simon Bolivar Youth Orchestra is from which country?

13. Which English composer wrote the opera Peter Grimes?

14. Which two Italian cities appear in the titles of plays by Shakespeare?

15. Who did Nick Clegg succeed as leader of the Liberal Democrat Party?

16. Which film director, using a specially adapted submarine, made a solo trip to the deepest point in the ocean, the Mariana Trench?

17. Who played Hannah Montana in the TV series of the same name?

18. At the 2010 VMAs Lady Gaga wore a dress made out of what?

19. Carry On star Sid James was born in which country?
    a) Australia
    b) New Zealand
    c) South Africa

20. Goliath, Bombardier and Asparagus are examples of what type of creature?
    a) beetle
    b) spider
    c) snake

MEDIUM

Answers to Quiz 100: Britain

1. Northumberland, Durham, North Yorkshire and Lancashire
2. Wakefield
3. Northamptonshire
4. The Cairngorms
5. Manchester
6. Edinburgh
7. Torquay, Paignton and Brixham
8. Nuclear power stations
9. Kent
10. Manchester
11. Southampton
12. Middlesbrough
13. Bournemouth
14. Chilterns
15. York
16. Bristol
17. Robert Burns
18. Nottingham
19. Worcester
20. Shetland

Quiz 102: Television part 1

1. Which actor plays Don Draper in Mad Men?

2. Which medical drama is set at Princeton-Plainsboro Teaching Hospital?

3. Wisteria Lane is the central location of which American drama?

4. In which children's programme will you find characters called Makka Pakka and The Tombliboos?

5. Who writes and stars in TV comedy Curb Your Enthusiasm?

6. Penelope Wilton plays which character in Downton Abbey?

7. Which British drama features a group of youngsters doing community service who get supernatural powers after a freak electrical storm?

8. What is the name of Brian's long-suffering wife in New Tricks?

9. Sarah Lund is the central character in which crime drama?

10. Philip Schofield presented which Saturday morning TV show from 1987 until 1993?

11. Which footballer is mentioned in the closing theme tune to Only Fools and Horses?

12. In sitcom The Good Life, what was Jerry and Margo's surname?

13. Which DJ was the winner of the first series of I'm A Celebrity Get Me Out Of Here?

14. Simon Gregson plays which soap character?

15. Way Down in the Hole is the theme tune to which American drama?

16. Who replaced Carol Vorderman on Countdown?

17. Which drama centred around the Mermaid Boatyard?

18. Scott Bakula played a time-travelling physicist in which drama?

19. What was the name of the pork store in The Sopranos?
    a) Altobelli's
    b) Baresi's
    c) Satriale's

20. Which presenter and DJ hosts a Beer and Pizza club?
    a) David Baddiel
    b) Frank Skinner
    c) Richard Bacon

MEDIUM

Answers to Quiz 101: Pot Luck

1. Baltimore
2. Corsica
3. Japan
4. Turin
5. Prickly heat
6. Courtney Cox
7. Harold Melvin and the Blue Notes
8. Oman
9. Apple
10. Aries, Leo, Sagittarius
11. Northern
12. Venezuela
13. Benjamin Britten
14. Venice and Verona
15. Menzies Campbell
16. James Cameron
17. Miley Cyrus
18. Meat
19. South Africa
20. Beetle

Quiz 103: Pot Luck

1. Maputo is the capital city of which African country?

2. 'The past is a foreign country, they do things differently there' is the opening line of which novel?

3. JM Coetzee and Peter Carey are the only double winners of which award?

4. 'Rosebud' is the opening line of which film classic?

5. Who, in 2003, became the artistic director of London's Old Vic theatre?

6. Tony Stark is the alter ego of which superhero?

7. Which philosopher said, 'There are no facts, only interpretations'?

8. Chinese musician Lang Lang is an internationally renowned player of which instrument?

9. Marjorie Allingham created which fictional sleuth?

10. On what day of the week does the budget speech take place?

11. The Kids Are Alright is a documentary about which band?

12. Vietnam was a former colony of which European country?

13. Who starred in and directed the films Super Size Me and The Greatest Movie Ever Sold?

14. Which Italian directed the 1960 classic La Dolce Vita?

15. In astrology what are the three water signs?

16. Reality TV star Pete Burns was the lead singer with which chart-topping group?

17. What is the only British place name mentioned in the title of a play by Shakespeare?

18. Lady Day was the nickname of which jazz singer?

19. What is the name of the largest sized beer barrel?
    a) tan
    b) tin
    c) tun

20. Who hangs off a clock face in the 1923 film Safety Last?
    a) Charlie Chaplin
    b) Buster Keaton
    c) Harold Lloyd

MEDIUM

Answers to Quiz 102: Television part 1

1. John Hamm
2. House
3. Desperate Housewives
4. In The Night Garden
5. Larry David
6. Isobel Crawley
7. Misfits
8. Esther
9. The Killing
10. Going Live
11. Trevor Francis
12. Leadbetter
13. Tony Blackburn
14. Coronation Street's Steve McDonald
15. The Wire
16. Rachel Riley
17. Howards' Way
18. Quantum Leap
19. Satriale's
20. Richard Bacon

Quiz 104: Law and Order

1. Lord Lovat was the last person in Britain to undergo what grizzly punishment?

2. Rogue trader Nick Leeson was instrumental in the collapse of which bank?

3. Which British politician faked his own death in 1974?

4. Which former Metropolitan Police Deputy Assistant Commissioner was the Liberal Democrat candidate in the 2012 London Mayoral election?

5. In what city did the St Valentine's Day Massacre take place?

6. The name of which prison appeared in the title of an album by The Smiths?

7. What do Han van Meegeren, John Myatt and Tom Keating have in common?

8. Which Oscar-winning actor served 32 days in jail in 1987 for hitting an extra?

9. Which English actor plays Al Capone in the TV series Boardwalk Empire?

10. Hawley Harvey were the Christian names of which physician-turned-murderer?

11. Who lived in an attic flat at 23 Cranley Gardens?

12. Which playwright was murdered by his lover, Kenneth Halliwell, in 1967?

13. Italian banker Roberto Calvi was found hanged in 1982 under which London bridge?

14. Who was the last inmate of Spandau Prison?

15. Which Israeli politician was assassinated by Yigal Amir in November 1995?

16. Which writer, actor and broadcaster spent three months in Pucklechurch Prison on remand in 1975?

17. What job connects Syd Dernley, Harry Allen and Albert Pierrepoint?

18. Which pair of Scottish body snatchers were the subject of a 2010 film?

19. In what year were betting shops legalised in Britain?
    a) 1950
    b) 1955
    c) 1960

20. In 1982, Michael Fagan broke into the bedroom of which notable figure?
    a) Archbishop of Canterbury
    b) Prime Minister
    c) The Queen

MEDIUM

Answers to Quiz 103: Pot Luck

1. Mozambique
2. The Go-Between by LP Hartley
3. The Booker Prize
4. Citizen Kane
5. Kevin Spacey
6. Iron Man
7. Friedrich Nietzsche
8. Piano
9. Campion
10. Wednesday
11. The Who
12. France
13. Morgan Spurlock
14. Federico Fellini
15. Cancer, Scorpio, Pisces
16. Dead Or Alive
17. Windsor
18. Billie Holliday
19. Tun
20. Harold Lloyd

Quiz 105: Pot Luck

1. Who was the Republican Vice-Presidential candidate in the 2008 US Presidential election?

2. Lusaka is the capital city of which African country?

3. 'Once there were four children whose names were Peter, Susan, Edmund and Lucy' is the opening line of which children's classic?

4. What are the four railways stations featured in the board game Monopoly?

5. The Kentucky Derby is run at which American racetrack?

6. A pentadecagon is a shape with how many sides?

7. In 1668, John Dryden became the first holder of which post?

8. Which ancient Greek said, 'The unexplained life is not worth living'?

9. What is the highest rank in the Royal Navy?

10. Zugzwang, en passant and zwischenzug are terms relating to which game?

11. On what side of the road do they drive in Brunei, Hong Kong and Japan?

12. Fingal O'Flahertie Wills were the middle names of which Irish writer?

13. What was The Beatles' last number one UK single?

14. Which cyclist won the Tour de France on five occasions between 1991 and 1995?

15. In what year did post World War II food rationing end?

16. Who did Jacob Zuma succeed as President of South Africa?

17. Who sang the theme tune to the James Bond film Licence To Kill?

18. Who played the famous fashion designer in the film Coco Before Chanel?

19. Which of the following was a real pope?
    a) Pope Kenobi
    b) Pope Lando
    c) Pope Solo

20. The Pillars of Hercules are more commonly known as what?
    a) Rock of Gibraltar
    b) Ayers Rock
    c) Alderney

MEDIUM

Answers to Quiz 104: Law and Order

1. Beheading
2. Barings
3. John Stonehouse
4. Brian Paddick
5. Chicago
6. Strangeways (Here We Come)
7. They're all renowned art forgers
8. Sean Penn
9. Stephen Graham
10. Dr Crippen
11. Serial killer Dennis Nilsen
12. Joe Orton
13. Blackfriars
14. Rudolf Hess
15. Yitzhak Rabin
16. Stephen Fry
17. Hangman
18. Burke and Hare
19. 1960
20. The Queen

Quiz 106: Song Opening Lines

Identify the songs from the following opening lines:

1. Go shorty, it's your birthday

2. Well, I guess it would be nice if I could touch your body

3. Tommy used to work on the docks

4. She was more like a beauty queen from a movie scene

5. There must be some kind of way out of here, said the joker to the thief

6. In the time of chimpanzees I was a monkey

7. I was born in a cross-fire hurricane

8. Picture yourself in a boat on a river / With tangerine trees and marmalade skies

9. How does it feel, to treat me like you do?

10. Down down, you bring me down / I hear you knocking at my door and I can't sleep at night

11. In my imagination there is no complication / I dream about you all the time

12. Is it my imagination / Or have I finally found something worth living for?

13. I heard that you're settled down / That you found a girl and you're married now

14. Oh, I could hide 'neath the wings / Of the bluebird as she sings

15. We're leaving together / But still it's farewell / And maybe we'll come back / To earth, who can tell?

16. Well we were born within an hour of each other / Our mothers said we could be sister and brother

17. The heart is a bloom / Shoots up through the stony ground / There's no room / No space to rent in this town

18. You've painted up your lips and rolled and curled your tinted hair

19. I remember when, I remember I remember when I lost my mind

20. Watching every motion in my foolish lover's game / On this endless ocean finally lovers know no shame

Answers to Quiz 105: Pot Luck

1. Sarah Palin
2. Zambia
3. The Lion, the Witch and the Wardrobe by CS Lewis
4. Fenchurch St, Marylebone, Liverpool St and King's Cross
5. Churchill Downs
6. 15
7. Poet Laureate
8. Socrates
9. Admiral of the Fleet
10. Chess
11. Left
12. Oscar Wilde
13. The Ballad of John and Yoko
14. Miguel Indurain
15. 1954
16. Thabo Mbeki
17. Gladys Knight
18. Audrey Tatou
19. Pope Lando
20. Rock of Gibraltar

MEDIUM

Quiz 107: Pot Luck

1. Who have been the victim of more assassinations, US Presidents or Popes?

2. Before finding success with Oasis, Noel Gallagher was a roadie with which band?

3. What is the second most commonly used letter in the English language?

4. What was the name of highwayman Dick Turpin's horse?

5. What comes after primary, secondary and tertiary?

6. Bumble is the nickname of which cricket commentator?

7. Which former Rolling Stone drowned in his own swimming pool, aged 27?

8. In weaponry, what do the initials ICBM stand for?

9. Which Ancient Greek lawgiver was known for the harshness of his punishments?

10. Which country won the World Cup in 1934 and 1938?

11. In a personal ad, what do the initials OHAC stand for?

12. What nationality was former UN Secretary General Kurt Waldheim?

13. What part of the body would suffer from a hallux valgus?

14. 'Thy choicest gifts in store / On her be pleased to pour' are the opening lines to the third verse of which song?

15. Jazz musician Dizzy Gillespie is associated with which instrument?

16. What is the first name of champion jockey AP McCoy?

17. What animals live in a sett?

18. Who was the first president of Turkey?

19. Which of the following isn't a Mr Man?
    a) Mr Chatterbox
    b) Mr Chirpy
    c) Mr Clumsy

20. Before becoming president, George H W Bush was Director of which organisation?
    a) CIA
    b) FBI
    c) NASA

Answers to Quiz 106: Song Opening Lines

1. In Da Club by 50 Cent
2. Faith by George Michael
3. Livin' On a Prayer by Bon Jovi
4. Billie Jean by Michael Jackson
5. All Along The Watchtower by Jimi Hendrix
6. Loser by Beck
7. Jumpin' Jack Flash by The Rolling Stones
8. Lucy In The Sky With Diamonds by The Beatles
9. Blue Monday by New Order
10. I Am The Resurrection by The Stone Roses
11. I Should Be So Lucky by Kylie Minogue
12. Cigarettes and Alcohol by Oasis
13. Someone Like You by Adele
14. Daydream Believer by The Monkees
15. The Final Countdown by Europe
16. Disco 2000 by Pulp
17. Beautiful Day by U2
18. Ruby, Don't Take Your Love to Town by Kenny Rogers
19. Crazy by Gnarls Barkley
20. Take My Breath Away by Berlin

MEDIUM

Quiz 108: Ireland

1. What was the name of the 1952 film starring John Wayne set in Innisfree?

2. Which Mayo town attracts 1.5m pilgrims each year?

3. The life of which writer is celebrated on Bloomsday?

4. What is the largest county in Ireland?

5. Which author wrote The Barrytown Trilogy?

6. What do the initials GAA stand for?

7. Which county has won the most All-Ireland Senior Football Championship titles?

8. Tolka Park is the home ground of which football club?

9. Which Irish comedian hosts TV comedy School of Hard Sums?

10. In what year did Ireland join the European Economic Community?

11. What is the largest park in Dublin?

12. Kenneth Branagh was born in which Irish city?

13. Which Irish political party's name translates into English as 'Tribe of the Irish'?

14. What was the pen name of author Brian O'Nolan?

15. Blowin' Your Mind was the debut album by which Irish singer?

16. Who was Ireland's second female president?

17. Kevin O'Brien, Ed Joyce and Boyd Rankin are notable Irish performers in which sport?

18. The River Corrib flows through which city?

19. The most easterly point in the Republic of Ireland is in which county?
    a) Dublin
    b) Louth
    c) Wicklow

20. Complete the title of the 2011 film: Killing…?
    a) Bono
    b) Geldof
    c) The Edge

Answers to Quiz 107: Pot Luck

1. Popes
2. Inspiral Carpets
3. A
4. Black Bess
5. Quaternary
6. David Lloyd
7. Brian Jones
8. Intercontinental Ballistic Missile
9. Draco
10. Italy
11. Own House And Car
12. Austrian
13. The foot (it's a bunion)
14. God Save the Queen
15. Trumpet
16. Anthony
17. Badgers
18. Kemal Ataturk
19. Mr Chirpy
20. CIA

Quiz 109: Pot Luck

1. Miss Lemon is the secretary of which fictional detective?

2. Which American president shares his name with a modern-day American composer?

3. Actor Michael Fassbender was born in which country?

4. The Battle of Worcester was the last battle in which war?

5. What is defenestration?

6. Which soul singer was tragically murdered by his father in 1984, at the age of just 44?

7. In golf, what do the initials R&A stand for?

8. Which Liverpool playwright wrote The Boys From The Blackstuff?

9. What is measured in ohms?

10. Yosemite Falls are in which American state?

11. What chemical element has the symbol K and the atomic number 19?

12. In what ocean does the island of Tristan da Cunha lie?

13. Who is fourth in line to the British throne?

14. What nationality is the Nobel prize-winning author Orhan Pamuk?

15. Arthur Wynne invented which type of popular puzzle?

16. In which country would you find the port of Fray Bentos?

17. Which Scottish city is nicknamed Auld Reekie?

18. TV show Top of the Pops was originally filmed in which city?

19. In 2009, British swimmer Lewis Gordon Pugh became the first person to swim where?
    a) North Pole
    b) South Pole

20. How many years did the 100 Years War last?
    a) 100 years
    b) 116 years
    c) 132 years

Answers to Quiz 108: Ireland

1. The Quiet Man
2. Knock
3. James Joyce
4. Cork
5. Roddy Doyle
6. Gaelic Athletic Association
7. Kerry
8. Shelbourne
9. Dara Ó Briain
10. 1973
11. Phoenix
12. Belfast
13. Fine Gael
14. Flann O'Brien
15. Van Morrison
16. Mary McAleese
17. Cricket
18. Galway
19. Wicklow
20. Bono

Quiz 110: History

MEDIUM

1. Who did Ban Ki-Moon succeed as Secretary General of the United Nations?

2. Which territory was ceded to Britain by the 1713 Treaty of Utrecht?

3. Who was the British monarch when the American Declaration of Independence was signed?

4. What is the name of the rocky plateau captured by Israel in the 1967 Six-Day War?

5. Who was Soviet leader during the Cuban Missile Crisis?

6. During World War II where did Bevin Boys work?

7. In which country did an uprising called The Boxer Rebellion take place?

8. Who was the head of the Argentine Military Junta during the Falklands War?

9. Which English king died at the Battle of Bosworth Field?

10. Archbishop Makarios III was the first President of which country?

11. The Dayton Agreement brought an end to conflict in which country?

12. Who was the German Chancellor during German reunification in 1990?

13. Allen Dulles was the first director of which organisation?

14. How many countries were in the original European Economic Community?

15. Which English monarch was crowned on Christmas Day?

16. In what year was the National Health Service launched?

17. Manuel II was the last king of which European country?

18. Which two countries were involved in the War of Jenkins' Ear?

19. In what year did the Boston Tea Party take place?
    a) 1773
    b) 1775
    c) 1777

20. In what century did the Hundred Years War begin?
    a) 14th
    b) 15th
    c) 16th

Answers to Quiz 109: Pot Luck

1. Hercule Poirot
2. John Adams
3. Germany
4. English Civil War
5. The act of throwing something or someone out of a window
6. Marvin Gaye
7. Royal and Ancient
8. Alan Bleasdale
9. Electrical resistance
10. California
11. Potassium
12. Atlantic Ocean
13. Prince Andrew
14. Turkish
15. Crossword
16. Uruguay
17. Edinburgh
18. Manchester
19. At the North Pole
20. 116 years

MEDIUM

Quiz 111: Pot Luck

1. Which TV adventurer is the Chief Scout?

2. The ATL union represents people working in which field?

3. Which former England international was banned from rugby for three years for his involvement in the 'Bloodgate' scandal?

4. Which social media news website was created by Scotsman Pete Cashmore?

5. The Rembrandts recorded the theme music to which long-running sitcom?

6. Barbara Vine is the pseudonym of which thriller writer?

7. The grouse-shooting season starts on the 12th of which month?

8. What size of paper measures 297mm x 420mm?

9. In the Dewey Decimal Classification system, books on what subject are numbered between 200 and 299?

10. What is the best possible hand in a game of Ohama poker?

11. What was the first Carry On film?

12. How many sides does a undecagon have?

13. What rank comes after Private in the British Army?

14. In Swift's Gulliver's Travels, what was Gulliver's first name?

15. What French phrase describes a painting style which deceives the eye?

16. The musical Cabaret is based on a novel by which author?

17. Which a cappella group had a Christmas number one in 1983 with Only You?

18. What instrument did jazz musician Count Basie play?

19. All snowflakes are what shape?
    a) pentagonal
    b) hexagonal
    c) octagonal

20. Who was the Bad Teacher in the 2011 film of the same name?
    a) Drew Barrymore
    b) Cameron Diaz
    c) Lucy Liu

MEDIUM

Answers to Quiz 110: History

1. Kofi Annan
2. Gibraltar
3. George III
4. Golan Heights
5. Nikita Khruschev
6. In mines
7. China
8. General Leopoldo Galtieri
9. Richard III
10. Cyprus
11. Bosnia
12. Helmut Kohl
13. The CIA
14. Six
15. William I, the Conqueror
16. 1948
17. Portugal
18. Great Britain and Spain
19. 1773
20. 14th

Quiz 112: Dogs

1. Which family owns a pet greyhound called Santa's Little Helper?

2. What was the name of Mark Haddon's award-winning 2003 novel?

3. Who had a number two hit in 2000 with Who Let The Dogs Out?

4. What is the name of the talkative dog in the animated comedy Family Guy?

5. True or false – there is a canine equivalent of the Oscars called the Golden Collars?

6. Which comedian and TV presenter owned a dog called Buster?

7. What did a dog call Pickles find in a garden hedge in South Norwood?

8. What breed of dog is Uggie, who appeared in the award-winning silent film The Artist?

9. Which former Blue Peter presenter now hosts One Man and His Dog?

10. What was the name of the first dog to travel in space?

11. Who was the owner of Spit The Dog?

12. What was the name of Wendy, John and Michael's dog in Peter Pan?

13. Who famously owns a Portuguese Water Dog named Bo?

14. Chef Rick Stein was often accompanied on his travels by a Jack Russell but what was his name?

15. The chihuahua is named after a region of which country?

16. In Homer's Odyssey, what was the name of Odysseus's canine companion?

17. What was the name of the 2008 film starring Owen Wilson and Jennifer Aniston and a labrador retriever?

18. Which fictional Basset Hound had brothers called Andy, Marbles, Olaf, and Spike and a sister called Belle?

19. What was the name of the dog in children's favourite The Littlest Hobo?
    a) Paris
    b) London
    c) Rome

20. A dog called Flash was a regular in which 1980s TV show?
    a) Knight Rider
    b) The Dukes of Hazzard
    c) The A Team

MEDIUM

Answers to Quiz 111: Pot Luck

1. Bear Grylls
2. Education
3. Dean Richards
4. Mashable
5. Friends
6. Ruth Rendell
7. August
8. A3
9. Religion
10. Royal flush
11. Carry On Sergeant
12. 11
13. Lance-Corporal
14. Lemuel
15. Trompe l'oeil
16. Christopher Isherwood
17. The Flying Pickets
18. Piano
19. Hexagonal
20. Cameron Diaz

Quiz 113: Pot Luck

1. In 2002, which former Shipping Forecast area was renamed FitzRoy?

2. Which loose association of early 20th-century writers and intellectuals included Virginia Woolf, E.M. Forster and Lytton Strachey?

3. Who said, 'A man cannot be too careful in his choice of enemies'?

4. Anthony Daniels played which character in the Star Wars films?

5. Velma Kelly, Billy Flynn and Mama Morton are characters in which musical?

6. Which South African athlete is nicknamed Blade Runner?

7. Who recorded the award-winning album Let England Shake?

8. The distance between the elbow and the tip of the middle finger gave its name to which ancient measurement?

9. Revolutionary leader Che Guevara was born in which country?

10. In what South American country did Che Guevara die?

11. In which American city would you find sports teams called Bears, Bulls and Cubs?

12. From 1928 to 1939, King Zog was the monarch of which country?

13. A torch is held by one hand of the Statue of Liberty but what object is in the other hand?

14. Who was the last British monarch from the House of Hanover?

15. The ancient city of Carthage is located in which modern-day country?

16. How many brothers did former US President John F Kennedy have?

17. A Stopfordian comes from which English town?

18. Who is referred to as Brenda in the satirical magazine Private Eye?

19. All Scotch Whisky has to be aged in oak barrels for a minimum of how many years?
    a) 1
    b) 2
    c) 3

20. Complete the name of the 2012 film starring Matt Damon and Scarlett Johansson: We Bought A...?
    a) Mansion
    b) Ferrari
    c) Zoo

MEDIUM

Answers to Quiz 112: Dogs

1. The Simpsons
2. The Curious Incident of the Dog in the Night-Time
3. Baha Men
4. Brian
5. True
6. Paul O'Grady
7. The World Cup
8. Jack Russell
9. Matt Baker
10. Laika
11. Bob Carolgees
12. Nana
13. Barack Obama
14. Chalky
15. Mexico
16. Argos
17. Marley & Me
18. Snoopy
19. London
20. The Dukes of Hazzard

Quiz 114: Spies

1. In which city will you find the International Spy Museum?

2. What was the Dutch woman Margaretha Geertruida 'Margreet' Zelle better known as?

3. Which married American couple were executed in 1953 on charges that they were Communist spies?

4. What do the initials GCHQ stand for?

5. What is the Secret Intelligence Service more commonly known as?

6. Which author created the character Harry Palmer?

7. Erin Watts, Zafar Younis and Ruth Evershed were characters in which TV drama?

8. Thames House is the headquarters of which organisation?

9. Alec Leamas is the central character in which spy fiction classic?

10. Which TV comedy follows the fortunes of of CIA agent Stan Smith?

11. The BND is the secret service of which European country?

12. What was the codename given to British World War Two spy Eddie Chapman?

13. Who was Queen Elizabeth I's Principal Secretary and is often described as her spymaster?

14. What was the name of the British pensioner who was exposed as a Soviet spy in 1999?

15. The Quiet American is a novel by which author?

16. Which art historian was exposed as the so-called 'Fourth Man' in 1979?

17. George Clooney won his only Oscar to date as a spy in which 2005 thriller?

18. Which actress played Connie Sachs in the 2011 film version of Tinker, Tailor, Soldier, Spy?

19. GCHQ is based in which English town?
    a) Cheltenham
    b) Gloucester
    c) Hereford

20. What was the name of the World War II decoding machine that helped crack German cyphers?
    a) Arcanum
    b) Enigma
    c) Stickler

MEDIUM

Answers to Quiz 113: Pot Luck

1. Finisterre
2. The Bloomsbury Group
3. Oscar Wilde
4. C-3PO
5. Chicago
6. Oscar Pistorius
7. PJ Harvey
8. Cubit
9. Argentina
10. Bolivia
11. Chicago
12. Albania
13. A book
14. Queen Victoria
15. Tunisia
16. Three
17. Shropshire
18. Queen Elizabeth II
19. 3
20. Zoo

Quiz 115: Pot Luck

1. In March 2012, actor and comedian David Mitchell announced his engagement to which writer and broadcaster?

2. Which actress and comedian's autobiography was called Look Back In Hunger?

3. The Oscar-winning film The Sting was set in which city?

4. Former Italian Prime Minister Silvio Berlusconi was the owner of which football club?

5. Tommy Cockles, Billy Bleach and Competitive Dad are characters created by which comedian?

6. What the real name of rapper The Streets?

7. Which notable figure of the contemporary art world wrote the book Be The Worst You Can Be?

8. Someone born on 22 March would have what star sign?

9. Freetown is the capital city of which African country?

10. The A1 road connects London with which Scottish city?

11. How many did children did Queen Victoria have?

12. Which three signs of the zodiac are known as the earth signs?

13. I Want To Know What Love Is was a number one hit in 1984 for which group?

14. Who played serial killer Fred West in TV drama Appropriate Adult?

15. In what year did Tony Blair resign as Prime Minister?

16. Which Scottish actor and comedian created a series of art works called Born on a Rainy Day?

17. Beatrice and Benedick are characters in which of Shakespeare's plays?

18. What character did Ruth Jones play in TV comedy Gavin and Stacey?

19. In what field of the arts is Wayne McGregor a notable name?
    a) dance
    b) sculpture
    c) photography

20. Which of these Madonna songs did not reach number 1 in the UK?
    a) Into The Groove
    b) Holiday
    c) American Pie

Answers to Quiz 114: Spies

1. Washington DC
2. Mata Hari
3. Julius and Ethel Rosenberg
4. Government Communications Headquarters
5. MI6
6. Len Deighton
7. Spooks
8. MI5
9. The Spy Who Came In From The Cold
10. American Dad!
11. Germany
12. Agent Zigzag
13. Francis Walsingham
14. Melita Norwood
15. Graham Greene
16. Anthony Blunt
17. Syriana
18. Cathy Burke
19. Cheltenham
20. Enigma

Quiz 116: Europe

1. Zealand is the largest island in which country?

2. Which city hosted the 2012 Eurovision Song Contest?

3. The French city of Bordeaux sits on which river?

4. What is the smallest republic in Europe?

5. Which country has been divided by a Green Line since 1974?

6. Liechtenstein shares borders with which two countries?

7. Which territory in mainland South America is part of the European Union?

8. Which Austrian topped the charts in 1985 with Rock Me Amadeus?

9. In which city will you find a monument called the Atomium?

10. What is the most northerly capital city in Europe?

11. Which influential German band recorded the album Trans-Europe Express?

12. What is the currency of Hungary?

13. Which river flows through Vienna, Bratislava, Budapest and Belgrade?

14. In which country is the city of Maastricht?

15. Which country plays host to the World Air Guitar Championships?

16. GBZ is the international vehicle registration code for which British Overseas Territory?

Answers - page 237

17. Mount Elbrus, the highest mountain in Europe, is in which country?

18. What country does manchego cheese come from?

19. In which city is Barajas Airport?
    a) Barcelona
    b) Madrid
    c) Lisbon

20. Which of the following countries wasn't an original member of the European Economic Community?
    a) Luxembourg
    b) Belgium
    c) Spain

MEDIUM

Answers to Quiz 115: Pot Luck

1. Victoria Coren
2. Jo Brand
3. Chicago
4. AC Milan
5. Simon Day
6. Mike Skinner
7. Charles Saatchi
8. Aries
9. Sierra Leone
10. Edinburgh
11. 9
12. Taurus, Capricorn, Virgo
13. Foreigner
14. Dominic West
15. 2007
16. Billy Connolly
17. Much Ado About Nothing
18. Vanessa 'Nessa' Jenkins
19. Dance
20. Holiday

Quiz 117: Pot Luck

1. Which superhero was born Kal-El?

2. In what establishment would you find guests called Miss Tibbs and Miss Gatsby?

3. Which Swedish singer took a Buffalo Stance in 1988?

4. Who played fictional US President Jack Stanton in the 1998 film Primary Colors?

5. The CN Tower is in which North American city?

6. What is the last book of the New Testament?

7. Which three Shakespeare plays have a woman's name in the title?

8. Who was the last leader of the Liberal Party before they merged with the SDP?

9. What element has the chemical symbol Hg?

10. Which writer did Nicole Kidman play in the 2002 film The Hours?

11. Which Scottish historian's works include Empire, The Ascent of Money and Civilisation: The West and the Rest?

12. What is the plant antirrhinum more commonly known as?

13. Who did Andrew Strauss succeed as captain of the England Test cricket team?

14. According to the musical, the mysterious town of Brigadoon appears for one day every how many years?

15. How many states of America are comprised of two words?

16. Worms is a city in which country?

17. A sommelier is someone with expertise in what?

18. In relation to the Internet, what do the initials SEO stand for?

19. What was the name of the public inquiry into the standards of the British press?
    a) Leveson Inquiry
    b) Taylor Inquiry
    c) Chilcot Inquiry

20. Which country won the first Eurovision Song Contest?
    a) UK
    b) France
    c) Switzerland

MEDIUM

Answers to Quiz 116: Europe

1. Denmark
2. Baku
3. Garonne River
4. San Marino
5. Cyprus
6. Austria and Switzerland
7. French Guiana
8. Falco
9. Brussels
10. Reykjavik
11. Kraftwerk
12. Forint
13. Danube
14. The Netherlands
15. Finland
16. Gibraltar
17. Russia
18. Spain
19. Madrid
20. Spain

Quiz 118: Animals

1. What creature lives in a holt?

2. A filly is a female horse that is under how many years old?

3. Are drone bees male or female?

4. A dog called Diefenbaker appeared in which police drama?

5. The leveret is the young of which animal?

6. What creatures live in a formicary?

7. What animal gives its name to a major river in Western Australia?

8. What type of animal is a dik dik?

9. How many hearts does an octopus have?

10. Shark skeletons are made of what material?

11. To what family of birds does the peacock belong?

12. Canis lupus is the Latin name of which animal?

13. What animal links a 2003 film by Gus Van Sant and a 2003 album by The White Stripes?

14. Who was the lead singer with 1960s rock group The Animals?

15. What is the fastest land animal in the world?

16. Morocco Mole was the sidekick of which animated secret agent?

17. Bos taurus is the scientific name for which creatures?

18. The larva of which insect is known as a leatherjacket?

19. What is the largest of the great apes?
    a) gorilla
    b) chimpanzee
    c) orangutan

20. What type of creature is a wigeon?
    a) duck
    b) eagle
    c) rabbit

Answers to Quiz 117: Pot Luck

1. Superman
2. Fawlty Towers
3. Neneh Cherry
4. John Travolta
5. Toronto
6. Revelation
7. Romeo and Juliet, Anthony and Cleopatra and Troilus and Cressida
8. David Steel
9. Mercury
10. Virginia Woolf
11. Niall Ferguson
12. Snapdragon
13. Kevin Pietersen
14. 100
15. Ten
16. Germany
17. Wine
18. Search engine optimisation
19. Leveson Inquiry
20. Switzerland

Quiz 119: Pot Luck

1. Which chef is the co-host of Masterchef: The Professionals?

2. Jo O'Meara, Rachel Stevens and Bradley McIntosh were members of which band?

3. Halifax is the capital city of which Canadian province?

4. An oak leaf is the emblem of which conservation organisation?

5. Who played Edith Piaf in the film La Vie en Rose?

6. In Are You Being Served?, what was Mrs Slocombe's first name?

7. Australian outlaw Ned Kelly was hanged at which prison?

8. What was the maiden name of William Shakespeare's mother?

9. Michelle Pfeiffer, Halle Berry, Eartha Kitt and Lee Merriweather have all played which fictional character?

10. In Germany, what is ein Handy?

11. Which British architect designed the Pompidou Centre in Paris?

12. What fruit is used to make calvados?

13. Which playwright's works include The Glass Menagerie, The Rose Tattoo and The Night of the Iguana?

14. TAP is the national airline of which country?

15. Who was Prime Minister for longer – Margaret Thatcher or Tony Blair?

16. Car manufacturer Tata Motors is based in which country?

17. Mrs Johnstone is the main character in which musical?

18. Odette is a queen in which ballet by Tchaikovsky?

19. Which of the following countries is not a monarchy?
    a) Finland
    b) Norway
    c) Sweden

20. Which actress's 2012 autobiography was called Where Have I Gone?
    a) Jo Brand
    b) Julia Bradbury
    c) Pauline Quirke

MEDIUM

Answers to Quiz 118: Animals

1. Otter
2. 4 years
3. Male
4. Due South
5. Hare
6. Ants
7. Swan
8. Antelope
9. 3
10. Cartilage
11. Pheasant
12. Wolf
13. Elephant
14. Eric Burdon
15. Cheetah
16. Secret Squirrel
17. Cattle
18. Crane fly (Daddy longlegs)
19. Gorilla
20. Duck

Quiz 120: Games

1. A full set of 28 dominoes contains how many pips?

2. FIDE is the governing body of which game?

3. Chris Moneymaker, Jonathan Duhamel and Pius Heinz have all been world champions in which game?

4. What popular game was invented by Alfred Mosher Butts?

5. The King's Indian Defence is a manoeuvre in which game?

6. What was the name of the computer that beat world chess champion Garry Kasparov?

7. In poker, what hand has the nickname Big Slick?

8. What is the game Roshambo known as in Britain?

9. What popular Asian game is played on a 19 x 19 square board with 181 black and 180 white stones?

10. In Monopoly, how much do the railway stations cost?

11. Richard Madeley and Chris Tarrant hosted a gameshow based on which board game?

12. What is the game Captain's Mistress more commonly known as?

13. Especially popular in China, what four-player game is played using 136 or 144 tiles?

14. What popular board game was devised by Anthony E. Pratt, a solicitor's clerk from Birmingham?

15. In Scrabble, how much is the letter X worth?

16. Leicester Square and Piccadilly are two of the three yellow squares on a Monopoly board but what is the third?

17. What version of baccarat shares its name with the French for railway?

18. What strategy board game was created by Albert Lamorisse and was originally called La Conquête du Monde?

19. How many holes are on a bar billiards table?
    a) 8
    b) 9
    c) 10

20. The card game Canasta was invented in which country?
    a) Italy
    b) Spain
    c) Uruguay

MEDIUM

Answers to Quiz 119: Pot Luck

1.	Michel Roux Jr.	11.	Richard Rogers
2.	S Club 7	12.	Apple
3.	Nova Scotia	13.	Tennessee Williams
4.	National Trust	14.	Portugal
5.	Marion Cottilard	15.	Margaret Thatcher
6.	Betty	16.	India
7.	Old Melbourne Gaol	17.	Blood Brothers
8.	Arden	18.	Swan Lake
9.	Catwoman	19.	Finland
10.	Mobile phone	20.	Pauline Quirke

Quiz 121: Pot Luck

1. What was reggae star Shaggy's first UK number one?

2. Which British band provided the theme tune to hit TV drama The Sopranos?

3. Tbilisi is the largest city in which former Soviet Republic?

4. Alex O'Loughlin, Scott Caan and Daniel Dae Kim star in the modern day version of which classic police show?

5. What is an archaeologist with the first names Henry Walton more commonly known as?

6. What was the Bee Gees first number one?

7. Al Pacino played which character in gangster classic Scarface?

8. The Rose Bowl is the home ground of which county cricket team?

9. Saint Helier is the capital of which of the Channel Islands?

10. Which country hosted the World Cup in 1970?

11. Which English city is situated at the confluence of the Rivers Ouse and Foss?

12. People Will Say We're In Love and The Farmer and the Cowman are songs from which Rodgers and Hammerstein musical?

13. What was the name of Billy J Kramer's backing band?

14. Sharleen Spiteri was the lead singer with which group?

15. Which dance act had top ten hits in the early 1990s with What Can You Do For Me, Something Good and Believe In Me?

16. Geno by Dexys Midnight Runners was a tribute to which soul singer?

17. Which playwright wrote A Streetcar Named Desire?

18. What is the only one of the Great Lakes that is wholly in America?
    a) Huron
    b) Michigan
    c) Superior

19. Which Tory politician hasn't appeared on Strictly Come Dancing?
    a) Virginia Bottomley
    b) Edwina Currie
    c) Ann Widdecombe

20. What is the connection between the above answers?

MEDIUM

Answers to Quiz 120: Games

1. 168
2. Chess
3. Poker
4. Scrabble
5. Chess
6. Deep Blue
7. Ace king
8. Rock paper scissors
9. Go
10. £200 each
11. Cluedo
12. Connect 4
13. Mahjong
14. Cluedo
15. 8
16. Coventry Street
17. Chemin de fer
18. Risk
19. 9
20. Uruguay

Quiz 122: Science

1. What is the chemical element wolfram more commonly known as?

2. What element has the chemical symbol Sb?

3. To the nearest degree, what temperature, in Celsius, is absolute zero?

4. What reaction is caused by passing electricity through a liquid?

5. Atoms are made up of which three basic parts?

6. What do the initials DNA stand for?

7. What is calcium oxide more commonly known as?

8. Which scientist is known for his laws of motion?

9. What was the name of the nuclear reactor damaged in the 2011 Japanese earthquake and tsunami?

10. Hydrargyrum is another name for which chemical element?

11. What are the constituent elements of the alloy brass?

12. Which science fiction writer devised the Three Laws of Robotics?

13. What is the first element on the Periodic Table?

14. HNO3 is the chemical formula for what acid?

15. What orbits the nucleus of an atom?

16. In computing, what do the initials ISDN stand for?

17. What word describes the process in which a substance changes from a solid to a gas without passing through a liquid phase?

18. Which Russian chemist created the Periodic Table?

19. Fluorine, Chlorine, Bromine and Iodine make up which chemical group?
    a) alkali metal group
    b) halogen group
    c) noble group

20. What name is also the SI unit of inductance?
    a) George
    b) Henry
    c) William

MEDIUM

Answers to Quiz 121: Pot Luck

1. Oh Carolina
2. Alabama 3
3. Georgia
4. Hawaii Five-O
5. Indiana Jones
6. Massachusetts
7. Tony Montana
8. Hampshire
9. Jersey
10. Mexico
11. York
12. Oklahoma!
13. The Dakotas
14. Texas
15. Utah Saints
16. Geno Washington
17. Tennessee Williams
18. Michigan
19. Virginia Bottomley
20. They all contain all or part of the name of an American state

Quiz 123: Pot Luck

1. Icthyology is the branch of zoology concerned with the study of what type of animals?

2. Brush Up Your Shakespeare is a song from which musical?

3. Key Lime Pie is the official dessert of which American state?

4. Children's classic Le Petit Prince was written by which author?

5. What are Univers, Johnston Sans and 2012 Headline?

6. In which film did a character eat 50 hard boiled eggs in an hour to win a bet?

7. Middlesex, Surrey and Cornwall are counties in which Caribbean country?

8. Which Roman emperor had a horse called Incitatus?

9. In what year did Hitler become Chancellor of Germany?

10. What is the name of the clown in a Punch and Judy show?

11. Narita International Airport is in which country?

12. The first section of motorway in Britain was a bypass around which northern town?

13. Phlebitis is an inflammation of what?

14. What was the first city outside Europe to host the Olympic Games?

15. The Ledge, The Mines of Sulphur and Penny for a Song are works by which British composer?

16. Which animated TV series is set in Quahog, Rhode Island?

17. Apiphobia is a fear of what type of creature?

18. In the TV comedy Friends, what was the name of Phoebe's identical twin sister?

19. Complete the title of the self-help book by Spencer Johnson: Who Moved My...?
    a) Job
    b) House
    c) Cheese

20. Which DJ competed in the 400m British Olympic trials in 2000?
    a) Nemone
    b) Sara Cox
    c) Zoe Ball

MEDIUM

Answers to Quiz 122: Science

1. Tungsten
2. Antimony
3. Minus 273C
4. Electrolysis
5. Protons, neutrons and electrons
6. Deoxyribonucleic acid
7. Quicklime
8. Isaac Newton
9. Fukushima I Nuclear Power Plant
10. Mercury
11. Copper and zinc
12. Isaac Asimov
13. Hydrogen
14. Nitric acid
15. Electrons
16. Integrated Services Digital Network
17. Sublimation
18. Dmitri Mendeleev
19. Halogen group
20. Henry

Quiz 124: Television part 2

1. Who co-wrote classic TV comedy Fawlty Towers with John Cleese?

2. Which newsreader won the first series of Strictly Come Dancing?

3. Who plays Mrs Lemon in the modern-day TV drama Sherlock?

4. Alys Fowler, Chris Beardshaw, Carol Klein and Rachel de Thame have all appeared on which TV series?

5. What was the name of the Only Fools and Horses prequel starring James Buckley?

6. Who hosted The South Bank Show?

7. Which comedian plays accountant Tim Adams in comedy Not Going Out?

8. Who provides the voice of Sideshow Bob in The Simpsons?

9. Connections, sequences, connecting wall and missing vowels are rounds in which quiz show?

10. Which Top Gear host presents Man Lab?

11. In Coronation Street, who killed Charlie Stubbs?

12. Wilson, Brewster, Koko, Hoot, Toot and Piper are trains in which animated children's programme?

13. In Outnumbered, what is dad Pete's occupation?

14. Chicago's County General Hospital was the setting for which long running-medical drama?

15. Who were the original hosts of The One Show?

16. Which Irish traveller won Celebrity Big Brother in 2011?

17. Roy Trenneman, Maurice Moss and Jen Barber were characters in which Channel 4 comedy?

18. American drama Treme is set in which city?

19. Who is in charge of the aftercare on The Jeremy Kyle Show?
    a) Greg
    b) Gordon
    c) Graham

20. What was the name of the owner of the Winchester Club in Minder?
    a) Dave
    b) John
    c) Mike

MEDIUM

Answers to Quiz 123: Pot Luck

1. Fish
2. Kiss Me Kate
3. Florida
4. Antoine de Saint-Exupéry
5. Typefaces
6. Cool Hand Luke
7. Jamaica
8. Caligula
9. 1933
10. Joey
11. Japan
12. Preston
13. A vein
14. St Louis
15. Richard Rodney Bennett
16. Family Guy
17. Bee
18. Ursula
19. Cheese
20. Nemone

Quiz 125: Pot Luck

1. Which American thriller writer shares his name with a former Labour Foreign Secretary?

2. The daughter of which musician played Snow White in the 2012 film Mirror, Mirror?

3. Jonathan Sacks is the holder of which religious post?

4. The M8 connects which two British cities?

5. Swimmer Eric 'The Eel' Moussambani represented which country in the Sydney Olympics?

6. What is the name of the baseball team in The Simpsons?

7. Who plays the title character in US medical drama Nurse Jackie?

8. Which poet wrote the famous line 'No man is an island'?

9. Eden Gardens is a cricket ground in which country?

10. What nationality was the South American political leader Simón Bolívar?

11. 61 Hours, The Persuader and Killing Floor are thrillers written by which British author?

12. The Wildcats are a rugby league team from which city?

13. 'The rest is silence' were the last words uttered by which Shakespearean character?

14. In technology, what do the initials VoIP stand for?

15. What is The Great Charter of the Liberties of England more commonly known as?

16. The Alamo is located in which modern-day Texas city?

17. What is aioli?

18. The Mantoux test is used to screen for what disease?

19. What is the national animal of Canada?
    a) beaver
    b) polar bear
    c) moose

20. Claire Petulengro and Shelley von Strunkel write what sort of newspaper columns?
    a) crosswords
    b) horse racing tips
    c) horoscopes

MEDIUM

Answers to Quiz 124: Television part 2

1. Connie Booth
2. Natasha Kaplinsky
3. Una Stubbs
4. Gardeners' World
5. Rock and Chips
6. Melvyn Bragg
7. Tim Vine
8. Kelsey Grammer
9. Only Connect
10. James May
11. Tracy Barlow
12. Chuggington
13. Teacher
14. ER
15. Adrian Chiles and Nadia Sawalha
16. Paddy Doherty
17. The IT Crowd
18. New Orleans
19. Graham
20. Dave

Quiz 126: First and Last

1. In 1967, Louis Washkansky became the first person to undergo what operation?

2. What does the Latin phrase 'Primus inter pares' mean?

3. Who was the first Briton to travel into space?

4. What aviation first was achieved by pilot Chuck Yeager in 1947?

5. How many people are present in Da Vinci's painting The Last Supper?

6. Which Manchester United player was the first man to be sent off in an FA Cup final?

7. What is the biggest-selling number two UK hit single of all time?

8. What 1992 film, starring Daniel Day-Lewis, was based on a novel by James Fenimore Cooper?

9. Who was the first black person to win a Best Actor Oscar?

10. Dewhurst, Simmonite and Clegg were the surnames of the main characters in which long-running sitcom?

11. Which female topped the charts in 1988 with First Time?

12. What was the name of the first mammal to be cloned?

13. Who was the first person to win the jackpot on Who Wants To Be A Millionaire?

14. Which action movie character made his debut in the 1982 film First Blood?

15. Complete the title of a 1989 hit by Morrissey: Last of the Famous...?

16. In 1986, Helen Dunmore became the first winner of which prize for her novel A Spell of Winter?

17. What was the name of the 2004 romantic comedy starring Adam Sandler and Drew Barrymore?

18. The first Commonwealth Games took place in which country?

19. The first branch of coffee shop Starbucks opened in which city?
    a) Denver
    b) New York
    c) Seattle

20. What sort of person would use a last?
    a) dressmaker
    b) hairdresser
    c) shoemaker

MEDIUM

Answers to Quiz 125: Pot Luck

1. Robin Cook
2. Phil Collins (his daughter is Lily)
3. Chief Rabbi
4. Glasgow and Edinburgh
5. Equatorial Guinea
6. Springfield Isotopes
7. Edie Falco
8. John Donne
9. India
10. Venezuelan
11. Lee Child
12. Wakefield
13. Hamlet
14. Voice Over Internet Protocol
15. The Magna Carta
16. San Antonio
17. Garlic mayonnaise
18. Tuberculosis
19. Beaver
20. Horoscopes

Quiz 127: Pot Luck

1. Barlinnie Prison is in which British city?

2. What medical condition is also known as Daltonism?

3. Prince Albert II is the monarch of which European country?

4. Which American city hosted the 2002 Winter Olympics?

5. Diplopia is the medical name for which condition?

6. Which mythological sprit's wailing warns of impending death?

7. Which Scot won the 2011 World Snooker Championship?

8. A Neapolitan is a person from which city?

9. Who had a Total Eclipse Of The Heart in 1983?

10. Which crime writer wrote romantic fiction under the pen name Mary Westmacott?

11. Love Is A Four Letter Word was a best-selling 2012 album by which American singer-songwriter?

12. A puree of which fruit is an ingredient in a bellini cocktail?

13. Encephalitis is an inflammation of what part of the body?

14. Readies was the working title of which long-running British comedy?

15. Which Canadian-born Hollywood star appeared on Timmy Mallett's Wide Awake Club?

16. Which group had a Christmas number one with Killing In The Name?

17. Who preceded Rowan Williams as Archbishop of Canterbury?

18. The Hour of Bewilderbeast was a Mercury Prize-winning album by which artist?

19. Which film did not win an Oscar for Best Picture?
a) The Shawshank Redemption
b) The Departed
c) Million Dollar Baby

20. The headquarters of football governing body FIFA are in which city?
a) Berne
b) Geneva
c) Zurich

MEDIUM

Answers to Quiz 126: First and Last

1. Heart transplant
2. First among equals
3. Helen Sharman
4. He broke the sound barrier
5. 13
6. Kevin Moran
7. Last Christmas by Wham!
8. The Last of the Mohicans
9. Sidney Poitier
10. Last of the Summer Wine
11. Robin Beck
12. Dolly the Sheep
13. Judith Keppel
14. John Rambo
15. International Playboys
16. The Orange Prize for Fiction
17. 50 First Dates
18. Canada
19. Seattle
20. Shoemaker

Quiz 128: Transport

1. Kia Motors are based in which Asian country?

2. Who starred as Buster Edwards in the 1983 film about The Great Train Robbery?

3. Logan International Airport is in which city?

4. Which motor manufacturer has produced models called Shogun, Lancer and Outlander?

5. What motorway links London and South Wales?

6. What was the name of the 1953 Ealing comedy about a group of villagers trying to stop the closure of a local branch line?

7. Captain Benjamin Briggs was the skipper of which mysterious ship?

8. Which London Underground line was inaugurated in May 1979?

9. How many sides does the STOP road sign have?

10. Which French railway station takes its name from the site of a famous 1805 battle won by Napoleon I?

11. What unofficial accolade was given to the passenger ship that crossed the Atlantic in the quickest time?

12. LOT is the national airline of which country?

13. In road signage, what shape are warning signs?

14. Ferries from Rosslare in Ireland sail to which Welsh port?

15. What sort of train did Liverpool popsters The Farm sing about on their 1990 top ten hit?

16. Which former politician presented the TV series Great British Railway Journeys?

17. In which European city is Kloten Airport?

18. What is the flag-carrying airline of Hong Kong?

19. In 2012, Gabor Rakonczay became the first person to cross the Atlantic in what?
    a) canoe
    b) glider
    c) barge

20. Which manufacturer produces the world's most expensive production car?
    a) Bugatti
    b) Ferrari
    c) Porsche

MEDIUM

Answers to Quiz 127: Pot Luck

1. Glasgow
2. Colour blindness
3. Monaco
4. Salt Lake City
5. Double vision
6. Banshee
7. John Higgins
8. Naples
9. Bonnie Tyler
10. Agatha Christie
11. Jason Mraz
12. Peach
13. Brain
14. Only Fools and Horses
15. Mike Myers
16. Rage Against The Machine
17. George Carey
18. Badly Drawn Boy
19. The Shawshank Redemption
20. Zurich

Quiz 129: Pot Luck

1. Which British author wrote the novels Money, Yellow Dog and The Pregnant Widow?

2. Another Way To Die was the theme song to which James Bond film?

3. What is allergic rhinitis more commonly known as?

4. Who played Foxy Cleopatra in Austin Power's Goldmember?

5. What was Disney's first full-length animated feature film?

6. What telephone number was used for the first time in 1937?

7. Which painter's works include Blue Nude, The Piano Lesson and The Rocaille Armchair?

8. Bobby Gillespie is the lead singer with which Scottish band?

9. Which controversial TV presenter lost a legal battle in 2012 in a dispute over public access to a path near his Isle of Man home?

10. Who was the first British monarch from the House of Windsor?

11. In what year did Channel 4 first appear on UK TV screens?

12. 'No man but a blockhead ever wrote, except for money' wrote which author?

13. The volcano Krakatoa is in which country?

14. Which American city is home to sports teams called Steelers, Pirates and Penguins?

15. Which Pacific island group was christened the Sandwich Islands by Captain Cook?

Answers - page 263

16. Which five James Bond films have one word titles?

17. US politician Mitt Romney's son shares a name with which long-running British detective drama?

18. Who played Control in the 2011 film version of Tinker, Tailor, Soldier, Spy?

19. Which city hosted the 2010 World Cup final?
    a) Cape Town
    b) Johannesburg
    c) Pretoria

20. What were All Saints drinking in their 2000 hit?
    a) Black Tea
    b) Black Coffee
    c) Black Russian

MEDIUM

Answers to Quiz 128: Transport

1. South Korea
2. Phil Collins
3. Boston
4. Mitsubishi
5. M4
6. The Titfield Thunderbolt
7. Marie Celeste
8. Jubilee Line
9. Eight
10. Austerlitz
11. Blue Riband
12. Poland
13. Triangular
14. Fishguard
15. Groovy Train
16. Michael Portillo
17. Zurich
18. Cathay Pacific
19. Canoe
20. Bugatti

Quiz 130: Books

1. Complete the title of the 2010 novel by Jennifer Egan: A Visit From The...?

2. A Time To Kill was the debut novel by which best-selling author?

3. Who wrote The Hunger Games trilogy?

4. The children's book Mr Stink was written by which comedian?

5. Who is the central character in the thriller The 39 Steps?

6. Goodbye, Columbus was the debut novel by which American author?

7. Who wrote the Flashman novels?

8. Which novel by George Eliot was subtitled A Study of Provincial Life?

9. Humbert Humbert is a character in which novel?

10. What was James Joyce's last novel?

11. Carlos Ruiz Zafón's The Shadow of the Wind is set in which country?

12. Which British Prime Minister wrote the novels Coningsby, Sybil and Tancred?

13. Complete the title of 1839 novel by Edgar Allan Poe: The Fall of the House of...?

14. In what genre of fiction is Iain M Banks a notable name?

15. What is the first name of Flaubert's Madame Bovary?

16. Who is the main protagonist in Anthony Horowitz's 2011 novel The House of Silk?

17. Which British author wrote The Thousand Autumns of Jacob de Zoet?

18. Which group, whose biggest hit was Born To Be Wild, took their name from a novel by Herman Hesse?

19. A Suitable Boy is by which author?
    a) Salman Rushdie
    b) Vikram Seth
    c) Arundhati Roy

20. Pulling Myself Together is the autobiography of which Loose Woman?
    a) Coleen Nolan
    b) Carol McGiffin
    c) Denise Welch

Answers to Quiz 129: Pot Luck

1. Martin Amis
2. Quantum of Solace
3. Hay fever
4. Beyonce Knowles
5. Snow White and the Seven Dwarfs
6. 999
7. Henri Matisse
8. Primal Scream
9. Jeremy Clarkson
10. George V
11. 1982
12. Dr Johnson
13. Indonesia
14. Pittsburgh
15. Hawaii
16. Moonraker, Thunderball, Octopussy, Goldfinger and Goldeneye
17. Taggart
18. John Hurt
19. Johannesburg
20. Black Coffee

Quiz 131: Pot Luck

1. On a radio, what do the initials AM stand for?

2. Invicta is the motto of which English county?

3. Why is Christmas sometimes shortened to Xmas?

4. What is the subject of Ernest Hemingway's book Death In The Afternoon?

5. A Varsovian is a person from which city?

6. Which Championship club did Liverpool beat on penalties to win the 2012 League Cup final?

7. Oliver Tambo Airport is in which country?

8. Which TV comedy was almost called The Fighting Tigers?

9. What is the first name of Georges Simenon's Inspector Maigret?

10. What is the only letter of the alphabet that doesn't feature in the name of any American state?

11. Americans call it the eggplant but what is it called in Britain?

12. What march is usually played to mark the arrival of the President of the United States?

13. The Daily Slate was the newspaper in which TV cartoon?

14. What is a merkin?

15. The highest mountain and largest lake in England are in which county?

16. Cesar Romero played which enemy of Batman in the 1960s TV series?

17. The name of which Rolling Stone appeared in the title of a number one hit by Cher Lloyd?

18. Set in Asia, what was George Orwell's debut novel?

19. Hayfever afflicts approximately what percentage of the UK population?
    a) 10%
    b) 20%
    c) 30%

20. Complete the title of the album by the Kings of Leon: Come Around...?
    a) Sometime
    b) Lonesome
    c) Sundown

MEDIUM

Answers to Quiz 130: Books

1. Goon Squad
2. John Grisham
3. Suzanne Collins
4. David Walliams
5. Richard Hannay
6. Philip Roth
7. George McDonald Fraser
8. Middlemarch
9. Lolita
10. Finnegans Wake
11. Spain
12. Benjamin Disraeli
13. Usher
14. Science fiction
15. Emma
16. Sherlock Holmes
17. David Mitchell
18. Steppenwolf
19. Vikram Seth
20. Denise Welch

Quiz 132: Sport part 2

1. Which Italian took over as manager of Swindon Town in 2011?

2. England became the number one-rated side in Test cricket in 2011 after beating which team?

3. In what sport is Michaela Tabb a referee?

4. The Padres are a Major League Baseball team from which American city?

5. Who did Sir Alex Ferguson succeed as manager of Manchester United?

6. Grace Road is the home ground of which county cricket team?

7. What is the only stadium to have hosted two World Cup finals?

8. Which Formula One Grand Prix takes place at the Marina Bay circuit?

9. Who knocked Ireland out of the 2011 Rugby World Cup?

10. Which city hosted the 1952 Olympic Games?

11. In what month does Royal Ascot take place?

12. Who was the last Englishman to win the Open Championship?

13. The Africa Cup of Nations takes place every how many years?

14. In darts, what is the only two-figure number that cannot be finished in two darts?

15. How many players are on an Australian Rules Football team?

16. In 2011, Cadel Evans became the first rider from which country to win the Tour de France?

17. The Manor Ground was the former home of which English football club?

18. The British Grand Prix motorcycle race takes place at which circuit?

19. Angelo Mathews is an international cricketer who represents which country?
    a) India
    b) South Africa
    c) Sri Lanka

20. What race is the traditional curtain raiser for the flat racing season?
    a) The Grantham
    b) The Lincoln
    c) The Doncaster

MEDIUM

Answers to Quiz 131: Pot Luck

1. Amplitude modulation
2. Kent
3. X is the first letter of the Greek word for Christ
4. Bull fighting
5. Warsaw
6. Cardiff City
7. South Africa
8. Dad's Army
9. Jules
10. Q
11. Aubergine
12. Hail to the Chief
13. The Flintstones
14. A pubic wig
15. Cumbria
16. The Joker
17. Jagger (Swagger Jagger)
18. Burmese Days
19. 20%
20. Sundown

Quiz 133: Pot Luck

1. Frederic Chopin Airport serves which city?

2. In which English county is the Forest of Dean?

3. Jonathan Ross and Russell Brand caused controversy after leaving a message on which actor's answering machine?

4. Who resigned as chairman of BSkyB in April 2012?

5. Who was the 16th President of the United States of America?

6. Which British monarch was nicknamed the Sailor King?

7. Which group won the Eurovision Song Contest in 1976?

8. Who played vigilante Robert McCall in 1980s TV drama The Equalizer?

9. Who plays Captain Jonathan Archer in Star Trek: Enterprise?

10. Kigali is the capital city of which African country?

11. Who stepped down as the manager of Barcelona at the end of the 2011/12 season?

12. Richard Bachman is the pseudonym of which American writer?

13. X Factor winners Little Mix reached number one with Cannonball but who recorded the original version?

14. Which famous radio DJ was a member of The Fall?

15. Which former boy band star played Sean Parker in the 2010 film The Social Network?

16. What girl's name was the title of a 2007 number one for Kaiser Chiefs?

17. Who designed the cover to the Beatles' Sergeant Pepper album?

18. What is the capital city of Botswana?

19. What is the name of the newspaper that features in the Spider Man films?
    a) Daily Planet
    b) Daily Bugle
    c) Daily World

20. In Greek mythology, how many eyes did Argus have?
    a) 1
    b) 2
    c) 100

MEDIUM

Answers to Quiz 132: Sport part 2

1. Paolo di Canio
2. India
3. Snooker
4. San Diego
5. Ron Atkinson
6. Leicestershire
7. Azteca Stadium, Mexico City
8. Singapore
9. Wales
10. Helsinki
11. June
12. Nick Faldo
13. Two
14. 99
15. 18
16. Australia
17. Oxford United
18. Silverstone
19. Sri Lanka
20. The Lincoln

Quiz 134: Famous Daves

1. Member of Nirvana and Foo Fighters?

2. Actor who plays Eddie Moon in EastEnders?

3. Former Foreign Secretary who is the MP for South Shields?

4. Comedian who enjoyed a Googlewhack Adventure?

5. Actor who played Fox Mulder in The X Files?

6. Guitarist and vocalist with rock group Pink Floyd?

7. TV presenter born David Gulesserian?

8. In 1999, became the first elected First Minister of Northern Ireland?

9. Actor who starred in Scream and had a brief career as a professional wrestler?

10. Lead singer with synth popsters Depeche Mode?

11. Topped the charts with When Love Takes Over and Sexy Chick?

12. Producer whose films included Bugsy Malone, Chariots of Fire, The Duellists and Local Hero?

13. Author whose works include A Heartbreaking Work of Staggering Genius and Zeitoun?

14. Leader of a Branch Davidian Cult, killed at the Waco siege?

15. Pulitzer Prize-winning playwright who wrote Glengarry Glen Ross?

16. He became the chairman of the Football Association in 2011?

17. Film director best known for The Fly, Crash and A History of Violence?

18. Name shared by a former England midfielder and a soap bad boy?

19. Led the England team to Ashes victory in 1985?

20. Famous British poker player nicknamed the Devilfish?

MEDIUM

Answers to Quiz 133: Pot Luck

1. Warsaw
2. Gloucestershire
3. Andrew Sachs
4. James Murdoch
5. Abraham Lincoln
6. William IV
7. Brotherhood of Man
8. Edward Woodward
9. Scott Bakula
10. Rwanda
11. Pep Guardiola
12. Stephen King
13. Damien Rice
14. Marc Riley aka Lard
15. Justin Timberlake
16. Ruby
17. Peter Blake
18. Gaborone
19. Daily Bugle
20. 100

DIFFICULT QUIZZES

Quiz 135: Pot Luck

1. Who hosted the 2009 revival of The Krypton Factor?

2. Which American state takes its name from the wife of King Charles II?

3. What is the shortest word in English that contains the letters a b c d e and f?

4. A person with turophobia fears what type of food?

5. What is the most landed-on square on a Monopoly board?

6. The longest journey without a change on the London Underground takes place on which line?

7. Roseau is the capital city of which Caribbean island?

8. Where in Australia would you find a cricket ground called the Bellerive Oval?

9. What can an MP say if he wants to empty the public galleries of the House of Commons?

10. Which monarch made the first Royal Christmas broadcast?

11. In 1969, which took countries were involved in the so-called Soccer War?

12. In 2001, which group became the first Western act to play in Cuba for more than 20 years?

13. What is the only country in South America that hosts Test match cricket?

14. Safar, Rajab and Shawwal are months in which calendar?

15. Athens was the first in 1985, Cork was in 2005 and Liverpool and Stavanger were in 2007? What were they?

16. How many letters are in the Hebrew alphabet?

17. What is the name of the owner of the comic book store in The Big Bang Theory?

18. What connects Winston Churchill, Raoul Wallenberg, William and Mary Penn and Mother Teresa of Calcutta?

19. The Gift was the only number one album for which group?
    a) The Who
    b) The Jam
    c) The Move

20. In German politics, what do the initials CDU stand for?
    a) Capitalist Democratic Union
    b) Christian Democratic Union
    c) Cultural Democratic Union

Answers to Quiz 200: Taking the Michael

1. Princess Michael of Kent
2. Michael McDonald
3. Michael Ignatieff
4. Michael Douglas
5. Mick Fitzgerald
6. Mickey Goldmill
7. Michael Bublé
8. Mikey Graham
9. Michael Stich
10. Michael Haneke
11. Michael Phelps
12. Michael Le Vell
13. Michael Bloomberg
14. Michael Flatley
15. Michael Portillo
16. Mickey Adams
17. Michael Imperioli
18. Michael Oher
19. Mickey Quinn
20. Michael Atherton

DIFFICULT

Quiz 136: Book Opening Lines

Identify the books from the following opening lines:

1. The sweat wis lashing oafay Sick Boy; He was trembling.

2. The hamlet stood on a gentle rise in the flat, wheat-growing north-east corner of Oxfordshire.

3. Mr. Utterson the lawyer was a man of a rugged countenance, that was never lighted by a smile; cold, scanty and embarrassed.

4. Well, Prince, so Genoa and Lucca are now just family estates of the Buonapartes.

5. 3 May. Bistritz. Left Munich at 8.35pm on 1st May, arriving at Vienna early next morning; should have arrived at 6.46, but the train was late.

6. When he was nearly thirteen, my brother Jem got his arm badly broken at the elbow.

7. Mother died today. Or perhaps it was yesterday, I don't know.

8. People do not give it credence that a fourteen-year-old girl could leave her home and go off in the wintertime to avenge her father's blood.

9. Lyra and her daemon moved through the darkening hall.

10. As Gregor Samsa awoke one morning from uneasy dreams, he found himself transformed into a giant insect.

11. This is the saddest story I have ever heard.

12. Abandon All Hope Ye Who Enter Here is scrawled in blood red lettering on the side of the Chemical Bank...

13. Miss Brooke had that kind of beauty which seems to be thrown into relief by poor dress.

14. The schoolmaster was leaving the village, and everybody seemed sorry.

15. The Mole had been working very hard all the morning, spring cleaning his little home.

16. Whether I shall turn out to be the hero of my own life, or whether that station will be held by anybody else, these pages must show.

17. A merry little surge of electricity piped by automatic alarm from the mood organ beside his bed awakened Rick Deckard.

18. Miss Jane Marple was sitting by her window.

19. I returned from the city about three o'clock on that May afternoon, pretty well disgusted with life.

20. There was no possibility of taking a walk that day.

Answers to Quiz 135: Pot Luck

1. Ben Shephard
2. Maryland (Queen Henrietta Marie)
3. Feedback
4. Cheese
5. Trafalgar Square
6. Central (West Ruislip to Epping)
7. Dominica
8. Hobart, Tasmania
9. I spy strangers
10. King George V
11. El Salvador and Honduras
12. Manic Street Preachers
13. Guyana
14. Islamic
15. European Capital of Culture
16. 22
17. Stuart
18. They were all granted honorary US citizenship
19. The Jam
20. Christian Democratic Union

DIFFICULT

Quiz 137: Pot Luck

1. Leviathan was the most famous work of which English philosopher?

2. Which American author is mentioned in the Beatles song I Am The Walrus?

3. Name the five UK towns and cities that have hosted the Eurovision Song Contest?

4. Which American president was the first to have been born in a hospital?

5. Which Scottish football club play their home games at Hampden Park?

6. Which popular 1980s group took its name from supporters of the 1871 Paris Commune?

7. Who was the Egyptian goddess of the rain?

8. What name links a Dickensian dog and a 1980s TV gameshow?

9. Banjul is the capital city of which African country?

10. Which Blue Peter presenter also hosted motorbike trials show Kick Start?

11. Who comes next in this list? Arnold Bax, Arthur Bliss, Malcolm Williamson?

12. What berry is made by crossing a raspberry with a blackberry?

13. Which Roman philosopher died after being given love potion by his wife Lucilia?

14. Which director's credits include Sideways, Election and The Descendants?

15. Who wrote the classic children's novel War Horse?

16. Russia has how many time zones?

17. In which Indian city would you find Dum Dum Airport?

18. Concord is the capital of which US state?

19. There are how many rooms in Buckingham Palace?
    a) 175 b) 650 c) 975

20. On a film set, what term describes the last shot of the day?
    a) Bourbon shot b) Martini shot c) Vodka shot

Answers to Quiz 136: Book Opening Lines

1. Trainspotting by Irvine Welsh

2. Lark Rise to Candleford by Flora Thompson

3. The Strange Case of Dr Jekyll and Mr Hyde by Robert Louis Stevenson

4. War and Peace by Leo Tolstoy

5. Dracula by Bram Stoker

6. To Kill A Mockingbird by Harper Lee

7. The Outsider (l'Étranger) by Albert Camus

8. True Grit by Charles Portis

9. Northern Lights by Philip Pullman

10. Metamorphosis by Franz Kafka

11. The Good Soldier by Ford Madox Ford

12. American Psycho by Brett Easton Ellis

13. Middlemarch by George Eliot

14. Jude The Obscure by Thomas Hardy

15. The Wind in the Willows by Kenneth Grahame

16. David Copperfield by Charles Dickens

17. Do Androids Dream of Electric Sheep? by Philip K Dick

18. The Mirror Crack'd by Agatha Christie

19. The Thirty-Nine Steps by John Buchan

20. Jane Eyre by Charlotte Bronte

DIFFICULT

Quiz 138: Flags and Emblems

1. The cedar tree appears on the flag of which country?

2. The Dominican Republic is the only country to have what on its flag?

3. How many stars are on the European Union flag?

4. What is the only country whose flag isn't a quadrilateral?

5. What bird appears on the flags of Mexico, Albania, Egypt and Serbia?

6. How many stars are on the flag of New Zealand?

7. Which African country's flag is made up of red and green horizontal halves with a yellow star in the middle?

8. The flags of Benin, Guinea, Mali, Cameroon and Congo are all made up of which three colours?

9. A dragon features on the flag of which Asian country?

10. In a motor racing Grand Prix, what does a yellow and red striped flag signify?

11. What object appears on the flags of Kenya and Swaziland?

12. The crane bird appears on the flag of which east African country?

13. Honomaru or Circle of the Sun is the name of the flag of which Asian country?

14. Which two states have square flags?

15. The flag of which country contains a globe, 27 stars and the words Ordem e Progresso?

16. The Union Flag appears on the flag of which American state?

17. Which Asian country's flag features a red circle on a dark green background?

18. Which part of the British Isles has a flag featuring a Triskelion?

19. A trident appears on the flag of which Caribbean country?
    a) Barbados
    b) Jamaica
    c) St Lucia

20. The flag of which country is the oldest still in use by an independent nation?
    a) Denmark
    b) Norway
    c) Sweden

Answers to Quiz 137: Pot Luck

1. Thomas Hobbes
2. Edgar Allan Poe
3. London, Harrogate, Birmingham, Edinburgh and Brighton
4. Jimmy Carter
5. Queen's Park
6. The Communards
7. Tefnut
8. Bullseye
9. Gambia
10. Peter Purves
11. Peter Maxwell Davies (Master of the Queen's Music)
12. Loganberry
13. Lucretius
14. Alexander Payne
15. Michael Morpurgo
16. Nine
17. Kolkata
18. New Hampshire
19. 650
20. Martini shot

DIFFICULT

Quiz 139: Pot Luck

1. Which Algerian-born, French writer and philosopher died in a car crash in 1960?

2. Which Australian rock band recorded the soundtrack to the 2010 film Iron Man 2?

3. What links the Caribbean island of Anguilla and Charlton Athletic FC?

4. What is the smallest of the Great Lakes?

5. Which layer of the earth's atmosphere lies between the mesosphere and exosphere?

6. Mark Rutte resigned as the Prime Minister of which country in April 2012?

7. The works of which composer have been chosen the most times by castaways on Desert Island Discs?

8. Who succeeded Kim Jong-Il as leader of North Korea?

9. In which country would you find Mount Ararat?

10. Yaounde is the capital city of which African country?

11. Who is TV's Restoration Man?

12. Rajya Sabha is the upper house of parliament in which country?

13. Lunchtime O'Boulez, Dr B Ching and Gavel Basher are columnists in which magazine?

14. Which former Soviet republic won the 2011 Eurovision Song Contest?

15. What is the capital of the US state of Wisconsin?

16. Catherine the Great ruled Russia in which century?

17. Chippy Minton, Mr Clamp, Mr Antonio and Miss Lovelace lived in which animated village?

18. The Homburg has was popularised by which English king?

19. The geographical centre of the USA is in which state?
    a) Kansas
    b) Kentucky
    c) Missouri

20. Who played Stephanie Zinone in Grease 2?
    a) Melanie Griffiths
    b) Jodie Foster
    c) Michelle Pfeiffer

Answers to Quiz 138: Flags and Emblems

1. Lebanon
2. A bible
3. Twelve
4. Nepal
5. Eagle
6. Four
7. Burkina Faso
8. Green, yellow and red
9. Bhutan
10. A slippery track
11. Shield
12. Uganda
13. Japan
14. Switzerland and Vatican City
15. Brazil
16. Hawaii
17. Bangladesh
18. Isle of Man
19. Barbados
20. Denmark

DIFFICULT

Quiz 140: Movies part 1

1. John Cusack played which author in the 2012 film Raven?

2. Which Swede directed the film version of Tinker, Tailor, Soldier, Spy?

3. Which British actor wrote and directed the film Adulthood?

4. In which adventure classic would you find a nightclub called Club Obi-Wan?

5. Randall, Fidgit, Strutter, Og, Wally and Vermin are characters in which fantasy film?

6. Which Oscar-winning actor has, since 1987, been the Ambassador of The Bahamas to Japan?

7. 'Madness. Madness' is the last line of which classic war film?

8. Four Lions was the directorial debut from which actor and satirist?

9. 'I was 12 going on 13 the first time I saw a dead human being' is the opening line of which coming-of-age movie?

10. Which 1984 film was known in Poland as Electronic Murderer?

11. In Back To The Future, what speed must Doc's Delorean reach in order to achieve time travel?

12. What were Dusty Bottoms, Lucky Day and Ned Nederlander collectively known as?

13. Starring Vincent Cassell, the 2008 film Killer Instinct was about which French gangster?

14. Philip John Clapp is the real name of which actor and stuntman?

15. Which actor played Eli in the 2010 film The Book Of Eli?

16. Who was the first American actress to appear on a postage stamp?

17. What film, about striking workers at a Ford factory, was known in Germany as We Want Sex?

18. Clint Eastwood played Walt Kowalski in which 2008 film?

19. What was the first word spoken by an ape in Planet of the Apes?
a) die
b) smile
c) please

20. Complete the title of the 2012 film: Martha Marcy May...?
a) Maria
b) Marlene
c) Miriam

Answers to Quiz 139: Pot Luck

1. Albert Camus
2. AC/DC
3. The Valley (the capital of Anguilla is The Valley. Charlton play at The Valley)
4. Ontario
5. Thermosphere
6. The Netherlands
7. Mozart
8. Kim Jong-un
9. Turkey
10. Cameroon
11. George Clarke
12. India
13. Private Eye
14. Azerbaijan
15. Madison
16. 18th
17. Trumpton
18. King Edward VII
19. Kansas
20. Michelle Pfeiffer

DIFFICULT

Quiz 141: Pot Luck

1. What fabric, invented in 1958 by Du Pont, was originally known as Fiber K?

2. Who played Laurence Olivier in the 2011 film My Week With Marilyn?

3. Toys featuring characters from which TV show were banned in Iran in 2012?

4. Who played the harmonica on the Eurythmics' hit There Must Be An Angel?

5. What is Donald Duck's middle name?

6. Velociraptor! was a number one album from which group?

7. Most of Belfast lies in which Irish county?

8. What do the intials WH in WH Auden stand for?

9. What nationality is the author Margaret Atwood?

10. In 1929, Emil Jannings became the first recipient of what award?

11. Opilio, Tanner and Dungeness are types of what creature?

12. Kingpin is a film about which sport?

13. What is the name of the university in comedy drama Fresh Meat?

14. Cheilitis is the inflammation of what part of the body?

15. What is the Irish singer Eithne ni Bhraonain better known as?

16. Captain Leland Francis Stottlemeyer appears in which US detective drama?

17. Jane Turner and Gina Riley played the title characters in which Australian comedy?

18. Which actor's last words were, 'I should have switched from Scotch to Martinis'?

19. Michael Jackson, Tina Turner, Whitney Houston and Eddie Murphy have all appeared on the stamps of which country?
    a) Tanzania
    b) Togo
    c) Tunisia

20. Who hasn't hosted the Oscars?
    a) Ellen Degeneres
    b) Ricky Gervais
    c) Paul Hogan

Answers to Quiz 140: Movies part 1

1. Edgar Allan Poe
2. Tomas Alfredson
3. Noel Clarke
4. Indiana Jones and the Temple of Doom
5. Time Bandits
6. Sidney Poitier
7. The Bridge On The River Kwai
8. Chris Morris
9. Stand By Me
10. The Terminator
11. 88mph
12. The Three Amigos
13. Jacques Mesrine
14. Johnny Knoxville
15. Denzel Washington
16. Grace Kelly
17. Made in Dagenham
18. Gran Torino
19. Smile
20. Marlene

DIFFICULT

Quiz 142: Written Word

1. In France and Belgium, what are Bandes Dessinées?

2. What do the JRR in JRR Tolkien stand for?

3. Sam Weller and Nathaniel Winkle are characters in which Dickens novel?

4. Which character appeared for the first time in a story called The Mysterious Affair at Styles?

5. What nationality is Gabriel Garcia Marquez?

6. The Gathering is a Booker Prize-winning novel by which author?

7. Which American author ran a Saab car dealership before finding success as a writer?

8. Oscar nominated film The Help is based on a 2009 novel by which author?

9. Les Rougon-Macquart is a collection of twenty novels by which author?

10. Which Scottish football club shares its name with an 1818 novel by Sir Walter Scott?

11. Gabriel Oak is a character in which novel by Thomas Hardy?

12. The creator of the Objectivist movement, which author's real name was Alisa Zinov'yevna Rosenbaum?

13. May I Have Your Attention, Please? was the 2011 autobiography of which comedian?

14. What is the name of the publishing house founded by author Dave Eggers?

15. In Oliver Twist, what is the Artful Dodger's real name?

16. Who is the owner of Manor Farm in George Orwell's Animal Farm?

17. Which broadcaster and journalist wrote the 2011 bestseller How To Be A Woman?

18. Who wrote the 2004 novel Small Island?

19. What is the name of the collection of Leonardo da Vinci's manuscripts that sold for $30.8m in 1994?
    a) Codex Derby
    b) Codex Leicester
    c) Codex Nottingham

20. Selling for over £7.3m in 2010, what is the name of the most expensive printed book in the world?
    a) Animals of America
    b) Birds of America
    c) Flowers of America

Answers to Quiz 141: Pot Luck

1. Spandex (Lycra)
2. Kenneth Branagh
3. The Simpsons
4. Stevie Wonder
5. Fauntleroy
6. Kasabian
7. Antrim
8. Wystan Hugh
9. Canadian
10. An Oscar
11. Crab
12. Ten-pin bowling
13. Manchester Medlock University
14. Lips
15. Enya
16. Monk
17. Kath and Kim
18. Humphrey Bogart
19. Tanzania
20. Ricky Gervais

DIFFICULT

Quiz 143: Pot Luck

1. May your God go with you was the catchphrase of which comedian?

2. What long-running TV programme was based on the French show 'Des Chiffres et Des Lettres'?

3. Chris Evans hosted a gameshow called Don't Forget Your what?

4. Wendi Deng is the wife of which famous person?

5. The constellation Hydra is named after what sort of creature?

6. Which country has the largest coastline in the world?

7. Between 1918 and 1943, Boris III was the king of which European country?

8. Which Hollywood superstar owned a 136kg pet pot-bellied pig called Max?

9. What do the initials JMW stand for in the painter JMW Turner's name?

10. Which actor, best known for playing a TV detective, had a 1975 number one hit with If?

11. Which fashion designer described singer Adele as 'a little too fat, but she has a beautiful face and a divine voice'?

12. Complete the title of the number one album by Bruno Mars: Doo-Wops and...?

13. Which doctor coined the word nerd in his 1950 book If I Ran The Zoo?

14. The Roman Road Ermine Street ran from London to which city?

15. The No. 1 Ladies' Detective Agency is set in which country?

16. What was the name of the womanising barman played by Ted Danson in sitcom Cheers?

17. Which former synchronised swimming champion succeeded Dominique Strauss-Khan as head of the International Monetary Fund in 2011?

18. Ceremonials was a number one album in 2011 by which group?

19. What product was the first to feature a bar code?
    a) chewing gum
    b) washing powder
    c) shampoo

20. Warsaw was the original name of which Manchester band?
    a) Happy Mondays
    b) Joy Division
    c) The Stone Roses

Answers to Quiz 142: Written Word

1. Comic books
2. John Ronald Reuel
3. The Pickwick Papers
4. Hercule Poirot
5. Colombian
6. Anne Enright
7. Kurt Vonnegut
8. Kathryn Stockett
9. Emile Zola
10. Heart of Midlothian
11. Far From The Madding Crowd
12. Ayn Rand
13. James Corden
14. McSweeney's
15. Jack Dawkins
16. Mr Jones
17. Caitlin Moran
18. Andrea Levy
19. Codex Leicester
20. Birds of America

DIFFICULT

Quiz 144: Television part 1

1. Which British actor plays CIA operative David Estes in US drama Homeland?

2. What was the name of the spacecraft in Blake's Seven?

3. In Downton Abbey, what is the first name of the Countess Dowager of Grantham?

4. Who played Bomber in 1980s classic Auf Wiedersehen Pet?

5. Which comedy drama is set in the fictional seaside town of Portwenn?

6. What is the name of the British supernatural comedy drama that features characters called Annie Sawyer, Tom McNair and Hal York?

7. Which group recorded the theme music to Father Ted?

8. What was the fashion house drama that starred Louise Lombard and Stella Gonet?

9. What is the name of the Australian actor who plays Patrick Jane in The Mentalist?

10. Which series is set at 165 Eaton Place?

11. Detective series Dirk Gently is based on the novels of which author?

12. What is the name of The Simpsons' pet cat?

13. 70s comedy George and Mildred was a spin-off from which series?

14. Which medical drama is set in the fictional Midland town of Letherbridge?

15. Who starred as Cecil Slinger in the supermarket-set comedy Slinger's Day?

16. On which sporting show will you find Rocket, Tubes and Baby Elvis?

17. Political drama Borgen is set in which country?

18. In Miami Vice, what was the name of Crockett's pet alligator?

19. US drama Suits is set in which profession?
    a) accountancy
    b) advertising
    c) law

20. TV comedy Sirens is about?
    a) the Ambulance service
    b) the Fire Service
    c) The Police

Answers to Quiz 143: Pot Luck

1. Dave Allen
2. Countdown
3. Toothbrush
4. Rupert Murdoch
5. Sea serpent
6. Canada
7. Bulgaria
8. George Clooney
9. Joseph Mallord William
10. Telly Savalas
11. Karl Lagerfeld
12. Hooligans
13. Dr Seuss
14. York
15. Botswana
16. Sam Malone
17. Christine Lagarde
18. Florence and the Machine
19. Chewing gum
20. Joy Division

DIFFICULT

Quiz 145: Pot Luck

1. Sherry derives its name from which Spanish city?

2. Which country's flag contains six colours, more than any other in the world?

3. Which EastEnders actress was Christopher Biggins' assistant on children's TV gameshow On Safari?

4. Sexy Boy and Kelly Watch The Stars were hits for which French duo?

5. The film Tom and Viv was about which poet?

6. What was the name of the dog in the Oscar-winning film The Artist?

7. Which food writer won the Beard of the Year award in 2011?

8. What is the female equivalent of brethren?

9. Princess Diana of Themyscira is the alter ego of which comic superheroine?

10. Which English town became a city as part of the Queen's Diamond Jubilee celebrations?

11. Who was the eldest of the literary Brontë sisters?

12. Which Portuguese football club knocked Manchester City out of the 2011/12 Europa League?

13. Thomasina Myers, Tim Anderson and Shelina Permalloo have all won which reality TV show?

14. Who composed symphonies called The Headmaster, The Philosopher, Maria Theresia and The Palindrome?

15. Which poet owned a cat called George Pushdragon?

16. The First Book of Nephi is the opening book in which religious text?

17. Which philosopher said, 'All noble things are difficult as they are rare'?

18. Hartford is the capital of which US state?

19. In Greek cuisine, baklava is a type of what?
    a) meat
    b) vegetable
    c) pastry

20. The Beatles made a guest appearance in which 1960s sci fi series?
    a) Star Trek
    b) Dr Who
    c) The Twilight Zone

Answers to Quiz 144: Television part 1

1. David Harewood
2. Liberator
3. Violet
4. Pat Roach
5. Doc Martin
6. Being Human
7. Divine Comedy
8. The House of Eliott
9. Simon Baker
10. Upstairs Downstairs
11. Douglas Adams
12. Snowball
13. Man About The House
14. Doctors
15. Bruce Forsyth
16. Soccer AM
17. Denmark
18. Elvis
19. Law
20. Ambulance service

DIFFICULT

Quiz 146: Politics part 1

1. Who succeeded Baroness Royall of Blaisdon as the Leader of the House of Lords in 2010?

2. How did farmer Craig Evans cause controversy during the 2001 General Election campaign?

3. Which Scottish politician was fined £3,000 in 2012 after admitting a charge of common assault in a House of Commons bar?

4. Who, in 1908, became the only British Prime Minister to assume office while on foreign soil?

5. Who is the official responsible for the security of the House of Commons?

6. Which boxer was elected to the national legislature of The Philippines in 2010?

7. T. Dan Smith was a council leader in which English city?

8. Who, in 2009, became the first full-time President of the European Council?

9. Ian Richardson played which politician in TV drama House of Cards?

10. José Manuel Barroso succeeded which Italian as President of the European Commission?

11. Which Prime Minister's wife was the niece of Winston Churchill?

12. Who was the Prime Minister at the start of the 20th century?

13. Paul Kagame is the president of which African country?

14. Who was the UKIP MEP for the East Midlands constituency from 2004 until 2009?

Answers - page 299

15. Who was the first US President to appear on television?

16. Chat show host Jerry Springer was previously the mayor of which American city?

17. At 6ft 4in, who was the tallest ever American president?

18. Who played the American president in the 1996 film Mars Attacks?

19. What is the smallest UK parliamentary constituency?
    a) Birmingham Ladywood
    b) Islington North
    c) Manchester Central

20. What was Michelle Gildernew's majority in the Fermanagh and South Tyrone seat in the 2011 General Election?
    a) 4
    b) 14
    c) 44

Answers to Quiz 145: Pot Luck

1. Jerez
2. South Africa
3. Gillian Taylforth
4. Air
5. TS Eliot
6. Uggie
7. Jay Rayner
8. A sistren
9. Wonder Woman
10. Chelmsford
11. Charlotte
12. Sporting Lisbon
13. Masterchef
14. Joseph Haydn
15. TS Eliot
16. The Book of Mormon
17. Benedict Spinoza
18. Connecticut
19. Pastry
20. Dr Who

DIFFICULT

Quiz 147: Pot Luck

1. Frankfort is the capital of which US state?

2. Blur have had two number one singles. Beetlebum was one but what was the other?

3. Almaty is the biggest city in which country?

4. What is the female equivalent of fraternal?

5. Which James Bond theme performed the best in the UK singles chart, reaching number two?

6. Kampuchea is the former name of which Asian country?

7. What is the highest rank in the RAF?

8. RENFE is the national railway of which country?

9. A band called Figrin D'an and the Modal Nodes appeared in which film?

10. Belgian priest Georges Lemaitre first advanced which theory of the universe?

11. Detective drama Murdoch Mysteries is set in which country?

12. The Primate of All Ireland is the Archbishop of where?

13. Edward Murdstone, Daniel Peggotty and James Steerforth are characters in which novel by Charles Dickens?

14. Which town in Wales became a city in 2012?

15. What colour flags are thrown by officials in American football matches to signify a penalty?

16. In the Bible, who was Jacob's youngest son?

17. Elim, Paarl and Constantia are wine-producing regions of which country?

18. What element has the chemical symbol W and the atomic number 74?

19. Don't It Make You Feel Good was a hit for which Aussie soap actor?
    a) Jason Donovan
    b) Stefan Dennis
    c) Craig McLachlan

20. What was the Greek philosopher Democritus known as
    a) the crying philosopher
    b) the laughing philosopher
    c) the smiling philosopher?

Answers to Quiz 146: Politics part 1

1. Lord Strathclyde
2. He threw an egg at John Prescott who subsequently punched him
3. Eric Joyce
4. Herbert Asquith
5. Serjeant-at-Arms
6. Manny Pacquiao
7. Newcastle
8. Herman Van Rompuy
9. Francis Urquhart
10. Romano Prodi
11. Anthony Eden
12. Marquis of Salisbury
13. Rwanda
14. Robert Kilroy-Silk
15. Franklin D Roosevelt
16. Cincinnati
17. Abraham Lincoln
18. Jack Nicholson
19. Islington North
20. 4

DIFFICULT

Quiz 148: Art and Architecture

1. Which Florentine artist was nicknamed 'Little Barrel'?

2. The Hepworth gallery is in which Yorkshire town?

3. View of Delft is by which Dutch master?

4. Who played Jackson Pollock in the 2000 film Pollock?

5. Which Scottish sculptor won the 2011 Turner Prize?

6. What is a maulstick?

7. What nationality was the painter Kandinsky?

8. Which Coventry-born contemporary artist is noted for his use of aircraft modelling paint?

9. The Schnütgen Museum is located in which German city?

10. What is the art movement Jugendstil more commonly known as?

11. Umberto Boccioni, Giacomo Balla and Gino Severini were associated with which 20th-century artistic movement?

12. Style magazine Dazed and Confused was co-founded by which Glasgow-born photographer?

13. Which British artist wore a bear costume in a Berlin museum for his work Sleeper?

14. Which architect designed Blenheim Palace?

15. El Greco was born on which Greek island?

16. In which British city would you find a modern art gallery called Ikon?

17. Benefits Supervisor Sleeping and Girl With A White Dog are works by which German-born British artist?

18. Which Dutch artist painted The Temptation of St Anthony and The Garden of Earthly Delights?

19. In which part of a building would you find a mullion?
    a) door
    b) roof
    c) window

20. Which Bulgarian-born artist famously wrapped the Reichstag in Berlin in polypropylene fabric?
    a) Christo
    b) Hristo
    c) Zlatyu

Answers to Quiz 147: Pot Luck

1. Kentucky
2. Country House
3. Kazakhstan
4. Sororal
5. A View To A Kill by Duran Duran
6. Cambodia
7. Marshall of the RAF
8. Spain
9. Star Wars
10. The Big Bang Theory
11. Canada
12. Armagh
13. David Copperfield
14. St Asaph
15. Yellow
16. Benjamin
17. South Africa
18. Tungsten
19. Stefan Dennis
20. The laughing philosopher

DIFFICULT

Quiz 149: Pot Luck

1. What type of acid is produced when milk goes sour?

2. Which technology company created the social network games FarmVille, CastleVille and Empires & Allies?

3. National Express was the only top ten hit for which group?

4. What is the nickname of the NBA basketball team in Detroit?

5. In which English coastal town is the Jerwood Gallery?

6. Posdnuos, Dave and Maseo are members of which hip hop group?

7. A carpet features on the flag of which former Soviet Republic?

8. What design classic was created by automotive engineer George Carwardine?

9. Singer and actor Noel Harrison represented Britain at the Olympics in which sport?

10. What are Scotland's seven cities?

11. Dana Owens is the real name of which actress and hip hop star?

12. What is the name of the rugby league Super League team based in Perpignan?

13. Fagus is the Latin name for which tree?

14. Chorophobia is an irrational fear of what activity?

15. What sort of creatures is a herpetologist interested in?

16. Sana'a is the capital city of which country?

17. What is the fifth book of the Old Testament?

18. The Mediterranean island of Painosa is the setting for which absurdist novel?

19. Which actor was nominated for the Waterstone's Children's Book Prize for The Windvale Sprites?
    a) Mackenzie Crook
    b) Ricky Gervais
    c) Martin Freeman

20. The gaffer is in charge of what on a film set?
    a) electrics
    b) sound
    c) props

Answers to Quiz 148: Art and Architecture

1. Botticelli
2. Wakefield
3. Vermeer
4. Ed Harris
5. Martin Boyce
6. A stick used by artists to steady the hand holding the brush
7. Russian
8. George Shaw
9. Cologne
10. Art Nouveau
11. Futurism
12. Rankin
13. Mark Wallinger
14. Sir John Vanbrugh
15. Crete
16. Birmingham
17. Lucian Freud
18. Hieronymus Bosch
19. Window
20. Christo

DIFFICULT

Quiz 150: Awards and Prizes

1. In what field are the TRIC Awards won?

2. Who is the only snooker player to win the BBC Sports Personality of the Year Award?

3. The Astrid Lindgren Memorial Award is a prize in which field?

4. In 2012, Sharmeen Obaid-Chinoy became the first person from which country to win an Oscar?

5. Sara-Jane Hutt was the last British winner of what contest?

6. The Carl Alan Awards honour people in which branch of the arts?

7. In 2005, Jonathan Coe won the Samuel Johnson Prize for his biography of which experimental writer?

8. With eight awards, who is the most successful female Brit Award winner?

9. In what country does the International Golden Orange Film Festival take place?

10. The Brownlow Medal is awarded to the best player in which sport?

11. Academy Awards are presented in how many competitive categories?

12. Which duo won the Album of the Year Grammy in 2009 for Raising Sand?

13. In 1969, P.H. Newby became the first winner of which award?

14. In international Rose d'Or television awards take place in which country?

15. Which UK city hosted the MTV Europe Music Awards in 2011?

16. Which controversial French writer won the French Prix Goncourt for the novel The Map and the Territory?

17. What is the South American equivalent of the UEFA Champions League?

18. The Polar Music Prize is an international award in which country?

19. What prize is awarded to the winner of the Best Film at the Locarno Film Festival?
    a) Golden Bear
    b) Golden Leopard
    c) Golden Lion

20. What is the highest award in scouting?
    a) The Prince's Scout Award
    b) The Duke of Edinburgh's Scout Award
    c) The Queen's Scout Award

Answers to Quiz 149: Pot Luck

1. Lactic
2. Zynga
3. Divine Comedy
4. Detroit Pistons
5. Hastings
6. De La Soul
7. Turkmenistan
8. Anglepoise Lamp
9. Ski-ing
10. Aberdeen, Dundee, Edinburgh, Glasgow, Inverness, Perth and Stirling
11. Queen Latifah
12. Catalan Dragons
13. Beech
14. Dancing
15. Reptiles and amphibians
16. Yemen
17. Deuteronomy
18. Catch-22
19. Mackenzie Crook
20. Electrics

DIFFICULT

Quiz 151: Pot Luck

1. Who won the 1994 Mercury Prize for the album Elegant Slumming?

2. Mount Meager is in which Commonwealth country?

3. Enver Hoxha was the Communist leader of which country?

4. What is the most popular non-classical piece chosen by castaways on Desert Island Discs?

5. At the Battle of Bannockburn, Robert the Bruce defeated which English monarch?

6. Who wrote the novels Black Spring, Tropic of Cancer and Tropic of Capricorn?

7. Dili is the capital of which Asian country?

8. 'I believe in America' is the opening of which classic movie?

9. Gephyrophobia is a fear of what types of structure?

10. How many universities make up the American Ivy League?

11. What is the lightest weight division in Olympic boxing?

12. Which two South American countries are members of OPEC?

13. Known and Unknown was a 2011 memoir by which American politician?

14. The award-winning musical duo Amadou and Mariam are from which African country?

15. Which prison reformer appears on the £5 note?

16. In musical notation, what does legato mean?

17. Which Briton won a Best Actor Oscar for his performance in Reversal of Fortune?

18. The Raptors are an NBA basketball team from which North American city?

19. Briana Corrigan, Jacqui Abbott and Alison Wheeler were female vocalists with which band?
    a) The Beautiful South
    b) Soul II Soul
    c) Portishead

20. Which film studio was founded by brothers Harry and Jack Cohn?
    a) MGM
    b) Columbia
    c) Paramount

Answers to Quiz 150: Awards and Prizes

1. Television and Radio
2. Steve Davis
3. Children's literature
4. Pakistan
5. Miss World
6. Dance
7. B.S. Johnson
8. Annie Lennox
9. Turkey
10. Australian Rules Football
11. 24
12. Robert Plant and Alison Krauss
13. The Booker Prize
14. Switzerland
15. Belfast
16. Michel Houellebecq
17. Copa Libertadores
18. Sweden
19. Golden Leopard
20. The Queen's Scout Award

DIFFICULT

Quiz 152: Astronomy and Space

1. Ceres is the largest example of what type of celestial body?

2. Which planet is sometimes known as the Evening Star and the Morning Star?

3. Miranda, Ariel, Titania and Oberon are moons of which planet?

4. What was the name of the ill-fated British spacecraft that was lost on a mission to Mars in 2003?

5. Phobos is one of Mars' two moons. What is the other called?

6. What are Arend-Roland, Shoemaker-Levy 9 and Swift-Tuttle?

7. Which constellation appears on Van Gogh's painting, Starry Night Over the Rhone?

8. The atmosphere of Mars is composed primarily of which gas?

9. What is astronaut Neil Armstrong's middle name?

10. Which planet is named after the father of the Roman god Saturn?

11. The Royal Greenwich Observatory was commissioned by which English monarch?

12. Which one-hit wonder topped the charts in 1996 with Spaceman?

13. Vladimir Remek, the first non-Russian or American to go into space, was from which country?

14. Which constellation is named after a vain Greek Queen who boasted about her beauty?

15. Sirius, the brightest star in the night sky, is part of which constellation?

16. Who directed the 2009 science fiction film Moon?

17. What word describes the point at which an orbiting object is closest to the earth?

18. True or false. Titan, the biggest moon of Saturn is larger than the planet Mercury?

19. All three astronauts on the first mission to the moon were born in what year?
    a) 1925
    b) 1930
    c) 1935

20. Halley's Comet orbits the sun once every how many years?
    a) 76
    b) 96
    c) 116

Answers to Quiz 151: Pot Luck

1. M People
2. Canada
3. Albania
4. Je ne Regrette Rien by Edith Piaf
5. Edward II
6. Henry Miller
7. East Timor
8. The Godfather
9. Bridges
10. 8
11. Light flyweight
12. Ecuador and Venezuela
13. Donald Rumsfeld
14. Mali
15. Elizabeth Fry
16. Smoothly
17. Jeremy Irons
18. Toronto
19. The Beautiful South
20. Columbia

DIFFICULT

Quiz 153: Pot Luck

1. Ervin Burrell and William Rawls were characters in which American drama?

2. Steve Rogers is the alter ego of which super hero?

3. Only artists under what age are eligible to be considered for art's Turner Prize?

4. Author V.S. Naipaul was born in which Commonwealth country?

5. Birkirkara is the largest city in which country?

6. 'It was a bright cold day in April, and the clocks were striking thirteen' is the opening line from which novel?

7. Who painted Venice, a View of the Rialto Bridge, Looking North from the Fondamenta del Carbon, which sold for £26.7m in 2011?

8. White City Blue, Rumours of a Hurricane and Under The Stars are novels by which contemporary author?

9. What is the lowest officer rank in the British Army?

10. Maseru is the capital city of which Commonwealth country?

11. Which composer wrote the opera Turandot?

12. Jamur Gemilang or 'Stripes of Glory' is the nickname of which country's flag?

13. What Gas Mark is equivalent to 190C and 375F?

14. What pseudonym is used by a film maker who has disowned a film?

15. Who was the last leader of the SDP before the party merged with the Liberals?

16. Acton Bell was the pen name of which author?

17. What is the penultimate book of the New Testament?

18. MDNA was a 2012 album by which music veteran?

19. In which English county would you find the River Piddle?
    a) Dorset
    b) Suffolk
    c) Norfolk

20. Which number one-selling singer worked as a pattern cutter for Savile Row tailor?
    a) Billy Ocean
    b) Eddy Grant
    c) Paul Weller

Answers to Quiz 152: Astronomy and Space

1. Asteroid
2. Venus
3. Uranus
4. Beagle 2
5. Deimos
6. Comets
7. The Plough (Big Dipper)
8. Carbon dioxide
9. Alden
10. Uranus
11. Charles II
12. Babylon Zoo
13. Czechoslovakia
14. Cassiopeia
15. Canis Major
16. Duncan Jones
17. Perigee
18. True
19. 1930
20. 76

DIFFICULT

Quiz 154: Colours

1. Which Swiss duo had a top ten hit in 1988 with The Race?

2. What 1985 sword and sorcery film starred Brigitte Nielsen and Arnold Schwarzenegger?

3. Red was the first top 40 single for which Manchester band?

4. What colour are the five rings on the Olympic flag?

5. Who founded the fashion label Red or Dead?

6. Hall Green, Acocks Green and Garretts Green are suburbs of which English city?

7. What was the name of the 2011 horror film that starred John Goodman and was directed by Kevin Smith?

8. Which actor played the title character in the 2011 film The Green Hornet?

9. Which US president appears on the Purple Heart military medal?

10. Which Yorkshire-born novelist wrote a series of novels called the Red Riding Quartet?

11. What was the nickname of German pilot Manfred Von Richthofen?

12. Somebody Else's Guy was the first UK hit for which soul singer?

13. Which organisation was founded in Loughgall, Co.Armagh in 1795?

14. Founded in 1693, what is the oldest gentlemen's club in London?

15. What type of animal is a Yellow-shafted Flicker?

16. Black Night and Strange Kind of Woman were the only top ten singles for which rock group?

17. What is the only Ivy League university that is in the state of Rhode Island?

18. Young At Heart was the only number one single for which group?

19. The president of which Asian country lives in the Blue House?
    a) China
    b) Japan
    c) South Korea

20. Blue (Da Ba Dee) was a 1999 hit for which Italian dance group?
    a) Eiffel 65
    b) Eiffel 75
    c) Eiffel 85

Answers to Quiz 153: Pot Luck

1. The Wire
2. Captain America
3. 50
4. Trinidad and Tobago
5. Malta
6. 1984
7. Francesco Guardi
8. Tim Lott
9. Second Lieutenant
10. Lesotho
11. Giacomo Puccini
12. Malaysia
13. Gas Mark 5
14. Alan Smithee
15. Robert Maclennan
16. Anne Brontë
17. Jude
18. Madonna
19. Dorset
20. Billy Ocean

DIFFICULT

Quiz 155: Pot Luck

1. The temple of Angkor Wat appears on the flag of which Asian country?

2. What are the only two predominantly Roman Catholic countries in Asia?

3. How many time zones are there in China?

4. At the age of 84, who was Britain's oldest Prime Minister?

5. How is the number 5 written in binary?

6. What is the penultimate letter of the Greek alphabet?

7. How many people are entitled to hold the Order of Merit at any one time?

8. Praia is the capital city of which African country?

9. In which Essex town will you find an amusement park called the Kursaal?

10. Which actor has played characters called Jack Byrnes, Paul Vitti and Neil McCauley?

11. In 2007, Donald Tusk became the Prime Minister of which country?

12. Which Scottish football club play their home games at McDiarmid Park?

13. Joanne Wheatley and Edd Kimber are former winners of which TV culinary contest?

14. Ian Watkins, Mike Lewis and Luke Johnson are members of which Welsh rock band?

15. 'Be afraid. Be very afraid' was the tagline to which 1986 film?

16. The Clayhanger Trilogy was written by which Staffordshire-born author?

17. Which group provided the theme tune to the James Bond film The World Is Not Enough?

18. What national radio station was launched on 11 March 2002?

19. Red Hand Day, marked annually on 12 February is a campaign to eradicate the use of what?
    a) child soldiers
    b) landmines
    c) nuclear weapons

20. What bird features on the flag of Dominica?
    a) Eagle
    b) Parrot
    c) Pigeon

Answers to Quiz 154: Colours

1. Yello
2. Red Sonja
3. Elbow
4. Blue, black, red, yellow, green
5. Wayne Hemingway
6. Birmingham
7. Red State
8. Seth Rogen
9. George Washington
10. David Peace
11. Red Baron
12. Jocelyn Brown
13. Orange Order
14. White's
15. Bird
16. Deep Purple
17. Brown
18. The Bluebells
19. South Korea
20. Eiffel 65

DIFFICULT

Quiz 156: Movies part 2

1. Who was the first act to appear in and sing the theme in the same James Bond film?

2. Who directed The Tree of Life?

3. What 2006 film starring Ben Stiller was based on a children's book by Milan Trenc?

4. Johnny Depp provided the voice of a chameleon in which 2011 animated film?

5. What was the sequel to Bill and Ted's Excellent Adventure?

6. In which film will you hear the words 'If you build it, he will come'?

7. Which actor's directorial debut was Looking For Richard?

8. What was the name of the character played by Cary Grant in North By Northwest?

9. Who played Tom Chaney in the 2010 version of True Grit?

10. It Had To Be Jew was a potential title for which 1970s comedy?

11. Who directed the 1997 film Good Will Hunting?

12. The Kid Stays in the Picture was a documentary about which film producer?

13. Who played the title role in the 2008 film biography of notorious British prisoner Charles Bronson?

14. Who provides the voice of smooth talking Ken in Toy Story 3?

15. Jurassic Park actor Sam Neill was born in which country?

16. Leonardo Dicaprio played US Marshal Teddy Daniels in which 2010 film directed by Martin Scorsese?

17. Which actress spent 17 days in jail in 1982 on tax evasion charges?

18. How old was Olivia Newton-John when she played schoolgirl Sandy in Grease?

19. Caryn Johnson is the real name of which actress?
    a) Demi Moore
    b) Whoopi Goldberg
    c) Queen Latifah

20. Which of the following isn't a genuine film?
    a) Abraham Lincoln vs. Zombies
    b) Abraham Lincoln: Vampire Hunter
    c) Abraham Lincoln vs. Alien Invaders

Answers to Quiz 155: Pot Luck

1. Cambodia
2. The Philippines and East Timor
3. One
4. Gladstone
5. 101
6. Psi
7. 24
8. Cape Verde
9. Southend-on-Sea
10. Robert De Niro
11. Poland
12. St Johnstone
13. The Great British Bake Off
14. Lostprophets
15. The Fly
16. Arnold Bennett
17. Garbage
18. BBC Radio 6 Music
19. Child soldiers
20. Parrot

DIFFICULT

Quiz 157: Pot Luck

1. In motor racing, what colour of flag is flown to warn a driver that he is about to be lapped?

2. Who was the female judge on the TV talent show Pop Idol?

3. Despite being the ninth largest state by area, what is the smallest US state by population?

4. In which country will you find the wine-producing regions of Danubian Plain, Rose Valley and Thrace?

5. Which four African countries are members of OPEC?

6. Basseterre is the capital of which Caribbean nation?

7. Which island is nicknamed the Apple Isle?

8. Who is the longest-serving President of France?

9. Whose rendition of the US national anthem at the 1991 Super Bowl proved so popular that it was released as a single and reached the Billboard top 10?

10. Which actor, best known for playing Jez Butterworth in the play Jerusalem, was the first artistic director of the Globe Theatre?

11. Boise is the capital of which state of America?

12. How many boroughs make up Greater London?

13. What is the northernmost borough of London?

14. The National Memorial Arboretum is in which English county?

15. Gus Van Sant's 2005 film Last Days is about which musician?

16. Which former footballer played a detective in the 2012 film Switch?

17. 'What is a city but the people' is a line from which Shakespeare play?

18. In which city is the Martin-Gropius-Bau Museum?

19. What organisation is the largest employer in the world?
    a) Indian Railways
    b) Chinese Army
    c) US Department of Defense

20. What was the first sequel to Planet of the Apes?
    a) Beneath...
    b) Escape From...
    c) Conquest Of...

Answers to Quiz 156: Movies part 2

1. Madonna in Die Another Day
2. Terence Malick
3. Night At The Museum
4. Rango
5. Bill and Ted's Bogus Journey
6. Field of Dreams
7. Robert De Niro
8. Roger O. Thornhill
9. Josh Brolin
10. Annie Hall
11. Gus Van Sant
12. Robert Evans
13. Tom Hardy
14. Michael Keaton
15. Northern Ireland
16. Shutter Island
17. Sophia Loren
18. 29
19. Whoopi Goldberg
20. Abraham Lincoln vs. Alien Invaders

DIFFICULT

Quiz 158: Sport part 1

1. In 1954, which athlete won the first Sports Personality of the Year award?

2. What nationality is Formula One driver Pastor Maldonado?

3. What is the only country not to win a gold medal in the Olympic Games it hosted?

4. In 1999, Lazio beat Real Mallorca in Birmingham to become the last winners of which competition?

5. Which sport has provided the most winners of the BBC Sports Personality of the Year Award?

6. What colour is the outer circle of an archery target?

7. FINA is the world governing body of which sport?

8. Which team conceded 3 own goals in their 6-1 FA Cup defeat against Liverpool in 2012?

9. Actor Jason Statham represented Great Britain in the World Championships at which sport?

10. Who, in 1986, became the first non-European to win the Tour de France?

11. Mark Loram was the last British world champion in which sport?

12. Which country won the 2011 Women's World Cup?

13. Which actor owns the racehorse Riverside Theatre, which won the 2012 Ryanair Chase at Cheltenham?

14. In 1872, Wanderers became the first winners of which competition?

15. In greyhound racing, the dog in which trap wears an orange jacket?

16. Who did India beat in the first ICC World Twenty20 competition in 2007?

17. Which female has won the most Tennis Grand Slam Singles titles?

18. After a six-year absence, which team returned to rugby league Super League in 2012?

19. Which Spanish club knocked Manchester United out of the 2011/12 Europa League?
    a) Atletico Madrid
    b) Athletic Bilbao
    c) Valencia

20. In what year did the first Winter Olympics take place?
    a) 1904
    b) 1924
    c) 1954

Answers to Quiz 157: Pot Luck

1. Blue
2. Nikki Chapman
3. Wyoming
4. Bulgaria
5. Algeria, Angola, Libya and Nigeria
6. St Kitts and Nevis
7. Tasmania
8. Francois Mitterand
9. Whitney Houston
10. Mark Rylance
11. Idaho
12. 32
13. Enfield
14. Staffordshire
15. Kurt Cobain
16. Eric Cantona
17. Coriolanus
18. Berlin
19. US Department of Defense
20. Beneath the Planet of the Apes

DIFFICULT

Quiz 159: Pot Luck

1. Dushanbe is the capital city of which former Soviet Republic?

2. In the 1990s, Sam Mendes was the artistic director of which London theatre?

3. James Bolger, Helen Clark and John Key have all served as Prime Minister in which country?

4. Ingemar Stenmark was Olympic and World champion in which sport?

5. Gillian Gilbert and Stephen Morris are the lesser-known members of which band?

6. Malacology is the study of what type of creatures?

7. What are Mauna Loa, Katmai and Kilauea?

8. The Caspian Sea has borders with which five countries?

9. In which country would you find the second highest waterfall in the world, the Tugela Falls?

10. What are the names of Prince Edward's two children?

11. Which two American states joined the USA in 1912?

12. Bandar Seri Begawan is the capital city of which country?

13. Who provided the voices for children's cartoons Mr Benn and King Rollo?

14. Which comedian hosted the modern-day version of the gameshows Bullseye?

15. John Griffith Chaney was the real name of which American author?

16. In what decade did the composer Puccini die?

17. Whitney Houston had the Christmas number one in 1992 with which song?

18. Edward White Benson, Frederick Temple and Randall Davidson have all held which post?

19. The Golden Shears is a competition in which discipline?
    a) hair dressing
    b) sheep shearing
    c) dress making

20. What is the name of the detective in Mark Billingham's crime novels?
    a) Tom Thorne
    b) Tom O'Sullivan
    c) Tom Hendry

Answers to Quiz 158: Sport part 1

1. Chris Chataway
2. Venezuelan
3. Canada (Montreal 1976)
4. European Cup Winners' Cup
5. Athletics
6. White
7. Swimming
8. Brighton and Hove Albion
9. Diving
10. Greg Lemond
11. Speedway
12. Japan
13. James Nesbitt
14. The FA Cup
15. Trap 4
16. Pakistan
17. Margaret Court
18. Widnes
19. Athletic Bilbao
20. 1924

DIFFICULT

Quiz 160: Musicals

1. What was the last musical written by Rodgers and Hammerstein?

2. Which musical is based on the life of Broadway star Fanny Brice?

3. Andrew Lloyd Webber worked alongside playwright Alan Ayckbourn on a musical based on the books of which comic writer?

4. A musical about Oscar Wilde that closed after just one day was written by which DJ and broadcaster?

5. The Phantom of the Opera is based on a novel by which French author?

6. Which Australian comedian wrote the music for the stage version of Matilda?

7. Guys and Dolls is based on short stories by which author?

8. Which Shakespearean play features in the musical Kiss Me, Kate?

9. What is the name of the professor in My Fair Lady?

10. Which musical was subtitled The American Tribal Love-Rock Musical?

11. Which actor, best known for appearing in The Wire, wrote Five Guys Named Moe?

12. The songs of which musician formed the basis of the musical Movin' Out?

13. Members of which band wrote the music for the musical Spider-Man: Turn Off The Dark?

14. In which musical would you hear songs called Dammit, Janet!, Sweet Transvestite and Rose Tint My World?

15. Spend, Spend, Spend was about which 1961 pools winner?

16. The song There's No Business Like Show Business originally appeared in which musical?

17. Who played Mama Morton in the 2002 film version of Chicago?

18. The Shirley Bassey hit Big Spender was originally written for which show?

19. What was the name of Andrew Lloyd Webber's Bollywood-themed musical?
    a) Bombay Dreams
    b) Calcutta Dreams
    c) Delhi Dreams

20. Which musical is based on Puccini's La Boheme?
    a) Rent
    b) Miss Saigon
    c) Blood Brothers

Answers to Quiz 159: Pot Luck

1. Tajikistan
2. Donmar Warehouse
3. New Zealand
4. Ski-ing
5. New Order
6. Molluscs
7. Volcanoes
8. Iran, Russia, Turkmenistan, Kazakhstan and Azerbaijan
9. South Africa
10. James and Louise
11. Arizona and New Mexico
12. Brunei
13. Ray Brooks
14. Dave Spikey
15. Jack London
16. 1920s
17. I Will Always Love You
18. Archbishop of Canterbury
19. Sheep shearing
20. Tom Thorne

DIFFICULT

Quiz 161: Pot Luck

1. The Voight Kampf Test was used to determine whether someone was a human in which classic film?

2. Who was the only British Prime Minister to serve under King Edward VIII?

3. What is the female equivalent of a misogynist?

4. The brother of which comedian was the lead singer with Manchester band The Mock Turtles?

5. What is the most westerly province of Canada?

6. 'People are always asking me if I know Tyler Durden' is the opening line of which film?

7. In Greek mythology, who was the messenger of the gods?

8. Bono and The Edge from U2 wrote the theme to which James Bond film?

9. What does a manometer measure?

10. Castries is the capital city of which Caribbean country?

11. What was the name of the 1801 agreement reached between the papacy and Napoleon Bonaparte?

12. William Addis was the inventor of which hygiene instrument?

13. What Jewish holiday is also known as the Festival of Lots?

14. Who designed the costumes for the film 2001: A Space Odyssey?

15. The Crystal Head Vodka company was co-founded by which Canadian actor?

16. Which British author described himself as the Don Juan of the intelligentsia?

17. What is the most westerly of London's boroughs?

18. Olympia is the capital of which US state?

19. What was Aneka's 1981 chart topper?
    a) Chinese Boy
    b) Japanese Boy
    c) Korean Boy

20. Which US state has provided the most American Presidents?
    a) Massachusetts
    b) Texas
    c) Virginia

Answers to Quiz 160: Musicals

1. The Sound of Music
2. Funny Girl
3. PG Wodehouse
4. Mike Read
5. Gaston Leroux
6. Tim Minchin
7. Damon Runyon
8. The Taming of the Shrew
9. Henry Higgins
10. Hair
11. Clarke Peters
12. Billy Joel
13. U2
14. The Rocky Horror Show
15. Viv Nicholson
16. Annie Get Your Gun
17. Queen Latifah
18. Sweet Charity
19. Bombay Dreams
20. Rent

DIFFICULT

Quiz 162: Geography

1. Which two countries in South America are landlocked?

2. The Vistula is the longest river in which country?

3. What is the most northerly Shipping Forecast area?

4. Which landlocked country in southern Africa is bordered by South Africa and Mozambique?

5. St George's is the capital city of which country in the Caribbean?

6. Northamptonshire has borders with how many counties?

7. Cobweb Bridge is in which English city?

8. Which Irish city is home to two cathedrals, both called St Patrick's?

9. Which two South American countries do not have a border with Brazil?

10. Vantaa Airport is in which city?

11. The Krubera-Voronja caves are in which former Soviet Republic?

12. The mountain Tirich Mir is located in which country?

13. Ipswich is located on the estuary of which river?

14. The Atacama Desert is in which South American country?

15. Which country is also known as Aotearoa?

16. Kodiak Island lies off the coast of which American state?

17. WAN is the international car registration of which country?

18. What is the most northerly populated island in the British Isles?

19. New York lies on the same latitude as which city?
    a) Naples
    b) Marseille
    c) Malaga

20. The Hoover Dam lies on which American river?
    a) Colorado
    b) Mississippi
    c) Missouri

Answers to Quiz 161: Pot Luck

1. Blade Runner
2. Stanley Baldwin
3. A misandrist
4. Steve Coogan
5. British Columbia
6. Fight Club
7. Hermes
8. GoldenEye (sung by Tina Turner)
9. Pressure
10. St Lucia
11. The Concordat
12. Toothbrush
13. Purim
14. Hardy Amies
15. Dan Aykroyd
16. H.G. Wells
17. Hillingdon
18. Washington
19. Japanese Boy
20. Virginia

DIFFICULT

Quiz 163: Pot Luck

1. 'Her life was in their hands. Now her toe is in the mail' is the tagline to which Coen Brothers film?

2. François-Marie Arouet was the real name of which author?

3. Which director's films include Carrie, Carlito's Way and The Black Dahlia?

4. Who was the Greek Goddess Muse of comedy?

5. What rank comes between Ordinary Rating and Leading Rating in the Royal Navy?

6. Bishkek is the capital of which former Soviet republic?

7. The words ombudsman and tungsten come from which European language?

8. FCO is the airport code for which European city?

9. Sleeping Murder was the last mystery novel to feature which detective?

10. What nationality was former UN Secretary General Javier Perez de Cuellar?

11. Which Birmingham-born industralist appears on the £50 note?

12. The Lucasian Chair of Mathematics is a professorship at which university?

13. Rupert Murdoch's wife Wendi was born in which country?

14. Which London borough was given Royal status in February 2012?

15. Charles Darwin was born in which English town?

Answers - page 333

16. Which fashion designer created the kit for the Great Britain team at the 2012 Olympics?

17. Vectis was the Roman name for where?

18. Simon Russell Beale, Jenny Éclair and Jenny Seagrove were all born in which Asian country?

19. What is the Franciscan order of monks also known as?
    a) Blackfriars
    b) Greyfriars
    c) Whitefriars

20. In TV comedy The Office, what was Tim's surname?
    a) Canterbury
    b) Chichester
    c) Colchester

Answers to Quiz 162: Geography

1. Paraguay and Bolivia
2. Poland
3. Southeast Iceland
4. Swaziland
5. Grenada
6. Eight
7. Sheffield
8. Armagh
9. Chile and Ecuador
10. Helsinki
11. Georgia
12. Pakistan
13. River Orwell
14. Chile
15. New Zealand
16. Alaska
17. Nigeria
18. Unst
19. Naples
20. Colorado

DIFFICULT

Quiz 164: Britain

1. The historic Pulteney Bridge is in which British city?

2. The Roman town of Verulamium was in which modern-day city?

3. What motorway runs for 59 miles from Sunbury-on-Thames to Southampton?

4. Forster Square and Interchange are railway stations in which English city?

5. Which UK National Park lies between Southampton Water, Avon Valley, the Wiltshire Chalk Downs and The Solent?

6. Plymouth is the capital of which British Overseas Territory?

7. What are Holloway, Drake Hall and Cornton Vale?

8. What are the three National Parks in Wales?

9. The Cathedral of St Mary and St Helen is in which Essex town?

10. What is the southernmost island of the Shetlands?

11. In which Scottish city will you see statues of comic characters Desperate Dan and Minnie The Minx?

12. The city of Norwich lies on which river?

13. Which Scottish football team play their home games at the Firhill Stadium?

14. In Bickenhill near Birmingham, there is a museum devoted to what form of transport?

15. Which London railway station was formerly known as St Paul's?

16. In which Yorkshire village will you find a reading room of the British Library?

17. Hoy is part of which island group?

18. The Scottish Grand National is run at which racecourse?

19. Leeds Castle is home to a museum featuring what objects?
    a) dog collars
    b) pencils
    c) prams

20. Which monarch was born in Pembroke Castle?
    a) Henry VI
    b) Henry VII
    c) Henry VIII

Answers to Quiz 163: Pot Luck

1. The Big Lebowski
2. Voltaire
3. Brian De Palma
4. Thalia
5. Able Rating
6. Kyrgystan
7. Swedish
8. Rome
9. Miss Marple
10. Peruvian
11. Matthew Boulton
12. Cambridge
13. China
14. Greenwich
15. Shrewsbury
16. Stella McCartney
17. Isle of Wight
18. Malaysia
19. Greyfriars
20. Canterbury

DIFFICULT

Quiz 165: Pot Luck

1. Ranidaphobia is a fear of what animal?

2. Broadcaster Louis Theroux and writer Leslie Charteris were born in which Asian country?

3. What is the lowest commissioned rank in the RAF?

4. John Gorton, Gough Whitlam and Malcolm Fraser have all served as Prime Minister in which country?

5. What were Gilbert and Sullivan's first names?

6. Which monarch was known as the Wisest Fool in Christendom?

7. Jazz musician Cannonball Adderley is associated with which instrument?

8. Two seahorses feature on the crest of which Premier League football club?

9. Who released an aftershave called Instinct in 2005?

10. Which politician did the late Tony Banks describe as having the 'sensitivity of a sex-starved boa constrictor'?

11. Salem is the capital of which US state?

12. Victoria Lucas was the pen name of which Boston-born poet?

13. The Nuggets are a basketball team from which American city?

14. FL is the international vehicle registration code for which European country?

15. The Straits Times is a newspaper based in which country?

16. The adrenal glands sit atop which organ of the body?

17. Which three Labour politicians were members of the Cabinet continuously from 1997 until 2010?

18. What was the sequel to the 2010 film Clash of the Titans?

19. The shortest war in the world was fought between England and which African country?
    a) Zanzibar
    b) Zimbabwe
    c) Zaire

20. How long did the war last?
    a) 38 minutes
    b) 38 hours
    c) 380 hours

Answers to Quiz 164: Britain

1. Bath
2. St Albans
3. M3
4. Bradford
5. The New Forest
6. Montserrat
7. Women's prisons
8. Snowdonia, Brecon Beacons, Pembrokeshire Coast
9. Brentwood
10. Fair Isle
11. Dundee
12. River Wensum
13. Partick Thistle
14. The motorcycle
15. Blackfriars
16. Boston Spa
17. Orkney Islands
18. Ayr
19. Dog collars
20. Henry VII

DIFFICULT

Quiz 166: Soap Operas

1. Which EastEnder was killed while Wham's Wake Me Up Before You Go Go was playing on her stereo?

2. In Coronation Street, what was Sally Webster's maiden name?

3. Bad boys Rob Hawthorn, Toby Mills and Andy Holt appeared in which soap?

4. Which Coronation Street actress is the daughter of a Lord and had a top 20 hit single with Where Will You Be?

5. In Emmerdale, who started the fire that killed Terry Woods and Viv Hope?

6. Which EastEnders character had a drug addict sister called Rainie?

7. Which Corrie baddie was run over by a Blackpool tram?

8. Ray Meagher plays which long-standing soap character?

9. Who is the only original Hollyoaks cast member to still appear in the show?

10. Coronation Street's Liam Connor had a dog named after which heavy metal star?

11. Which Emmerdale character died after being hit over the head with a statue of a horse?

12. Which former Neighbour appeared in the Oscar-winning films The King's Speech and LA Confidential?

13. Who shared Neighbours' first lesbian kiss?

14. Which member of the Monty Python team has been in Home and Away?

15. Who played literary con artist Mel Hutchwright in Coronation Street?

16. Paul Usher played which Brookside rogue?

17. Which comedian made a guest appearance in Coronation Street as fitness fanatic Ernie Crabbe?

18. Which EastEnder was killed after being hit by a dog-shaped doorstop?

19. Who composed the theme tunes to Emmerdale Farm, Neighbours and Crossroads?

20. How did Ian Beale's wife Laura die?
    a) hit by a car
    b) fell down the stairs
    c) electrocuted

21. How many times has Ken Barlow been married?
    a) three
    b) four
    c) five

Answers to Quiz 165: Pot Luck

1. Frog
2. Singapore
3. Pilot Officer
4. Australia
5. William and Arthur
6. James I (James VI of Scotland)
7. Saxophone
8. Newcastle United
9. David Beckham
10. Margaret Thatcher
11. Oregon
12. Sylvia Plath
13. Denver
14. Liechtenstein
15. Singapore
16. Kidney
17. Gordon Brown, Jack Straw and Alistair Darling
18. Wrath of the Titans
19. Zanzibar
20. 38 minutes

DIFFICULT

Quiz 167: Pot Luck

1. The Rum Rebellion took place in which country?

2. Which four common English words end with the letters -dous?

3. A clowder is the collective noun given to a group of what animal?

4. In which American state would you find the Space Needle?

5. In binary, what number is written 1010?

6. Teddy Pendergrass was the lead singer with which group?

7. In 2010, an anonymous bidder paid £78,000 for a racy dress worn by which model at a 2002 student fashion show?

8. In Greek mythology, which playwright died after an eagle dropped a tortoise on his head?

9. How many bridges do the Boat Race crews row under during the annual race?

10. In 2012 Joachim Gauck was elected as president of which country?

11. Who is the husband of politician Yvette Cooper?

12. Chestnut was the middle name of which American gangster?

13. Rath Yatra is a major festival in which religion?

14. The Alan Bennett play The History Boys is set in which city?

15. Fantasy drama Game of Thrones is based on books by which author?

16. What is the only Alfred Hitchcock-directed film to win a Best Picture Oscar?

17. The Monmouth Rebellion was an attempt to overthrow which monarch?

18. Jeff Bezos founded which company?

19. For what is the Diagram Prize awarded?

20. Which cartoon villain's real name is Edward Nigma?
    a) The Joker
    b) The Penguin
    c) The Riddler

21. Which Formula One world champion has the middle name Devereux?
    a) Nigel Mansell
    b) Lewis Hamilton
    c) Damon Hill

Answers to Quiz 166: Soap Operas

1. Heather Trott
2. Sally Seddon
3. Hollyoaks
4. Sue Nicholls
5. Nick Henshall
6. Tanya Branning
7. Alan Bradley
8. Alf Stewart from Home and Away
9. Tony Hutchinson
10. Ozzy Osbourne
11. Tom King
12. Guy Pearce
13. Sky Mangel and Melanie Pearson
14. Michael Palin
15. Sir Ian McKellan
16. Barry Grant
17. Norman Wisdom
18. Den Watts
19. Tony Hatch
20. Fell down stairs
21. Four times

DIFFICULT

Quiz 168: Crime

1. In 1968, Valerie Solanas attempted to murder which famous artist?

2. What was the name of the forensic psychologist played by Robbie Coltrane in TV drama Cracker?

3. Ronnie Kray murdered George Cornell in which London pub?

4. A Deemster is a judge in which part of the British Isles?

5. Altcourse, the first private prison in England, is in which city?

6. Which female rapper served 10 months for perjury and conspiracy in 2005?

7. Barristers traditionally wear wigs made from what material?

8. Which British serial killer lived at 10 Rillington Place?

9. Who played Mr Pink in the film Reservoir Dogs?

10. Which political leader was killed by Nathuram Godse in 1948?

11. What was the American murderer David Berkowitz better known as?

12. Which former armed robber's life story was turned into a film starring Roger Daltrey?

13. Which three Pakistani cricketers were jailed for their involvement in the 2010 spot fixing scandal?

14. Who shot and killed bank robber Jesse James?

15. Which Lord Chief Justice led the series of trials known as The Bloody Assizes?

Answers - page 343

16. Highwayman Dick Turpin was hanged in which northern city?

17. What is the real name of the American mail bomber known as The Unabomber?

18. How did John and Anne Darwin hit the headlines in 2007?

19. In which Asian country is Changi prison?
    a) China
    b) Japan
    c) Singapore

20. What is the name of the detective in Dostoevsky's Crime and Punishment?
    a) Porfiry Petrovich
    b) Lev Myshkin
    c) Pyotr Kirilovich

Answers to Quiz 167: Pot Luck

1. Australia
2. Tremendous, horrendous, stupendous, hazardous
3. Cats
4. Washington
5. 10
6. Harold Melvin and the Blue Notes
7. Kate Middleton
8. Aeschylus
9. Two (Hammersmith and Barnes)
10. Germany
11. Ed Balls
12. Clyde Barrow
13. Hinduism
14. Sheffield
15. George R.R. Martin
16. Rebecca
17. James II
18. Amazon
19. The oddest book title of the year
20. The Riddler
21. Damon Hill

DIFFICULT

Quiz 169: Pot Luck

1. The planets Bespin, Dagobah and Hoth appear in which film?

2. Reginald Hill created which detective double act?

3. Which English word contains five consecutive vowels?

4. What is the name of the track that hosts the Melbourne Cup horse race?

5. Which US president wrote Profiles in Courage?

6. Bangui is the capital of which African country?

7. Winchester was the capital of which ancient Anglo-Saxon kingdom?

8. What was the first name of the cookery author Mrs Beeton?

9. Which 20th-century British Prime Minister is the only one to serve under three different monarchs?

10. Which TV cop drove a vintage, burgundy Triumph Roadster?

11. Which Scottish town became a city in honour of the Queen's Diamond Jubilee in 2012?

12. Roddy Frame was the founder of which Scottish band?

13. How many triangular faces does an icosahedron have?

14. Which amendment of the US constitution abolished slavery?

15. Where would you find the Mount of Jupiter, Mount of Saturn and Mount of the Sun?

16. Which female singer-songwriter released the 2012 album Little Broken Hearts?

17. In internet dating, what do the initials FWB stand for?

18. Elliot Gleave is the real name of which British singer and rapper?

19. What literary award was won by Adam Mars-Jones in 2012?
    a) Booker Prize
    b) Hatchet Job of the Year
    c) Richard and Judy Prize

20. Who was the most borrowed author in UK libraries in 2011?
    a) James Patterson
    b) JK Rowling
    c) Stieg Larsson

Answers to Quiz 168: Crime

1. Andy Warhol
2. Dr Edward 'Fitz' Fitzgerald
3. The Blind Beggar
4. Isle of Man
5. Liverpool
6. Lil' Kim
7. Horsehair
8. John Christie
9. Steve Buscemi
10. Mahatma Gandhi
11. Son of Sam
12. John McVicar
13. Salman Butt, Mohammad Amir and Mohammad Asif
14. Robert Ford
15. Judge Jeffreys
16. York
17. Ted Kaczynski
18. They faked his death to claim insurance policy payouts
19. Singapore
20. Porfiry Petrovich

DIFFICULT

Quiz 170: Pop Music

1. What nationality is singer, songwriter and producer Basshunter?

2. Who recorded The Wizard, the long-time theme of Top of the Pops?

3. The first episode of Top of the Pops aired in which year?

4. Our Version of Events was a number one-selling album in 2012 by which female singer?

5. Which British singer topped the charts in 1968 with The Ballad of Bonnie and Clyde?

6. What was Madonna's first UK chart hit?

7. The Dirt: Confessions of the World's Most Notorious Rock Group is a book about which band?

8. Which group topped the charts in 1990 with Dub Be Good To Me?

9. Orville Burrell is the real name of which Jamaican-born singer and rapper?

10. Which female singer topped the UK singles charts in 1971 with I'm Still Waiting then had to wait over 14 years for her next chart topper?

11. Who is the wife of jazz musician Jamie Cullum?

12. Whose debut number one single was Forever Love?

13. Which boy band were Hangin' Tough in 1990?

14. Which 1977 single was the first in the UK to sell two million copies?

15. What was Right Said Fred's only number one single?

16. Which group had the most number one hit singles in the 1970s?

17. What is Hawaiian-born singer, songwriter and producer Peter Gene Hernandez better known as?

18. Sonik Kicks was a 2012 album by which veteran male singer?

19. How many top ten singles did The Clash have?
    a) 0
    b) 1
    c) 2

20. A member of which group wrote the score for the film There Will Be Blood?
    a) Blur
    b) Radiohead
    c) Pulp

Answers to Quiz 169: Pot Luck

1. The Empire Strikes Back
2. Dalziel and Pascoe
3. Queueing
4. Flemington
5. John F Kennedy
6. Central African Republic
7. Wessex
8. Isabella
9. Stanley Baldwin
10. Jim Bergerac
11. Perth
12. Aztec Camera
13. 20
14. 13th
15. On a hand (they're areas used by palm readers)
16. Norah Jones
17. Friends With Benefits
18. Example
19. Hatchet Job of the Year
20. James Patterson

DIFFICULT

Quiz 171: Pot Luck

1. Running at just 35 seconds, who wrote the play Breath?

2. Bologna Airport is named after which Italian inventor?

3. In the novel by DH Lawrence, what is Lady Chatterley's first name?

4. In 2012, Bradley Wiggins became the second Briton to win the Paris-Nice bike race but who was the first?

5. Asleep In The Back was the debut album by which British group?

6. What is British singer, rapper and actor Ben Drew better known as?

7. Holding over 32m books, the largest library in the world is in which city?

8. In what year did Queen Victoria accede to the throne?

9. What is the sixth letter of the Greek alphabet?

10. Which legendary music producer murdered his landlady before turning the gun on himself?

11. The Colossus of Rhodes was a statue of which Ancient Greek Titan?

12. Former UN Secretary General Dag Hammarskjöld was from which country?

13. What is the penultimate event of a decathlon?

14. Which American president appears on the $50 bill?

15. Kate Kane is the alter ego of which superhero?

16. Coulrophobia is a fear of what?

17. How wide is each lane in an Olympic-size swimming pool?

18. What type of fastener takes its name from a combination of the French words for velvet and hook?

19. What nationality is the author Paulo Coelho?
    a) Brazilian
    b) Colombian
    c) Venezuelan

20. What is the name of the terrifying PE teacher in US drama Glee?
    a) Tracy Thornton
    b) Sue Sylvester
    c) Mary McCarthy

Answers to Quiz 170: Pop Music

1. Swedish
2. Paul Hardcastle
3. 1964
4. Emeli Sandé
5. Georgie Fame
6. Holiday
7. Motley Crue
8. Beats International
9. Shaggy
10. Diana Ross
11. Sophie Dahl
12. Gary Barlow
13. New Kids On The Block
14. Mull of Kintyre by Wings
15. Deeply Dippy
16. Abba (with 7)
17. Bruno Mars
18. Paul Weller
19. 1
20. Radiohead (Jonny Greenwood)

DIFFICULT

Quiz 172: Song Opening Lines

Identify the songs from the following opening lines:

1. Son, I'm 30/I only went with your mother 'cause she's dirty

2. Sweetness, I was only joking when I said / I'd like to smash every tooth in your head

3. Libraries gave us power, then work came and made us free

4. There lived a certain man in Russia long ago / He was big and strong in his eyes a flaming glow

5. I hear the train a comin' / It's rollin' round the bend

6. I've been really tryin' baby / Tryin' to hold back this feeling for so long

7. Once upon a time / You dressed so fine / Threw the bums a dime / In your prime

8. I, I love the colorful clothes she wears / And the way the sunlight plays upon her hair

9. Trudging slowly over wet sand / Back to the bench where your clothes were stolen

10. For each a road / For everyman a religion

11. I met him on a Monday and my heart stood still

12. Bernie Rhodes knows don't argue

13. You spurn my natural emotions / You make me feel like dirt / And I'm hurt

14. Stop dreaming of the quiet life cos it's the one we'll never know

15. Load up on guns and bring your friends / It's fun to lose and to pretend

16. The silicon chip inside her head gets switched to overload / And nobody's gonna go to school today / She's gonna make them stay at home

17. Sometimes you're better off dead / There's a gun in your hand and it's pointing at your head

18. Fire in the disco! Fire in the Taco Bell!

19. Four letter word just to get me along / It's a difficulty and I'm biting on my tongue and I / I keep stalling, keeping me together

20. This was never the way I planned, not my intention / I got so brave, drink in hand, lost my discretion / It's not what I'm used to, just wanna try you on

Answers to Quiz 171: Pot Luck

1. Samuel Beckett
2. Guglielmo Marconi
3. Constance
4. Tommy Simpson
5. Elbow
6. Plan B
7. Washington DC
8. 1837
9. Zeta
10. Joe Meek
11. Helios
12. Sweden
13. Javelin
14. Ulysses S Grant
15. Batwoman
16. Clowns
17. 2.5m
18. Velcro
19. Brazilian
20. Sue Sylvester

DIFFICULT

Quiz 173: Pot Luck

1. The CAC40 is a stock exchange in which country?

2. At The Castle Gate by Sibelius is the theme music to what long-running TV show?

3. Which two African countries have hosted a Formula One Grand Prix?

4. Pauline Black was the lead singer with which Two Tone band?

5. Which Hollywood superstar was arrested in 2012 while protesting outside the Sudanese Embassy in Washington?

6. Who did Julia Gillard succeed as Prime Minister of Australia in 2010?

7. Which American humourist wrote Dress Your Family In Corduroy and Denim?

8. In Pride and Prejudice, what is Mr Darcy's Christian name?

9. Peter Firth played which character in TV drama Spooks?

10. In what country does the Fallas Festival take place?

11. Tar Heel is a nickname given to people from which US state?

12. James Osterberg is the real name of which veteran American rocker?

13. What is the second largest city in Germany by population?

14. Which monarch founded the Order of the Garter?

15. Garuda is the flag-carrying airline of which country?

16. What is categorised using the Torino Scale?

17. Which veteran soul singer released a 2012 album called Tuskegee?

18. Where would you find Humboldt's Sea and The Marginal Sea?

19. Where does Karlheinz Stockhausen's opera Mittwoch aus Licht take place?
    a) on a boat
    b) in a car
    c) in a helicopter

20. What fruit was added to the Office of National Statistics' basket of goods used to calculate the cost of living in March 2012?
    a) banana
    b) melon
    c) pineapple

Answers to Quiz 172: Song Opening Lines

1. Kinky Afro by the Happy Monday
2. Bigmouth Strikes Again by The Smiths
3. Design For Life by Manic Street Preachers
4. Rasputin by Boney M
5. Folsom Prison Blues by Johnny Cash
6. Let's Get It On by Marvin Gaye
7. Like A Rolling Stone by Bob Dylan
8. Good Vibrations by The Beach Boys
9. Every Day is Like Sunday by Morrissey
10. F.E.A.R. by Ian Brown
11. Da Doo Ron Ron by The Crystals
12. Gangsters by The Specials
13. Ever Fallen In Love by Buzzcocks
14. A Town Called Malice by The Jam
15. Smells Like Teen Spirit by Nirvana
16. I Don't Like Mondays by The Boomtown Rats
17. West End Girls by The Pet Shop Boys
18. Danger! High Voltage! by Electric Six
19. That's Not My Name by The Ting Tings
20. I Kissed A Girl by Katy Perry

DIFFICULT

Quiz 174: Politics part 2

1. Who was the youngest Prime Minister of the 20th century?

2. Countess Markievicz, the first woman elected to the House of Commons, represented which party?

3. Which 20th-century British Prime Minister was in office for the shortest time?

4. The Eduskunta is the parliament of which country?

5. Who was the first woman to take up a seat as a Member of Parliament?

6. 'Would you buy a used car from this man?' was a slogan on a poster campaigning against which US politician?

7. Who was Britain's first openly gay MP?

8. Who was the most recent British Prime Minister to die in office?

9. How many years does the French President serve in each term?

10. Nelson Rockefeller was the Vice President alongside which US President?

11. For 14 years, Winston Churchill was an MP in which Scottish city?

12. William Lyon McKenzie King was the longest-serving Prime Minister of which country?

13. Todor Zhivkov was the long-time leader of which European country?

14. Which European country has a legislature called the Storting?

15. Which 19th-century politician served as Prime Minister four separate times?

16. Kwame Nkrumah was the first president of which African country?

17. Which technocrat succeeded Silvio Berlusconi as Italian Prime Minister in 2011?

18. Which Irish political party's name translates into English as Warriors of Destiny?

19. In what decade were MPs paid a salary for the first time?
    a) 1910s
    b) 1920s
    c) 1930s

20. For how many years was Winston Churchill an MP?
    a) 44
    b) 54
    c) 64

Answers to Quiz 173: Pot Luck

1. France
2. The Sky At Night
3. Morocco and South Africa
4. The Selecter
5. George Clooney
6. Kevin Rudd
7. David Sedaris
8. Fitzwilliam
9. Sir Harry Pearce
10. Spain
11. North Carolina
12. Iggy Pop
13. Hamburg
14. Edward III
15. Indonesia
16. The risk posed by a celestial body such as a comet hitting the earth
17. Lionel Richie
18. On the moon
19. In a helicopter
20. Pineapple

Quiz 175: Pot Luck

1. In which country will you find the cricket ground Eden Park?

2. In 2012, Leanne Wood became the leader of which British political party?

3. The so-called Wonga Coup was a plot to overthrow the government of which country?

4. Who did Hu Jintao succeed as leader of the Communist Party of China?

5. In America, Martin Luther King Day is celebrated in which month?

6. Lester Bowles Pearson, Paul Martin and Stephen Harper have all been prime minister in which Commonwealth country?

7. The River Kwai is in which country?

8. Composer Frederick Delius was born in which English city?

9. 'We all go a little mad sometimes' is a line from which Hitchcock chiller?

10. Which Dutchman won the 2012 BDO World Darts Championship?

11. What is the disease onchocerciasis more commonly known as?

12. Dipsomania is an uncontrollable craving for what?

13. What was the first name of Kentucky Fried Chicken founder Colonel Sanders?

14. In December 2011, Elio Di Rupo became Prime Minister of which country?

15. Complete the name of the French musical: The Umbrellas of...?

16. Larry Mullen and The Edge from rock band U2 were born in which country?

17. Joyce Frankenberg is the real name of which British actress?

18. Marilyn Monroe died during the shooting of which film?

19. In what year was Queen Victoria born?
    a) 1809
    b) 1814
    c) 1819

20. Puppeteer and Muppets creator Frank Oz was born in which English city?
    a) Gloucester
    b) Hereford
    c) Norwich

Answers to Quiz 174: Politics part 2

1. Tony Blair
2. Sinn Fein
3. Andrew Bonar Law
4. Finland
5. Nancy Astor
6. Richard Nixon
7. Chris Smith
8. Henry Temple, 3rd Viscount Palmerston
9. Five years
10. Gerald Ford
11. Dundee
12. Canada
13. Bulgaria
14. Norway
15. William Gladstone
16. Ghana
17. Mario Monti
18. Fianna Fáil
19. 1910s
20. 64

DIFFICULT

Quiz 176: History

1. John Ball and Wat Tyler were leaders of which uprising?

2. The International Monetary Fund and International Bank for Reconstruction and Development were set up at a conference in which American town?

3. The Rye House Plot was a conspiracy to assassinate which King of England?

4. Who was the West German Chancellor when the Berlin Wall was erected?

5. What was the name of the atomic bomb dropped on Nagasaki?

6. Austerlitz, the scene of a famous victory by Napoleon's army, is in which modern-day country?

7. Which Indian city was the scene of a massive chemical leak in 1984 that killed more than 2,000 people?

8. Who was the last king of Rome?

9. Who did Mikhail Gorbachev succeed as leader of the Soviet Union?

10. What did the 19th amendment of the US constitution ensure?

11. The Battle of Blenheim was fought during which war?

12. What was the royal family of France from 1582 to 1789?

13. The StB was the secret police in which Communist country?

14. Which Turkish-born politician was the the French Prime Minister from March 1993 until May 1995?

15. What nationality was the 15th-century explorer Bartolomeu Dias?

16. Which Nazi architect went on to become the German Minister of Armaments and War Production?

17. Who was the mother of King Arthur?

18. Who was the dictator of Portugal from 1933 to 1968?

19. What was the US policy doctrine that opposed European attempts to colonise the American continent?
a) Adams Doctrine
b) Monroe Doctrine
c) Braxton Doctrine

20. Hastings Banda was the long-time leader of which country?
a) Mauritania
b) Mali
c) Malawi

Answers to Quiz 175: Pot Luck

1. New Zealand
2. Plaid Cymru
3. Equatorial Guinea
4. Jiang Zemin
5. January
6. Canada
7. Thailand
8. Bradford
9. Psycho
10. Christian Kist
11. River blindness
12. Alcohol
13. Harland
14. Belgium
15. Cherbourg
16. England
17. Jane Seymour
18. Something's Got To Give
19. 1819
20. Hereford

DIFFICULT

Quiz 177: Pot Luck

1. In what year was the first national UK Census carried out?

2. Which author created the fictional universe Cthulhu Mythos?

3. Who are the first British group to go straight to number one in the US charts with their debut album?

4. In the arts, what do the initials BIPP stand for?

5. Which institution won its third University Challenge title in seven years in 2012?

6. In which American city will you find a baseball team called the Brewers?

7. What genre of music would you expect to hear at a music festival at Cherry Hinton Hall?

8. Which politician did Harriet Harman describe as a 'ginger rodent'?

9. Which Austrian artist painted Houses with Colourful Laundry, Suburb II, which sold for £24.7m in 2011?

10. Roy of the Rovers first appeared in which comic?

11. Keelmen Heaving Coals by Night is by which British artist?

12. Hispalis was the Roman name for which Spanish city?

13. Heathrow Airport is in which London borough?

14. Politician Peter Hain and biologist Richard Dawkins were born in which African country?

15. Which punk legend was born in Ankara, Turkey in 1952?

16. In what country is the Islamist movement Boko Haram based?

17. Michael Frayn's play 'Democracy' centres on which European politician?

18. In which English town is the mayor 'weighed in' on taking office?

19. The highest military and civilian award in Russia is the Order of...?
    a) St Andrew
    b) St Basil
    c) St Ivan

20. What is the name of DJ Simon Mayo's debut novel?
    a) Scratch
    b) Itch
    c) Snitch

Answers to Quiz 176: History

1. Peasants' Revolt
2. Bretton Woods
3. King Charles II
4. Konrad Adenauer
5. Fat Man
6. Czech Republic
7. Bhopal
8. Lucius Tarquinius Superbus
9. Konstantin Chernenko
10. Nationwide suffrage for women
11. War of Spanish Succession
12. The Bourbons
13. Czechoslovakia
14. Édouard Balladur
15. Portuguese
16. Albert Speer
17. Igraine of Cornwall
18. Antonio de Oliveira Salazar
19. Monroe Doctrine
20. Malawi

DIFFICULT

Quiz 178: Europe

1. In which European capital would you find Bromma Airport?

2. The 'Ndrangheta criminal organisation is centred in which region of Italy?

3. What German city is known in French as Aix-la-Chapelle?

4. Øresund Bridge links which two countries?

5. What nationality are the film-making Dardenne brothers?

6. Which European capital lies on the Dnieper River?

7. Wilhelmus is the national anthem of which country?

8. The Swedish krona is divided into 100 what?

9. Massilia was the Roman name for which French city?

10. Which two countries are linked by the Simplon Tunnel?

11. Who did Mariano Rajoy succeed as Spanish Prime Minister in 2011?

12. The German city of Hamburg lies on which river?

13. Tokaji and Bull's Blood are wines from which country?

14. What is the largest of the Greek Dodecanese islands?

15. BIH is the international vehicle registration code for which European country?

16. The Mecsek Mountains are in which country?

17. What is the southernmost region of mainland Spain?

18. Which country joined the European Union in 1981?

19. In 2004, Ivan Gašparovič became the head of state of which country?
    a) Slovakia
    b) Slovenia
    c) Czech Republic

20. What nationality were the rock band Europe?
    a) Denmark
    b) Norway
    c) Sweden

Answers to Quiz 177: Pot Luck

1. 1801
2. HP Lovecraft
3. One Direction
4. British Institute of Professional Photography
5. Manchester University
6. Milwaukee
7. Folk
8. Danny Alexander
9. Egon Schiele
10. Tiger
11. JMW Turner
12. Seville
13. Hillingdon
14. Kenya
15. Joe Strummer
16. Nigeria
17. Willy Brandt
18. High Wycombe
19. St Andrew
20. Itch

DIFFICULT

Quiz 179: Pot Luck

1. What was the first video shown on MTV Europe?

2. In the nursery rhyme Cock Robin, who made the shroud?

3. Which bridge was designed by Dr JJC Bradfield and is nicknamed 'The Coathanger'?

4. In astronomy, what type of celestial bodies are the Vesta family?

5. What is London's most southerly borough?

6. Sudeley Castle is in which English county?

7. In 2012, what film became the first to sweep the board at the Razzies?

8. What is the fifth largest country in the world by area?

9. Who sang the theme tune to the James Bond film The Man With the Golden Gun?

10. British author Hector Hugh Munroe wrote under which pen name?

11. Which American state is named after a non-English monarch?

12. Gordon Jackson played which character in TV drama The Professionals?

13. Which two Spanish clubs reached the final of the 2012 Europa League?

14. The annual bank holiday cheese-rolling event takes place in which county?

15. Lesser Horseshoe, Noctule and Nathusius' Pipistrelle are examples of what type of animal?

16. The Scheme For Full Employment, Three to See The King and The Restraint of Beasts are novels by which British author?

17. Which punk's real name was John Ritchie?

18. Which element of the Periodic Table has the atomic number 5 and the chemical symbol B?

19. The 1987 film Robocop was set in which city?
    a) Detroit
    b) Cleveland
    c) Pittsburgh

20. Why was Kazakhstan's Maria Dmitrienko unimpressed after winning gold at the Arab Shooting Championships?
    a) she was the only competitor
    b) organiser's played the spoof national anthem from the film Borat
    c) she was deported

Answers to Quiz 178: Europe

1. Stockholm
2. Calabria
3. Aachen
4. Denmark and Sweden
5. Belgian
6. Kiev
7. The Netherlands
8. Ore
9. Marseille
10. Italy and Switzerland
11. Jose Luis Zapatero
12. River Elbe
13. Hungary
14. Rhodes
15. Bosnia and Herzegovina
16. Hungary
17. Andalucia
18. Greece
19. Slovakia
20. Swedish

DIFFICULT

Quiz 180: Money

1. The Lek is the currency of which European country?

2. Which reggae artist had a top 20 single in 1979 with Money In My Pocket?

3. What is the United States Bullion Depository more commonly known as?

4. In which country is the MICEX-RTS stock exchange?

5. 'If you want a friend, get a dog' is a line from which financially inspired film?

6. In finance, what do the initials ROI stand for?

7. Which British novelist wrote Whoops!: Why everyone owes everyone and no one can pay?

8. What was the name of the 2011 film starring Paul Bettany, Demi Moore and Kevin Spacey about an investment bank on the verge of collapse?

9. Which composer appeared on the British £10 note between 1999 and 2010?

10. What British coin ceased being legal tender on 31 December 1960?

11. In the board game Monopoly, how much is the fine for being drunk in charge?

12. Which author wrote the financial thriller The Fear Index?

13. Much heard of during the financial crisis, what do the initials CDS stand for?

14. What was the name of the long running daytime finance programme hosted by Adrian Chiles and Declan Curry?

15. Which historian famously described economics as 'the dismal science'?

16. Which celebrity won Strictly Come Dancing in 2004?

17. What is the currency of Brazil?

18. In which century was the Bank of England founded?

19. In 2008, which Sussex town launched its own currency?
a) Hastings
b) Hove
c) Lewes

20. Where is the oldest stock exchange in the world?
a) Amsterdam
b) London
c) New York

Answers to Quiz 179: Pot Luck

1. Money For Nothing by Dire Straits
2. The Beetle
3. Sydney Harbour Bridge
4. Asteroids
5. Croydon
6. Gloucestershire
7. Jack and Jill
8. Brazil
9. Lulu
10. Saki
11. Louisiana
12. George Cowley
13. Atletico Madrid and Athletic Bilbao
14. Gloucestershire
15. Bat
16. Magnus Mills
17. Sid Vicious
18. Boron
19. Detroit
20. Organiser's played the spoof national anthem from the film Borat

DIFFICULT

Quiz 181: Pot Luck

1. The film Big Wednesday is about which sport?

2. Augusta is the capital of which US state?

3. Who is the only actress to win an Oscar playing someone who had also won an Oscar?

4. Fitzcarraldo, Into The Abyss and Cobra Verde are films by which director?

5. In March 2012, Mike Nesbitt became the leader of which UK political party?

6. Andros is the largest island of which country?

7. Who rode a horse called Bucephalus?

8. The Palk Strait separates which two countries?

9. An hendecagon is a shape with how many sides?

10. Nephrology is a branch of medicine dealing with which organ?

11. The first Winter Olympics were held in which country?

12. Which composer, whose works include Punch and Judy, The Minotaur and The Last Supper, was knighted in 1998?

13. The fictional island of Sodor was the setting for which collection of children's books that were later turned into a TV series?

14. What is the name of the town featured in the classic Christmas film It's A Wonderful Life?

15. In which popular sitcom are the main characters named after serial killers?

16. Who plays Sergeant Hathaway in detective drama Lewis?

17. Walter Gay, Louisa Chick, Lucretia Tox, Susan Nipper, Polly Toodle are characters in which novel by Charles Dickens?

18. Ginni Rometty was the first woman to head which technology company?

19. What was Ben-Hur's first name?
    a) Nathan
    b) Judah
    c) Ezekiel

20. Which newspaper columnist wrote the best selling book For Richer For Poorer: Confessions of a Player?
    a) Amanda Platell
    b) Caitlin Moran
    c) Victoria Coren

Answers to Quiz 180: Money

1. Albania
2. Dennis Brown
3. Fort Knox
4. Russia
5. Wall Street
6. Return on investment
7. John Lanchester
8. Margin Call
9. Edward Elgar
10. Farthing
11. £20
12. Robert Harris
13. Credit Default Swap
14. Working Lunch
15. Thomas Carlyle
16. Jill Halfpenny
17. Real
18. 17th
19. Lewes
20. Amsterdam

DIFFICULT

Quiz 182: Firsts and Lasts

1. What 1996 gangster film starring Bruce Willis is a remake of the Japanese film Yojimbo?

2. Murder From The Past was the last novel by which crime author?

3. In 1963, Frank Wathernam was the last inmate to leave which prison?

4. Which Olympic event took place for the last time at the 1920 games in Antwerp?

5. The Battle of Columbus was the last battle in which conflict?

6. Who said the first words on BBC Radio One?

7. It took just 25 hours, 17 minutes for which celebrity to gain 1 million followers on Twitter?

8. First Of The Gang To Die was a 2004 hit for which singer?

9. Which actor won an Oscar for his portrayal of an African leader in the film The Last King of Scotland?

10. In what year did the first FA Cup Final at Wembley take place?

11. Rudolf Hess was the last inmate of which prison?

12. What was the first American state to ratify the Constitution of the United States?

13. Who was the first footballer to attract 10 million Twitter followers?

14. The first television interracial kiss occurred on which programme?

15. The Last Broadcast was number 1 album for which group?

16. Who played Jesus in the 1988 film The Last Temptation of Christ?

17. In which decade did the first Oscar ceremony take place?

18. Complete the title of the 2010 film directed by M Night Shyamalan: The Last...?

19. In what year was the last person executed in the Tower of London?
    a) 1741
    b) 1841
    c) 1941

20. King Michael was the last king of which European country?
    a) Bulgaria
    b) Croatia
    c) Romania

Answers to Quiz 181: Pot Luck

1. Surfing
2. Maine
3. Cate Blanchett as Katharine Hepburn in The Aviator
4. Werner Herzog
5. Ulster Unionist Party
6. The Bahamas
7. Alexander the Great
8. India and Sri Lanka
9. 11
10. Kidney
11. France
12. Harrison Birtwistle
13. The Railway Series (Thomas The Tank Engine and Friends)
14. Bedford Falls
15. Gavin and Stacey
16. Lawrence Fox
17. Dombey and Son
18. IBM
19. Judah
20. Victoria Coren

DIFFICULT

Quiz 183: Pot Luck

1. Who wrote the 2010 Booker Prize shortlisted novel Room?

2. Which musician's debut live album was subtitled The 12-Year Old Genius?

3. Draco dormiens nunquam titilandus is the motto of which school?

4. Which Spinal Tap actor provides the voices of Principal Skinner and Mr Burns on The Simpsons?

5. What is the medical condition lateral epicondylitis more commonly known as?

6. What world championship event takes place annually at Waen Rhydd, Llanwrtyd Wells in Wales?

7. Who, in 2011 became the first artist to win the Mercury Music Prize twice?

8. Shas, Balad and Kadima are political parties in which country?

9. Portrait of George Dyer in a Mirror, Study of a Baboon and Study from the Human Body are works by which Dublin-born painter?

10. Which four British racecourses do not contain any of the letters of the word race in their name?

11. Andris Nelsons is the principal conductor with which British orchestra?

12. 'I've heard there was a secret chord / That David played, and it pleased the Lord' are the opening lines to which much covered song?

13. Plymouth Raiders, Leicester Rider and Newcastle Eagles are teams that play which sport?

14. Which Midlands town is home to an arboretum and illuminations?

15. Robert James Ritchie is the real name of which US musician whose albums include Cocky and Rock n Roll Jesus?

16. Which contemporary author's works include Moon Palace, The Book of Illusions and The New York Trilogy?

17. Christian Louboutin is a noted make of what?

18. Which Peruvian-born lay brother is the patron saint of barbers, hairdressers and racial harmony?

19. Someone who is sinistral is?
    a) left handed b) right handed c) ambidextrous

20. A Turkish shampoo advert featuring which dictator was banned in 2012?
    a) Hitler b) Mussolini c) Chairman Mao

Answers to Quiz 182: Firsts and Lasts

1. Last Man Standing
2. Agatha Christie
3. Alcatraz
4. Tug of war
5. American Civil War
6. Tony Blackburn
7. Charlie Sheen
8. Morrissey
9. Forest Whitaker
10. 1923
11. Spandau
12. Delaware
13. Kaka
14. Star Trek
15. Doves
16. Willem Defoe
17. 1920s
18. Airbender
19. 1941
20. Romania

DIFFICULT

Quiz 184: Transport

1. Which 1987 film comedy starred Steve Martin as a man struggling to get home for Thanksgiving with only John Candy for company?

2. In what year did Concorde make its final flight?

3. The M11 motorway links London and which city?

4. Which rock group had a 1973 top ten hit with Paper Planes?

5. In which European city is Gardermoen Airport?

6. Which gang drove a car called the Bulletproof Bomb?

7. The car manufacturer Proton is from which country?

8. Which British philosopher wrote The Art of Travel?

9. What number was Herbie in the films featuring the anthropomorphic Volkswagen Beetle?

10. In what decade of the 20th century was the driving test introduced?

11. What is the oldest national airline in the world?

12. Which Asian car manufacturer produces models called Santa Fe and Veloster?

13. Where in the British Isles will you find Ronaldsway Airport?

14. Which Middle Eastern country has the international car registration code of RL?

15. What sort of train were Madness waiting for in their 1986 top 20 hit?

16. Which author said, 'When I see an adult on a bicycle, I do not despair for the future of the human race'?

17. Zoom Zoom is a slogan used by which motor manufacturer?

18. Avianca is the flag-carrying airline of which country?

19. Vintage cars are ones built before which year?
    a) 1920
    b) 1930
    c) 1940

20. What car succeeded the Ford Model T?
    a) Model A
    b) Model B
    c) Model C

Answers to Quiz 183: Pot Luck

1. Emma Donoghue
2. Stevie Wonder
3. Hogwarts
4. Harry Shearer
5. Tennis elbow
6. The World Bog Snorkelling Championship
7. PJ Harvey
8. Israel
9. Francis Bacon
10. Goodwood, Huntingdon, Ludlow and Plumpton
11. City of Birmingham Symphony Orchestra
12. Hallelujah
13. Basketball
14. Walsall
15. Kid Rock
16. Paul Auster
17. Shoes
18. St Martin de Porres
19. Left handed
20. Hitler

DIFFICULT

Quiz 185: Pot Luck

1. Which five towns are mentioned in the titles of plays by Shakespeare?

2. What was the family name of the members of 80s pop group Five Star?

3. Bamako is the capital city of which African country?

4. Composer Ludwig van Beethoven was born in which German city?

5. What was The Police's first number one hit single?

6. Jean Baptiste Poquelin was the real name of which 17th-century French actor and playwright?

7. Comedian Miranda Hart, writer Agatha Christie and satirist Peter Cook were all born in which town?

8. Which US President said, 'Nothing in the world can take the place of persistence'?

9. The biggest selling newspaper in the world is in which country?

10. Actor Michael Gambon and author Bram Stoker were born in which city?

11. Complete the title of the 2005 number one from Oasis: The Importance of Being...?

12. Who was the lead actress in the Oscar-winning film The Artist?

13. What are the only two countries on the American continent that drive on the left?

14. What is the English equivalent of the Italian name Guglielmo?

15. Memoirs of a Fox Hunting Man and The Old Huntsman are works by which English writer who died in 1967?

16. Cluj is the second largest city in which European country?

17. Novelist JRR Tolkien, England cricket captain Andrew Strauss and actor Anthony Sher were born in which country?

18. Mr Pecksniff and his daughters Charity and Mercy are characters from which Dickens novel?

19. What animal featured in Mark Wallinger's Turner Prize nominated piece A Real Work Of Art?
    a) cow
    b) horse
    c) sheep

20. Which country covers a larger area?
    a) India
    b) Australia

Answers to Quiz 184: Transport

1. Planes, Trains and Automobiles
2. 2003
3. Cambridge
4. Status Quo
5. Oslo
6. The Ant Hill Mob
7. Malaysia
8. Alain de Botton
9. 53
10. 1930s
11. KLM
12. Hyundai
13. Isle of Man
14. Lebanon
15. Ghost
16. HG Wells
17. Mazda
18. Colombia
19. 1930
20. Model A

DIFFICULT

Quiz 186: Movie Taglines

Can you identify the movie from the tagline?

1. The Earth's darkest day will be man's finest hour.

2. His genius undeniable. His evil unspeakable.

3. An adventure 65 million years in the making.

4. See our family and feel better about yours.

5. He's having the worst day of his life....over and over.....

6. Makes Ben Hur look like an epic.

7. There's something about your first piece.

8. His story will touch you, even though he can't.

9. The first casualty of war is innocence.

10. She brought a small town to its feet and a huge corporation to its knees.

11. She gets kidnapped. He gets killed. But it all ends up okay.

12. On every street in every city, there's a nobody who dreams of being a somebody.

13. 3 Casinos. 11 Guys. 150 Million Bucks. Ready To Win Big?

14. They're young...they're in love...and they kill people.

15. Five good reasons to stay single.

16. This is Benjamin. He's a little worried about his future.

17. Even a hit man deserves a second shot.

18. Everyone has one special thing.

19. The year's most revealing comedy.

20. With the right song and dance, you can get away with murder.

Answers to Quiz 185: Pot Luck

1. Windsor, Verona, Venice, Tyre and Athens
2. Pearson
3. Mali
4. Bonn
5. Message In A Bottle
6. Molière
7. Torquay
8. Calvin Coolidge
9. Japan
10. Dublin
11. Idle
12. Berenice Bejo
13. Guyana and Suriname
14. William
15. Siegfried Sassoon
16. Romania
17. South Africa
18. Martin Chuzzlewit
19. Horse
20. Australia

DIFFICULT

Quiz 187: Pot Luck

1. A film adaptation of which Shakespeare play was banned by authorities in Thailand in 2012?

2. She's Strange, Word Up and Back and Forth were hits for which group?

3. The father of which British comic actress commanded HMS Coventry in the Falklands War?

4. In Internet dating, what do the initials HWP stand for?

5. The tenge is the currency of which former Soviet republic?

6. Which 1971 crime film was based on a novel called Jack's Return Home?

7. On the BBC charity version of Lou Reed's Perfect Day, who sang the line 'And then later, when it gets dark...'?

8. Which US President owned a dog called Checkers?

9. The name of which Arab capital translates into English as 'Father of Gazelle'?

10. Blagoevgrad, Pernik and Varna are regions of which European country?

11. What is the name of the pig in the children's favourite Charlotte's Web?

12. Vladimir Kramnik and Viswanathan Anand are recent world champions in which game?

13. What is a tonsure?

14. In relation to the trade union, what does the acronym BECTU stand for?

15. In The Simpsons, what is the name of Chief Wiggum's wife?

16. Kit Nubbles, Daniel Quilp and Dick Swiveller are characters in which Dickens novel?

Answers - page 381

17. Wyatt's Rebellion was a popular uprising against which English monarch?

18. Juba is the capital of which recently created country?

19. Gaz and Rob Coombes, Danny Goffey and Mick Quinn are members of which band?

20. Catoptrophobia is the fear of what?
    a) cats
    b) mirrors
    c) trees

21. Prunus armeniaca is the Latin name for which fruit?
    a) apricot
    b) pomegranate
    c) satsuma

Answers to Quiz 186: Movie Taglines

1. Armageddon
2. Hannibal
3. Jurassic Park
4. The Simpsons Movie
5. Groundhog Day
6. Monty Python and the Holy Grail
7. American Pie
8. Edward Scissorhands
9. Platoon
10. Erin Brokovich
11. The Princess Bride
12. Taxi Driver
13. Ocean's Eleven
14. Bonnie and Clyde
15. Four Weddings and a Funeral
16. The Graduate
17. Grosse Point Blank
18. Boogie Nights
19. The Full Monty
20. Chicago

DIFFICULT

Quiz 188: Food and Drink

1. Which alcoholic drink is nicknamed The Green Fairy?

2. Charles Alderton invented which soft drink?

3. What fish is traditionally used in the Scandinavian dish gravlax?

4. Pimenton is another name for what spice?

5. Cabbage, kale and broccoli are part of which plant family?

6. Vicia faba is the Latin name for which legume?

7. Paul Hollywood is a judge on which culinary television show?

8. Farleigh, Merryweather and Shropshire are varieties of which fruit?

9. What is a brochette?

10. Comice is a variety of which fruit?

11. What are the real names of TV's Hairy Bikers?

12. Sapsago cheese comes from which country?

13. Golden Ball, Green Globe and Tokyo Cross are types of what vegetable?

14. What is the Cajun equivalent of the Spanish dish paella?

15. Atacama, Central Valley and Coquimbo are wine growing regions in which country?

16. What fish is traditionally eaten at a Christmas meal in Poland?

17. What type of food is Monterey Jack?

18. The wine-growing Moselle Valley region lies in which three countries?

19. Ribes Grossularia is the Latin name for which berry?
    a) blackberry
    b) loganberry
    c) gooseberry

20. What type of meat is used in Italian bresaola?
    a) beef
    b) chicken
    c) pork

Answers to Quiz 187: Pot Luck

1. Macbeth
2. Cameo
3. Miranda Hart
4. Height and weight proportional
5. Kazakhstan
6. Get Carter
7. Bono
8. Richard Nixon
9. Abu Dhabi
10. Bulgaria
11. Wilbur
12. Chess
13. The shaved crown of a monk's or priest's head
14. Broadcasting, Entertainment, Cinematograph and Theatre Union
15. Sarah
16. The Old Curiosity Shop
17. Queen Mary
18. South Sudan
19. Supergrass
20. Mirrors
21. Apricot

DIFFICULT

Quiz 189: Pot Luck

1. In non-leap years, what is the middle day of the year?

2. Sabah, Sarawak and Perak are states in which Asian country?

3. Al Pacino's only Best Actor Oscar was for his performance in which film?

4. Which guitarist, who died in 2012, wrote the best-selling book Play In A Day?

5. Born in 1832, Charles Dodgson was the real name of which author?

6. Spitting Image topped the charts in 1986 with what animal inspired song?

7. Question Time was broadcast from what unusual location for the first time in May 2011?

8. John Galliano was fired from which fashion house after an anti-semitic rant?

9. In what year did the Pilgrim Fathers first set sail for America?

10. Zaire is the former name of which African country?

11. Aconcagua, the highest mountain in the Americas, is in which country?

12. What was the name of the eye patch-wearing Sunday Times journalist who was killed while covering the siege of Homs in 2012?

13. Which actor plays Frank Gallagher in the US version of TV drama Shameless?

14. Who was India's first Prime Minister?

DIFFICULT

15. The huge Cerne Giant hill figure is in which English county?

16. The fictional town of Hill Valley, California is the setting for which film trilogy?

17. Which 1933 film had the tagline 'The strangest story ever conceived by man'?

18. Who lives at 744 Evergreen Terrace, Springfield?

19. Dave and Ansell Collins topped the charts in 1971 with
    a) Double Trouble
    b) Double Barrel
    c) Double Dutch

20. What unit is used as payment in livestock sales?
    a) guinea
    b) farthing
    c) shilling

Answers to Quiz 188: Food and drink

1. Absinthe
2. Dr Pepper
3. Salmon
4. Smoked paprika
5. Brassica
6. Broad bean
7. The Great British Bake Off
8. Damson
9. A skewer for cooking
10. Pear
11. David Myers and Si King
12. Switzerland
13. Turnip
14. Jambalaya
15. Chile
16. Carp
17. Cheese
18. France, Germany and Luxembourg
19. Gooseberry
20. Beef

DIFFICULT

Quiz 190: Human Body

1. A cholecystectomy is the removal of what organ?

2. Where in the human body will you find the pituitary gland?

3. Dyspnea is another name for what?

4. What is a naevus more commonly known as?

5. Where on the body is the glabella?

6. An MRI is often used to determine an injury to the body but what do the initials MRI stand for?

7. What is the name of the structure that separates the nostrils?

8. How many valves does the human heart have?

9. Bile is produced by which organ of the body?

10. What do the initials CPR stand for?

11. What glands are responsible for producing tears?

12. Oncology is the branch of medicine that deals with which disease?

13. Which illness is also known as pertussis?

14. What tissue connects bones to one another?

15. In 2005, Frenchwoman Isàbelle Dinoire became the first person to undergo what operation?

16. Where in the body will you find the sclera?

17. The gallbladder is attached to the underside of which organ?

18. What do the initials HIV stand for?

19. How many bones make up the human hand?
    a) 17
    b) 27
    c) 37

20. The gastrocnemius muscle is also known as what?
    a) calf
    b) hamstring
    c) thigh

Answers to Quiz 189: Pot Luck

1. 2nd July
2. Malaysia
3. Scent of a Woman
4. Bert Weedon
5. Lewis Carroll
6. The Chicken Song
7. Wormwood Scrubs Prison
8. Dior
9. 1620
10. Democratic Republic of Congo
11. Argentina
12. Marie Colvin
13. William H Macy
14. Jawaharlal Nehru
15. Dorset
16. Back To The Future
17. King Kong
18. Ned Flanders (The Simpsons live at 742)
19. Double Barrel
20. Guinea

DIFFICULT

Quiz 191: Pot Luck

1. Which Premier League footballer won two episodes of Countdown in 2010?

2. The Casa Rosada (Pink House) is the official residence of the President of which South American country?

3. Which actor played Prince Philip in the 2006 film The Queen and Clifton the driver in The Artist?

4. What English stately home shares its name with the estate in the TV drama Shameless?

5. Which English rugby union team plays its home games at Kingsholm Stadium?

6. John Palmer was the alias of which English outlaw?

7. Democrats 66, Party For Freedom and Party For Animals are political parties in which country?

8. The Strait of Bonifacio lies between which two European islands?

9. What dinosaur provided the title of a 2011 album by Kasabian?

10. Which group collaborated with Tom Jones on his 1988 version of Kiss?

11. Britain's Malcolm Cooper was a double Olympic gold medallist in which sport?

12. Which politician wrote the diaries A Walk On Part, A View From The Foothills and Decline and Fall?

13. What is the county town of Derbyshire?

14. Which TV family lived at 633 Stag Trail Road, North Caldwell, New Jersey 07006?

15. Renwick is the middle name of one half of a popular double act. Can you name him?

Answers - page 389

16. The French call them Coquilles St. Jacques but what are they known as in English?

17. Olympic skater Robin Cousins, comedian Lee Evans and actor Michael Redgrave were born in which city?

18. Mary Queen of Scots was executed at which Northamptonshire castle?

19. In what year was Twitter launched?
    a) 2005
    b) 2006
    c) 2007

20. Which country withdrew its 1 cent coin in March 2012?
    a) Australia
    b) Canada
    c) New Zealand

Answers to Quiz 190: Human Body

1. Gallbladder
2. At the base of the brain
3. Shortness of breath
4. A mole or birthmark
5. The gap between the eyebrows
6. Magnetic resonance imaging
7. Septum
8. 4
9. Liver
10. Cardiopulmonary Resuscitation
11. Lachrymal glands
12. Cancer
13. Whooping cough
14. Ligament
15. Face transplant
16. Eyes
17. Liver
18. Human Immunodeficiency Virus
19. 27
20. Calf

DIFFICULT

Quiz 192: Books

1. Which science fiction writer wrote the Foundation Trilogy?

2. What nationality was the Nobel Prize winning author Jose Saramago?

3. Rock band The Doors took their name from a novel by which author?

4. John Willet, Gabriel Vardon and Sir John Chester are characters in which Dickens novel?

5. What does the TC in TC Boyle stand for?

6. The detective novels of George Pelecanos are primarily set in which city?

7. Caroline Graham created which literary-turned-TV detective?

8. Having A Lovely Time and Camberwell Beauty are novels by which comedian and actress?

9. Ambition, Grit and a Great Pair of Heels is the autobiography of which businesswoman?

10. What is the third book in the Harry Potter series?

11. Adam Fenwick-Symes is the main protagonist in which novel by Evelyn Waugh?

12. Which 1929 French novel was called The Holy Terrors in America?

13. Coming Back To Me was an award-winning autobiography by which cricketer?

14. Various Pets Alive Or Dead is by which award-winning author?

Answers - page 391

15. Journey Into Fear, Uncommon Danger and Epitaph For A Spy are by which thriller writer?

16. Changing My Mind: Occasional Essays is a non fiction collection from which award winning British writer?

17. Dangling Man was the debut novel by which Canadian-born American author?

18. Who wrote The Memory Keeper's Daughter?

19. Call For The Dead was the debut novel from which author?
    a) Stephen King
    b) Len Deighton
    c) John Le Carré

20. What is the name of the student murderer in Dostoevsky's Crime and Punishment?
    a) Raskolnikov
    b) Yepanchin
    c) Koznyshev

Answers to Quiz 191: Pot Luck

1. Clarke Carlisle
2. Argentina
3. James Cromwell
4. Chatsworth
5. Gloucester
6. Dick Turpin
7. The Netherlands
8. Corsica and Sardinia
9. Velociraptor
10. The Art of Noise
11. Rifle shooting
12. Chris Mullin
13. Matlock
14. The Sopranos
15. Bob Mortimer
16. Scallops
17. Bristol
18. Fotheringay Castle
19. 2006
20. Canada

DIFFICULT

Quiz 193: Pot Luck

1. What do the CS in novelist CS Lewis stand for?

2. Which band was the first to reach 1m followers on Google+?

3. Whitehorse is the capital city of which Canadian territory?

4. Who plays Lee's dad in the sitcom Not Going Out?

5. Who was the first British monarch to visit the USA?

6. In relation to the industrial equipment manufacturer, what do the initials JCB stand for?

7. Which female band was the first to top the UK single, album and download charts simultaneously?

8. The Folketing is the parliament of which country?

9. Which contact sport takes place in a ring called a dohyo?

10. Wantage Road is the home ground of which county cricket team?

11. A Fart in a Colander is the autobiography of which veteran British comedian, actor and broadcaster?

12. Jackson is the capital of which US state?

13. King Alexander of Greece died after being bitten by which animal?

14. In mobile phone technology, what do the initials WAP stand for?

15. A rare comic featuring which superhero sold for $1.1m when auctioned in 2011?

16. What is the second largest city in Japan by population?

17. What does a cruciverbalist enjoy doing?

18. The Beatles last concert took place in which American city?

19. Retinol is a form of which vitamin?
    a) A
    b) D
    c) E

20. What is the currency in Kenya, Tanzania and Uganda?
    a) dollar
    b) franc
    c) shilling

Answers to Quiz 192: Books

1. Isaac Asimov
2. Portuguese
3. Aldous Huxley (The Doors of Perception)
4. Barnaby Rudge
5. Tom Coraghessan
6. Washington DC
7. Inspector John Barnaby from Midsomer Murders
8. Jenny Éclair
9. Karren Brady
10. Harry Potter and the Prisoner of Azkaban
11. Vile Bodies
12. Les Enfants Terribles by Jean Cocteau
13. Marcus Trescothick
14. Marina Lewycka
15. Eric Ambler
16. Zadie Smith
17. Saul Bellow
18. Kim Edwards
19. John Le Carre
20. Raskolnikov

DIFFICULT

Quiz 194: Television part 2

1. What is the name of the character played by Rebecca Front in The Thick of It?

2. Which actor plays Ian Fletcher in Olympics inspired TV comedy Twenty Twelve?

3. In which sci-fi series will you see aliens called The Ood, The Ogrons and The Autons?

4. What is Judith Sheindlin more commonly known as?

5. Brian Capron played which soap opera villain?

6. What character did Stephen Merchant play in TV comedy Extras?

7. Mr Doovdé, George Agdgdgwngo and Brian Badonde were characters in which prank based comedy show?

8. Who plays Liz Lemon in the hit US comedy 30 Rock?

9. Tamsin Greig and Stephen Mangan starred alongside Matt LeBlanc in which comedy about a pair of British writers trying to make it in LA?

10. Walford, the fictional location of EastEnders, takes its name from which two London locations?

11. What was Grandad Trotter's first name in Only Fools and Horses?

12. Which actress plays Peggy Olsson in US drama Mad Men?

13. Who plays the title character's mother in TV comedy Miranda?

14. What names links a Formula One driver and the soothsayer in Roman-era comedy Up Pompeii?

15. Oliver Peyton is a judge on which TV competition?

16. What is the name of the incompetent lawyer in The Simpsons?

17. Which Spice Girl auditioned for the part of Bianca Jackson in EastEnders?

18. Who plays Adam's wife Alex, in the sitcom Rev?

19. Julianna Margulies plays Alicia Florick in which American drama?
    a) Dexter
    b) The Good Wife
    c) Breaking Bad

20. In what year was the Television Licence introduced?
    a) 1946
    b) 1951
    c) 1956

Answers to Quiz 193: Pot Luck

1. Clive Staples
2. Coldplay
3. Yukon
4. Bobby Ball
5. King George VI
6. Joseph Cyril Bamford
7. Sugababes
8. Denmark
9. Sumo wrestling
10. Northamptonshire
11. Roy Hudd
12. Mississippi
13. Monkey
14. Wireless Application Protocol
15. Spider Man
16. Yokohama
17. Crossword puzzles
18. San Francisco
19. Vitamin A
20. Shilling

DIFFICULT

Quiz 195: Pot Luck

1. The Waitresses recorded which Christmas song?

2. What are the names of the two mascots for the 2012 London Olympic Games?

3. Which actor created the Twitter hashtag #tigerblood which became the most popular hashtag of 2011?

4. The Spanish knight Ignatius of Loyola was the founder of which religious organisation?

5. Which Premier League striker has 'Ma Vie, Mes Régles' tattooed on his neck?

6. What nationality is the musician-turned-politician Youssou N'Dour?

7. Which contemporary American writer's works include I Am Charlotte Simmons, The Bonfire of the Vanities and A Man In Full?

8. Tagalog is an official language in which Asian country?

9. Euphorbia pulcherrima is the Latin name for which species of popular Christmas flower?

10. Which English football club's ground has a pub on each corner?

11. The 2011 English riots started after a shooting in which part of London?

12. John Le Carre's A Small Town in Germany is set in which town?

13. What is the aboriginal name for Ayers Rock?

14. Liberty or Death is the motto of which South American country?

15. What do the initials JD in the reclusive author JD Salinger stand for?

16. In which Asian city will you see the Petronas Towers?

17. Chatsworth House is in which English county?

18. Which band had eight consecutive number one albums between 1970 and 1979 but didn't release their first UK single until 1997?

19. Sid James made his Carry On debut in which film?
    a) Sergeant
    b) Constable
    c) Teacher

20. Which actor is the eldest?
    a) Ben Affleck
    b) Jude Law
    c) Ewan McGregor

Answers to Quiz 194: Television part 2

1. Nicola Murray
2. Hugh Bonneville
3. Dr Who
4. Judge Judy
5. Coronation Street's Richard Hillman
6. Agent Darren Lamb
7. Fonejacker
8. Tina Fey
9. Episodes
10. Walthamstow and Stratford
11. Edward
12. Elisabeth Moss
13. Patricia Hodge
14. Senna
15. The Great British Menu
16. Lionel Hutz
17. Emma Bunton
18. Olivia Colman
19. The Good Wife
20. 1946

DIFFICULT

Quiz 196: Sport part 2

1. Who were the only team to beat India in the 2011 Cricket World Cup?

2. Who was the champion flat jockey in 2010 and 2011?

3. Which countries will host the 2015 Cricket World Cup?

4. Langtree Park is the home ground of which rugby league team?

5. The 2018 Commonwealth Games will be held in which country?

6. Who was the last rider not named Tony McCoy to win the jump racing Champion Jockey title?

7. British cyclists came second and third in the 2011 Tour of Spain cycle race. Can you name them?

8. Andy Turner won a bronze medal at the 2011 World Athletics Championships in which event?

9. The massive Rungrado May Day stadium is in which country?

10. Who was the last Frenchman to win the Tour de France?

11. What is the name of Tiger Woods' former caddie who hit the headlines after making a racist comment about his former boss?

12. The last ever European Cup Winners' Cup final was held in which city?

13. Who won the 100m at the 2011 World Athletics Championships in Korea?

14. The Bobcats are an NBA basketball team from which American city?

15. The FA rowed with FIFA about the wearing of poppies on shirts prior to England's match against which team?

16. Which two golfers were involved in the so called 'Duel in the Sun' at the 1977 Open Golf Championship?

17. Who was the first tennis player born in the 1990s to win a Wimbledon title?

18. Primarily used for football, the 120,000 capacity Salt Lake Stadium is in which country?

19. What is the smallest winning margin in Tour de France history?
    a) 8 seconds
    b) 28 seconds
    c) 48 seconds

20. Which country did not take part in the 2011 Cricket World Cup?
    a) United Arab Emirates
    b) Canada
    c) Holland

Answers to Quiz 195: Pot Luck

1. Christmas Wrapping
2. Wenlock and Mandeville
3. Charlie Sheen
4. The Jesuits (Society of Jesus)
5. John Carew
6. Senegalese
7. Tom Wolfe
8. The Philippines
9. Poinsettia
10. Brentford's Griffin Park
11. Tottenham
12. Bonn
13. Uluru
14. Uruguay
15. Jerome David
16. Kuala Lumpur
17. Derbyshire
18. Led Zeppelin
19. Carry On Constable
20. Ewan McGregor

DIFFICULT

Quiz 197: Pot Luck

1. In which country will you find an 85m floating Christmas tree?

2. Washington National Airport is named after which US President?

3. Cebolla is the Spanish word for what vegetable?

4. Which chart topping singer started his career in a boy band called Menudo?

5. In what sport are Ken Bradshaw, Laird Hamilton and Kelly Slater notable names?

6. The flag of which European country features two cows?

7. Who was born first – Shakespeare or Michelangelo?

8. Four Darks in Red and Slate Blue and Brown on Plum are works by which painter?

9. FBI Special Agent Seeley Booth and Dr. Temperance Brennan are the central characters in which US crime drama?

10. How many sonnets did William Shakespeare write?

11. Gutzon Borglum created which famous American landmark?

12. Victoria Park is the home ground of which English football club?

13. Which British band, whose albums include Dummy and Third, take their name from a town 8 miles west of Bristol?

14. What is the name of David and Victoria Beckham's daughter who was born in 2011?

15. What organ of the body provided the title of a number one album by Florence and the Machine?

16. Also the title of a fiendish TV quiz show, what was the epigraph to EM Forster's novel Howards End?

17. Les Wallace, John Walton and Tony David have all been world champions in which sport?

18. Jason Crump, Tomasz Gollob and Greg Hancock are recent world champions in which sport?

19. What is Riboflavin also known as?
    a) vitamin B1
    b) vitamin B2
    c) vitamin B3

20. Kingsford Smith Airport serves which Australian city?
    a) Brisbane
    b) Melbourne
    c) Sydney

Answers to Quiz 196: Sport part 2

1. South Africa
2. Paul Hanagan
3. Australia and New Zealand
4. St Helens
5. Australia
6. Richard Dunwoody
7. Chris Froome and Bradley Wiggins
8. 110m hurdles
9. North Korea
10. Bernard Hinault
11. Steve Williams
12. Birmingham
13. Yohan Blake
14. Charlotte
15. Spain
16. Tom Watson and Jack Nicklaus
17. Petra Kvitova
18. India
19. 8 seconds
20. United Arab Emirates

DIFFICULT

Quiz 198: Births, Marriages and Deaths

1. Which singer gave birth to twins in 2011 called Moroccan and Monroe?

2. Two different songs called Happy Birthday reached number 2 in the charts in 1981. Who were they by?

3. Death and the Maiden is a play by which South American writer?

4. Which Hollywood actor named his son Kal-El (Superman's original name)?

5. Which England cricketer died in a car crash in Perth, Australia in 2002?

6. What was the name of the comedy starring Bruce Willis, Goldie Hawn and Maryl Streep about a pair who drink a potion promising everlasting youth?

7. Which supermodel tied the knot with Jamie Hince in 2011?

8. Who composed the opera Death In Venice?

9. Which former British Prime Minister died on 24 May 1995?

10. Stairway To Heaven was the American title of which 1946 film?

11. Funeral Pyre was a number 4 hit for which group?

12. James Bond actor Daniel Craig is married to which actress?

13. Which Nobel and Pulitzer Prize-winning author was born Chloe Ardelia Wofford?

14. Mary Anne Evans was the birth name of which 19th-century British novelist?

15. Diva Thin Muffin Pigeen is the daughter of which American musician who died in 1993?

16. Two racing drivers died at the Imola Grand Prix in 1994. Ayrton Senna was one, who was the other?

17. Which British driver and double Indy 500 winner died in a multiple car pile-up in a race in Nevada in 2011?

18. Tom Cruise gained his first Academy Award nomination for which film?

19. How did Nazi Josef Mengele, drummer Dennis Wilson and singer songwriter Jeff Buckley die?
    a) electrocution
    b) drowning
    c) car crash

20. Who designed Kate Middleton's wedding dress?
    a) Sarah Burton
    b) Vivienne Westwood
    c) Oscar de la Renta

Answers to Quiz 197: Pot Luck

1. Brazil
2. Ronald Reagan
3. Onion
4. Ricky Martin
5. Surfing
6. Andorra
7. Michelangelo
8. Mark Rothko
9. Bones
10. 154
11. The President's heads at Mount Rushmore
12. Hartlepool United
13. Portishead
14. Harper Seven
15. Lungs
16. Only Connect
17. Darts
18. Speedway
19. Vitamin B2
20. Sydney

DIFFICULT

Quiz 199: Pot Luck

1. André Cassagnes invented which mechanical drawing toy?

2. Which American actor directed the 2007 comedy Run Fatboy Run?

3. The 1932 Summer Olympic Games were hosted in which city?

4. Carioca is the nickname given to people from which city?

5. Which Hollywood star is the god daughter of psychedelic author Timothy Leary?

6. Who is the the only US President to have served two non-consecutive terms?

7. Which pirate captained a ship called Queen Anne's Revenge?

8. What famous battle took place on 11 July 1690?

9. What Australian city lies on the River Torrens?

10. Which poet features in the Alan Bennett play The Habit of Art?

11. In what year did Channel 5 makes its debut?

12. Roger Daltrey played the lead role in a 1975 film about which composer?

13. Which author was George Orwell's French teacher at Eton?

14. What is the most popular Beatles song chosen by castaways on Desert Island Discs?

15. The White Peacock was the first published novel by which author?

16. 'Above us, only sky' is the motto of which airport?

17. Who played Karla in the TV version of John Le Carre's Smiley's People?

18. The Holy Thorn Tree, said to be grown from the staff of Joseph of Arimathea, is in which Somerset town?

19. In what year was the 1/2p coin withdrawn from circulation?
    a) 1981
    b) 1984
    c) 1987

20. In which area of the arts was Elizabeth Catlett a noted name?
    a) dance
    b) literature
    c) sculpture

Answers to Quiz 198: Births, Marriages and Deaths

1. Mariah Carey
2. Stevie Wonder and Altered Images
3. Ariel Dorfman
4. Nicolas Cage
5. Ben Hollioake
6. Death Becomes Her
7. Kate Moss
8. Benjamin Britten
9. Harold Wilson
10. A Matter of Life and Death
11. The Jam
12. Rachel Weisz
13. Toni Morrison
14. George Eliot
15. Frank Zappa
16. Roland Ratzenberger
17. Dan Wheldon
18. Born on the Fourth of July
19. Drowning
20. Sarah Burton

DIFFICULT

Quiz 200: Taking the Michael

Identify the famous Michaels from the clues below:

1. Royal whose real name is Marie Christine Anna Agnes Hedwig Ida von Reibnitz?

2. Vocalist with the Doobie Brothers?

3. Author who was leader of Canada's Liberal Party from 2009 until 2011?

4. Son of the actor born Issur Danielovitch?

5. Jockey who won the 1996 Grand National riding Rough Quest?

6. Character who trained Sylvester Stallone in the Rocky films?

7. Recorded albums called It's Time and Call Me Irresponsible?

8. Member of Irish boyband Boyzone?

9. Won Wimbledon Men's Singles title in 1991?

10. Award-winning director whose films include The White Ribbon and Caché?

11. Winner of 16 Olympic medals including eight at the Beijing games?

12. Plays Kevin Webster in Coronation Street?

13. Succeeded Rudy Giuliani as Mayor of New York?

14. Dazzled the crowds in the interval at the 1994 Eurovision Song Contest?

15. Former Cabinet minister whose middle names are Denzel Xavier?

16. Football manager whose clubs include Leicester, Coventry, Sheffield United and Port Vale?

17. Played Christopher Moltisanti in The Sopranos?

18. American footballer who was the subject of the Oscar nominated film The Blind Side?

19. Footballer whose autobiography was called Who Ate All The Pies?

20. Holds the record for the most Test matches as England cricket captain?
    a) Michael Atherton
    b) Mike Brearley
    c) Michael Vaughan

Answers to Quiz 199: Pot Luck

1. Etch A Sketch
2. David Schwimmer
3. Los Angeles
4. Rio de Janeiro
5. Winona Ryder
6. Grover Cleveland
7. Blackbeard
8. Battle of the Boyne
9. Adelaide
10. WH Auden
11. 1997
12. Franz Liszt (Lisztomania)
13. Aldous Huxley
14. Yesterday
15. DH Lawrence
16. Liverpool John Lennon Airport
17. Patrick Stewart
18. Glastonbury
19. 1984
20. Sculpture

DIFFICULT

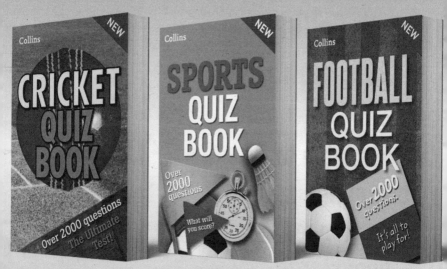